KAROL WOJTYŁA'S
PERSONALIST PHILOSOPHY

KAROL WOJTYŁA'S
PERSONALIST PHILOSOPHY

Understanding *Person* & *Act*

MIGUEL ACOSTA & ADRIAN J. REIMERS

THE CATHOLIC UNIVERSITY OF AMERICA PRESS
Washington, D.C.

Deisgn and typesetting by Kachergis Book Design

Library of Congress Cataloging-in-Publication Data
Names: Acosta, Miguel (Miguel Andres Acosta Lopez), author.
Title: Karol Wojtyla's personalist philosophy : understanding
Person and act / Miguel Acosta and Adrian J. Reimers.
Description: Washington, D.C. : The Catholic University of
America Press, 2016. | Includes bibliographical references
and index.
Identifiers: LCCN 2016012327 | ISBN 9780813231976 (pbk : alk.
paper)
Subjects: LCSH: John Paul II, Pope, 1920–2005. Osoba i czyn. |
Act (Philosophy) | Personality. | Philosophical anthropology.
| Phenomenological anthropology.
Classification: LCC B105.A35 J6423 2016 | DDC 128—dc23
LC record available at http://lccn.loc.gov/2016012327

CONTENTS

ACKNOWLEDGMENTS

For my part (Miguel Acosta), I want to thank the University of Notre Dame for its hospitality, for the university welcomed me as a Visiting Scholar during the 2010–2011 academic year. In particular, I thank Professors Alfred Freddoso, John O'Callaghan, and Montey Holloway, assisted by LinDa Grams, Catherine DeFauw, and Alice Osberger, for receiving me in the Department of Philosophy. I also thank the team at the Nanovic Institute for European Studies: Director John McAdams, Monica Caro, and Sharon Konopka. Thanks also to my scholarly colleagues José Luis Widow, Lee M. Cole, and Federico Tedesco.

I thank, too, the Universidad CEU San Pablo and the Instituto CEU de Humanidades Ángel Ayala, which allowed me to take this time for research abroad. I owe especial thanks to Adrian J. Reimers, a good friend, who helped me to discover new light in Karol Wojtyła's philosophy and who then translated a great deal of this text, and to his wife, Marie, who always made us feel at home.

Finally and most important, I am grateful for the constant support of my wife, María, who, besides being always by my side, has helped me with enlightening commentaries and as a reviewer of the Spanish manuscript.

ᢙ

For my part (Adrian J. Reimers), I first thank the Fulbright Scholar Program, which awarded a grant for six months' research in Kraków, Poland, which made possible the research and opportunity to prepare my portion of this work. I also thank the San Pablo CEU

University in Madrid for inviting me to present these essays as lectures to their professors and students. And finally, I thank Miguel Acosta, not only for inviting me to Spain to present these lectures and for helping me render them in good Spanish, but also for his advice and collaboration on this present work. It would be amiss not also to mention the help of colleagues in Poland, both at the Pontifical University of John Paul II in Kraków (especially Fr. Prof. Grzegorz Hołub), and in the Catholic University of Lublin (especially Fr. Prof. Alfred Wierzbicki), whose invitations to lecture on these themes and critical feedback from the faculties at their respective universities enabled me to sharpen some of the arguments that appear in the present volume. My wife, Marie, companion on these journeys and constant friend, has been an immense help—supporting me, enduring the mental distraction of an academic, and offering helpful, intelligent comments on the lectures themselves.

ABBREVIATIONS

LR	*Love and Responsibility*
AR	*Amor y Responsabilidad*
OC	*Osoba i czyn*
AP	*The Acting Person*
PA	*Persona y Acción*
PA (1982)	*Persona y Acción, ed. 1982*
PEA	*Persona e Atto*

KAROL WOJTYŁA'S
PERSONALIST PHILOSOPHY

INTRODUCTION

How can we say that we are fully alive if we do not even know ourselves well? Can anyone say that he thoroughly knows himself? The discovery of our personal identity is one of the most difficult tasks that we have, and we cannot escape it if we desire to live to the fullest. What is the "full life" if not the continual discovery of the meaning of our existence and its completeness? This is the heart of the question John Paul II addressed in his encyclical on faith and reason.

The admonition *Know yourself* was carved on the temple portal at Delphi, as testimony to a basic truth that must be adopted as a minimal norm by those who seek to set themselves apart from the rest of creation as "human beings," that is, as those who "know themselves."[1]

Socrates, the paradigmatic philosopher, exhorted his fellow Athenians: "The unexamined life is not worth living."[2]

Why do we need to know ourselves interiorly? In reality we always know "something" of the interior, but it is often a superficial knowledge. There is much more to seek in order to find our own identity. But we must learn to do this if we want to take advantage of that which we call "life." This is the object of philosophical anthropology, not only to know "what" we are but especially to know "who"

---

1. John Paul II, *Encyclical Fides et Ratio* (Vatican City: Librería Editrice Vaticana, 1998), no. 1 (henceforth *Fides et Ratio*).

2. Plato, *Apology of Socrates* 38a, from *The Collected Dialogues*, ed. Edith Hamilton and Huntington Cairns (Princeton, N.J.: Princeton University Press, 1980).

we are. It is a part of philosophy that intends to assemble the puzzle of every human being from the pieces provided by experience, science, and even faith. But let us not be deceived. There is not a closed answer. Life is not a problem to be solved and then put on the shelf. It is a mystery which opens up more and more in the measure that we live.

Karol Wojtyła—poet, philosopher, theologian—was one of those persons who sought the keys to these questions. He was a humanist deeply concerned with the secret of the human heart. A witness to the greatest genocide in recorded history, which occurred just a few miles from his home, he also served as a Catholic priest under an oppressive and avowedly atheistic Communist regime. As pope he was shot and badly wounded by a self-proclaimed Muslim assassin. Personally he faced the mystery of human evil and its consequences. How can persons do such evils? Why? What is the solution?

"The most tragic experience of our century, with the cruelties of "total" war, the extermination of tens of millions of people, the frightful experiments in the death camps, the programs of genocide, the explosion of the first atomic bomb. . . . People must have understood after this tragedy that at the centre of the danger which threatens us there stands first of all man himself. People must have also understood that the renewal of the nations and of the whole human family must be based on man in all his truth and dignity."[3]

The better to understand the human being and himself, Karol Wojtyła sought reasons in a philosophy illumined and supported by Christian faith. For Wojtyła, philosophy was to be an instrument, not an end in itself. He was not particularly concerned (as is common enough in much of our contemporary academic scene) with solving the puzzles posed in the premier journals. His scholarship was always focused on the question of the human being, on the nature and reality of the person. In this work we will speak of the road

3. André Frossard, *"Be Not Afraid": Pope John Paul II Speaks Out on His Life, His Beliefs, and His Inspiring Vision for Humanity*, trans. J. R. Foster (New York: St. Martin's Press, 1984), 208.

that he took, the characteristics of his philosophy, and his principal anthropological conclusions.

As John Paul II, he gave himself entirely to his task as pastor, including toward persons who did not belong to the Catholic Church. His attitude was not only peaceful but reconciliatory. We have the example of Mehmet Ali Agca, the man who attempted to assassinate him and whom he forgave publicly. In the name of the Church he also asked pardon of Galileo Galilei. One could tell thousands of anecdotes and details that show the exceptional personality of John Paul II. He led the faithful of the Catholic Church toward the new twenty-first century and implemented the ecclesial reforms proposed by the Second Vatican Council. His moral influence contributed, for example, to the overthrow of the Communist regimes in Europe,[4] especially in his native Poland. Objectively speaking, no one who has known his work can deny the worldwide influence that this man has had in contemporary history.

His papacy was the third longest in history, and during it many administrative and pastoral innovations were effected: The new *Catechism of the Catholic Church* was published, and a revised code of canon law put into effect. Various episcopal synods were held, as well as plenary meetings of the college of cardinals. He wrote fourteen encyclicals, fourteen apostolic exhortations, forty-two apostolic letters, eleven apostolic constitutions, and twenty-eight *motu proprio* (documents on questions of governance of the Church). He proclaimed 482 new saints and 1,330 new beatifications. Toward the end of the 1990s he began to show symptoms of Parkinson's disease, which became especially noticeable in 1999. He struggled with this illness until the end of his life in 2005. We can say that he amply fulfilled the mission that the Polish primate, Cardinal Wyszyński, announced to the newly elected pope in 1978: God had chosen him to lead the Church into the third millennium. In 2011 he was pro-

---

4. Concerning this, see George Weigel, *The Final Revolution: The Resistance Church and the Collapse of Communism* (New York: Oxford University Press, 1992).

claimed "Blessed" by his successor, Benedict XVI, after the verification of his charity and heroic virtues and the confirmation of a miracle by the Congregation for the Causes of the Saints, and, with the confirmation of a second miracle, he was canonized by Pope Francis in 2014.

This work aims to present the principal aspects of the philosophical thought of Karol Wojtyła/John Paul II. If one can speak of the "personalist philosophy of Karol Wojtyła," in what does this philosophy consist? What is the nucleus of his thought? To what extent is it relevant to our conception of the human being? These are some of the question that we wish to answer.

The authors of this work met in 2010, when Miguel Acosta undertook a research residency in the department of philosophy at the University of Notre Dame. There he observed Adrian Reimers's classes in philosophy of human nature, which included a study of Karol Wojtyła's *Love and Responsibility*. The remarkable fact about this book in the undergraduate setting is that Wojtyła's reflections concerning love and sexuality were of great interest to the young university students, who were surprised to discover its transcendental dimensions. As a matter of course, they had come to accept many taboos and clichés about sex and love, misinterpreting the meaning of human love and its relationship with sex. *Love and Responsibility* introduced a different dimension and at the same time one full of meaning to help them to reflect in a new way.

This is what is found in Wojtyła's philosophy: a different panorama, a point of view that makes one think in a different way with sometimes surprising and sometimes enlightening insights and nuances, never closed but always open to the truth. Rather than thinking from a single system, his philosophy seeks to dialog with experience and intends to recover that which is true in different philosophical currents and systems. However it is by no means a kind of eclecticism. His principles are clear and always rooted in the *philosophia perennis*, developed in a contemporary way.

Adrian Reimers is a specialist in the philosophical work of Karol Wojtyła. He has many publications, and in 2011 he received a Fulbright research fellowship to Poland, to the sites where Karol Wojtyła lived and worked prior to his election as John Paul II. During that stay in Europe, Miguel Acosta invited him to give a seminar on central aspects of the philosophy of Karol Wojtyła/John Paul II at the Universidad CEU San Pablo in Madrid. Given the interest of the participants, we thought it fitting to publish the three lectures of this seminar together with a more systematic introductory study. The result is this present work.

Purpose of the Work

This book is meant to spread the principal ideas of Karol Wojtyła's philosophy, enabling the reader to understand its characteristics and purpose and perhaps be inspired to undertake research and teaching about the philosophy.

This book comprises three parts: first, Miguel Acosta's introduction to Karol Wojtyła the philosopher; second, Adrian J. Reimers's three loosely connected essays on Wojtyła's personalism; and third, Miguel Acosta's *overview* of Wojtyła's key concepts and arguments, especially as developed in his main philosophical work *Osoba i czyn*.

The essay in chapter 3 on experience and knowledge may facilitate the understanding of the philosophical arguments discussed in part 3, in particular, Wojtyła's rejection of the reduction of knowledge to sense-experience or to the contents of consciousness. The argument from *Osoba i czyn* is related to that in the opening chapters of *Love and Responsibility*.[5]

To speak of *knowledge of the person* is a curious matter. Classically, knowledge is of universals, and the singular as such is not knowable. However, anyone who has been in love can testify to the joy of coming to know another person. When we know someone, what is

5. Karol Wojtyła, *Osoba i czyn: oraz inne studia antropologiczne* [Person and Act: and other anthropological studies] (Lublin: Towarzystwo Naukowe KUL, 2000); and *Love and Responsibility*, trans. H. T. Willetts (San Francisco, Calif.: Ignatius Press, 1993).

it we know? The essay in chapter 4 addresses this question primarily from the perspective of a work, *Man and Woman He Created Them*,[6] which Karol Wojtyła wrote in the 1970s but did not publish until after his election to the papacy, when he presented it in the famous Theology of the Body series of audiences.[7]

Chapter 5, the essay on *nihilism*, analyzes themes that John Paul II developed in his encyclical *Fides et Ratio*, particularly concerning the corrosive effects of scientism in relation to ethical utilitarianism and the denial of any true meaning to human life. This essay is arguably more theological than philosophical, drawing as it does on John Paul II's Christocentrism.

In chapter 6, Miguel Acosta begins part 3 by offering a general and synthetic overview of Wojytła's philosophical history and the trajectory of his thought, situating him within the Polish academic context and the broader context of Catholic thought. Acosta's intention is to show the close relationship of Wojtyła's life and thought. To facilitate philosophical study, he offers an explanation of Wojtyła's methodology, followed by a basic introduction to his anthropology.

Finally, Acosta develops the principal themes of Wojtyła's philosophical anthropology in the same sequence as they appear in *Osoba i czyn*.[8] Chapters 8 through 11—"Consciousness and Operativity," "Transcendence," "Integration," and "Participation"—focus on Wojytła's realist engagement with contemporary thought in this reflection on the human person.

The conception based on traditional metaphysics and realist

6. John Paul II, *Man and Woman He Created Them: A Theology of the Body*, trans. Michael Waldstein (Boston, Mass.: Pauline Books & Media, 2006).

7. On the history of this book and its use in John Paul II's general audiences, see Michael M. Waldstein, introduction to *Man and Woman* by John Paul II, 3–11. See also Cezary Ritter, afterword [in Polish] to *Mężczyzną i niewiastą stworzył ich: Odkupienie ciała a sakramentalność małżeństwa* [Man and woman he created them: The redemption of the body and the sacramentality of marriage], by Karol Wojtyła, 399–400 (Lublin: KUL, 2008).

8. The authors have chosen not to use *The Acting Person*, the English translation of Wojtyła's main philosophical work, *Osoba i czyn* [*Person and Act*]. See the end of this introduction for the sources we do use and an explanation of our reasons for this choice.

phenomenology is seen from the first moment of his analysis of *consciousness and operativity* (the free human act). These two concepts work together, revealing the importance of personal human experience and deepening the essential characteristics of our nature. This pair of concepts yields the necessary link for an epistemological focus and for ethics, for the purpose of understanding why morality is a direct consequence of the conscious human act.

Transcendence follows logically upon the foregoing. Experiencing the attraction of values in the world, the person is induced to action, to transcend his inner world toward his environment to engage with things around him ("horizontal transcendence"). However, because he is capable of knowing truth, he can also transcend his natural tendencies and direct himself toward truth, by which he can judge the values that attract him. This is "vertical transcendence," and it lies at the root of human freedom. By this transcendence the person directs himself to what really perfects him.

The section on *Integration* addresses a neuralgia that has plagued modern philosophy since Descartes and Hume: the relationship of consciousness with our physical nature, the so-called mind-body problem. Interestingly, Karol Wojtyła does not address the problem in those terms, which, despite Gilbert Ryle's warnings about "category mistakes,"[9] continue to frame the discussion; there is a body and somehow the mind affects it (or does not). Wojtyła, to avoid falling into dualist reductionism, chooses to move instead on the level of the person's experience of his bodiliness—its instincts, drives, emotions, excitabilities, and so on—as he exercises his efficient causality (operativity) in the world.

In the analysis of *Participation* lie some of the historically most important conceptions in Wojtyła's thought. Here the Polish pastor and thinker develops an analysis that would guide his actions as archbishop of Kraków under Communism and later his expansion and development of the Catholic Church's social teaching through

---

9. Gilbert Ryle, *The Concept of Mind* (New York: Barnes & Noble, 1949), 18ff.

his social encyclicals. In this post-Enlightenment era of the autonomous individual, Wojtyła defended the notion that the life of the person is a life with others, a participation in their life.

The scope of Wojtyła's philosophy is not limited to the Catholic or Christian sphere. Like any philosophy, it intends to be universal. The only requirement that Wojtyła makes is the reasonability of arguments based on reality. His principal goal is a profound knowledge of the human person. His anthropology is neither essentialist nor existentialist but combines both in a personalism based on a realist metaphysics and phenomenology.

It is uncertain whether Wojtyła's philosophy would have developed as it did, had it not been for the universal status that Karol Wojtyła received as John Paul II. Certainly the simple fact that his work was done in the Polish language prevented it from being widely known. However, beginning in 1978—and as we will see, even before—his philosophy was incorporated into hundreds of magisterial documents of the Catholic Church and thus it has a worldwide influence. The teachings of the pope are imbued with Wojtyła's philosophical concepts. This philosophy has spread throughout the world and is being developed in institutes, research centers, and universities, where year after year the number of publications and doctoral theses grows.

Comments on the Sources

The scholar seeking to address Karol Wojtyła's philosophical thought must address himself to his subject's longest and most fundamental philosophical work: *Osoba i czyn* (*Person and Act*), which Wojtyła published in Poland in 1969. It was subsequently translated and published in German, French, Italian, Spanish, and English. The English translation, *The Acting Person*, was published in 1979 as volume 10 of the series *Analecta Husserliana*, with the notation on the copyright page "Translated and revised from the 1969 Polish edition *Osoba i czyn*. This definitive text of the work established in collaboration with the author by Anna-Teresa Tymieniecka. Translated and revised from the 1969 Polish edition, *Osoba i czyn*."[10] The implicit claim here is that *Osoba i czyn* is a kind of preliminary edition to what subsequently appeared as a collaboration between Wojtyła and Dr. Tymieniecka. The Polish original is twice referred to as the "Polish edition." As others have noted, *The Acting Person* unfortunately does not faithfully or accurately render the thought of Karol Wojtyła;[11] English-speaking scholars and students, at least at the graduate level of studies, should probably avoid using this translation. For the sake of clarity and precision, we shall in this volume refer to Wojtyła's book as *Person and Act*.

Fortunately, in this undertaking we have been able to avail ourselves of the growing expertise in Wojtyła's philosophy, and together we have taken time to analyze the most contentious and elusive points of his anthropology. As we plunged into this work, we have had to deal with some confusing concepts from the languages of the translations. This arises especially from subtleties in the original Polish that may not admit of exact rendering in the Western languages. We have had access to an excellent Italian translation, *Persona e atto* by Giuseppe Girgenti and Patrycja Mikulska,[12] as well as the original, *Osoba i czyn*, which we used for the most serious checking of vocabulary and key concepts. During the course of writing this book, our work was greatly simplified by the appearance of a new Spanish translation, *Persona y acción*, translated from the Pol-

10. Karol Wojtyła, *The Acting Person*, ed. Anna-Teresa Tymieniecka, trans. Andrzej Potocki (Boston, Mass.: D. Reidel, 1979).

11. See Rocco Buttiglione, *Karol Wojtyła: The Thought of the Man Who Became Pope John Paul II*, trans. Paolo Guietti and Francesca Murphy (Grand Rapids, Mich.: Eerdmans, 1997), 117; Kenneth Schmitz, *At the Center of the Human Drama: The Philosophical Anthropology of Karol Wojtyła/Pope John Paul II* (Washington, D.C.: The Catholic University of America Press, 1993), 58–61; and Hans Köchler, "Karol Wojtyła's Notion of the Irreducible in Man and the Quest for a Just World Order," in *Karol Wojtyła's Philosophical Legacy*, ed. Nancy Mardas Billias, Agnes B. Curry, and George F. McLean (Washington D.C.: The Council for Research in Values and Philosophy, 2008), 171–72.

12. Karol Wojtyła, *Metafisica della persona: Tutti le opera filosofiche e saggi integrative* [Metaphysics of the person: The complete philosophical works and complementary essays], ed. Giovanni Reale, 3rd ed. (Milan: Bompiani, 2005).

ish by Rafael Mora.[13] Where necessary, we have adapted the Spanish by directly comparing it with the Polish original. Unless otherwise stated, citations are translated into English principally from this Spanish edition, but in comparison with other sources, especially the Italian, *Persona e atto*, and the Polish original. The principal reference is ordinarily the Spanish version from 2011.

13. Karol Wojtyła, *Persona y acción*, ed. Juan Manuel Burgos and Rafael Mora, trans. Rafael Mora (Madrid: Ediciones Palabra, 2011).

PART I

KAROL WOJTYŁA, PHILOSOPHER

MIGUEL ACOSTA

I &

WOJTYŁA'S PHILOSOPHICAL DEVELOPMENT

In this chapter, I will focus on showing some landmarks pertaining to Karol Wojtyła/John Paul II's philosophical development.[1] I do not pause to analyze his characteristics as poet, dramatist, or theologian, although it would be more precise to show how all these stand in strong relationship with his philosophical writings, because Wojtyła maintained great coherence and vital unity in all his work. Literature was a fine ally to his phenomenology as he perfected an existential anthropological description or account, and theology was present throughout his entire life as priest, bishop, and supreme pontiff, illuminating his philosophical intuitions.

As we know from his biography, Karol Wojtyła's many personal qualities developed throughout a life that was not exempt from suffering and persecution. He had a passionate temperament and was gifted with high intelligence; he was a good athlete and enjoyed a facility for languages. His physical strength helped him to endure intensive days of work, especially in his voyages as pope. From his infancy, such tragic events as the deaths of his parents (in 1929 and 1941) and his brother (in 1932), which left him without a family, as

---

1. For further penetration into the philosophical thought of Karol Wojtyła/John Paul II, we suggest Rocco Buttiglione, *Karol Wojtyła: The Thought*. We also recommend for contrast and comparison: Peter L. P. Simpson, *On Karol Wojtyła* (Belmont, Calif.: Wadsworth, 2001).

well as the massacre and occupation that Poland experienced during World War II, revealed to him one of the most mysterious aspects of being human: the meaning of suffering. Instead of shrinking into insipidity and falling prisoner to a bitter and hopeless view of existence, he came to rely on God and to recognize that, in some strange way, suffering forms part of life and love. "Suffering seems to belong to man's transcendence: it is one of those points in which man is in a certain sense 'destined' to go beyond himself, and he is called to this in a mysterious way."[2]

In his own case, the manifestation of love was not toward a unique and exclusive person but, by his priestly vocation, toward his spiritual children. His genuine concern for people, and his facility in getting along with them, enabled him to win the confidence of those who surrounded him. His concern for them was genuine, because he knew how to love them. In everything he was a joyous, happy person and at the same time a profound one. He knew how to unite the intellectual realm with practical action. His principal focus was his pastoral ministry, but he never left aside the intellectual search for the truth in his pursuit of the Truth with a capital "T" (God).[3] That is, he combined the way of natural reason (philosophy) with that of the supernatural (mysticism and theology).

In his introductory essay to the book by Karol Wojtyła, *Metafisica della persona*,[4] Giovanni Reale says that the human being approaches the truth along three ways: art, philosophy, and religion, and this through the poetic intuition, reason, and faith, respectively. He argues that the first philosopher to undertake this triad was Plato. He then proceeds to analyze these three paths of Karol Wojtyła, showing how he formed his search for truth by following these roads. In-

2. John Paul II, *Apostolic Letter Salvifici Doloris* (Vatican City: Librería Editrice Vaticana, 1984), no. 2 (henceforth: *Salvifici Doloris*).

3. See Adrian J. Reimers, "Karol Wojtyła's Aims and Methodology," in *Christian Wisdom Meets Modernity*, ed. Kenneth Oakes (London, New York: Bloomsbury Academic Press, forthcoming).

4. See Giovanni Reale, "Introductory essay" to *Metafisica della persona: Tutti le opera filosofiche e saggi integrative*, by Karol Wojtyła, (Milan: Bompiani, 2005), xii.

deed, Wojtyła's intellectual trajectory encompasses those realms of knowledge; we, though, will center our attention on the philosophical way. And to begin, it is appropriate to emphasize a distinctive characteristic that Jarosław Merecki brings out in a study concerning the sources of Karol Wojtyła's philosophy. Merecki states: "To me it seems just to say that his primordial source is not the thought of one or another philosopher, but rather the very experience of man."[5]

So it is that we find ourselves before a man who knew how to integrate different forms of expression of the human spirit into a unity and, at the same time, maintain a close relationship with his contemporaries through sincere friendship. His closeness and openness were manifest in his manner of listening attentively and respectfully, allowing others to be able to express their ideas in freedom and without any compulsion by his rank or position, even if he did not agree with them.[6] This manner of being influenced his manner of philosophizing. We are not faced with an intellectualist elaborating theories about man, the world, and God far from mundane concerns, nor with a mystic or poet who appears miserable from his brilliant intuitions, which distance him from ordinary matters. We are dealing with a man who has seen human miseries and glories and who, in order to understand himself and others better, desires to compose a philosophical explanation that begins with man himself.

In order to unite tradition and the present day, Wojtyła establishes a new method, one that forges a union between the wisdom of the *philosophia perennis* and actual contemporary currents. He himself says that he seeks to give an account of human action that starts

5. Jarosław Merecki, "Las fuentes de la filosofía de Karol Wojtyla," in *La filosofía personalista de Karol Wojtyla* [The personalist philosophy of Karol Wojtyła], ed. Juan Manuel Burgos (Madrid: Palabra, 2007), 14. Merecki has studied and treated of the direct disciples and friends of Karol Wojtyła—Professors Tadeusz Styczeń, Andrzej Szostek, Stanisław Grygiel, and Rocco Buttiglione.

6. In his biography of John Paul II, George Weigel illustrates this explicitly by telling of the 1970 debate about Wojtyła's (at the time) recent book, *Osoba i czyn*, among members of the faculty of philosophy of the Catholic University of Lublin (KUL). See George Weigel, *Witness to Hope: The Biography of Pope John Paul II* (New York: Harper Collins, 1999), 213, 883n90.

from an ethics based on Scholastic metaphysics and realist phenomenology. This union gives rise to his own style of personalism.

So there were two stages to my intellectual journey: In the first I moved from literature to metaphysics, while the second led me from metaphysics to phenomenology.... [I]n my reading and in my studies I always tried to achieve a harmony between faith, reason, and the heart. These are not separate areas, but are profoundly interconnected, each giving life to the other. This coming together of faith, reason, and the heart is strongly influenced by our sense of wonder at the miracle of the human person—at man's likeness to the Triune God, at the immensely profound bond between love and truth, at the mystery of mutual self-giving and the life that it generates.[7]

Like the philosophy of Thomas Aquinas, Wojtyła's philosophy is open to theology, and in some points the faith illuminates his philosophical conceptions. Therefore he acknowledges that faith has cognitive value, albeit of different form than philosophical discourse. It is a matter of a supra-rational, but not an irrational, realm. Indeed, from its beginnings philosophy has been served by religious or mystical contributions, and by those of faith, and has tried to understand them rationally. This happened with Plato, with Augustine of Hippo, with Kierkegaard; this also happened with Wojtyła, who proposes a Christian philosophy.[8] For this reason, we see a natural dialogue and compenetration between philosophical anthropology and the theological, which is clear from his early writings for

---

7. John Paul II, *Rise, Let Us Be on Our Way*, trans. Walter Zięmba (New York: Warner Books, 2004), 95, 97.

8. Concerning Christian philosophy, John Paul II writes: "In itself, the term is valid, but it should not be misunderstood: it in no way intends to suggest that there is an official philosophy of the Church, since the faith as such is not a philosophy. The term seeks rather to indicate a Christian way of philosophizing, a philosophical speculation conceived in dynamic union with faith. It does not therefore refer simply to a philosophy developed by Christian philosophers who have striven in their research not to contradict the faith. The term Christian philosophy includes those important developments of philosophical thinking which would not have happened without the direct or indirect contribution of Christian faith." *Fides et Ratio*, no. 76. For a reflection on the faith-reason relationship and Christian philosophy in Karol Wojtyła, see Reale's "Introductory essay," in Wojtyła's *Metafisica della persona*, xxviii–xxxviii.

both scholarly and ecclesiastical audiences.[9] We can note this especially from the moment that Wojtyła became John Paul II, Bishop of Rome and Pontiff of the Catholic Church, even though from this time onward, his production is above all theological and pastoral. Underlying these writings are always the principles that he had been developing from his earliest philosophical works. For example, we can observe this concordance in the general audiences now called the "Theology of the Body,"[10] which are reflections on theological anthropology and which harmonize fully with what he developed in his more strictly philosophical work *Love and Responsibility*.

However, just as we cannot speak of a total "separation" of ways of knowing—philosophical and theological—neither can we speak of a confused mixture of concepts and arguments. In his philosophical writings he does not ordinarily make explicit reference to texts from sacred Scripture, the Church's Magisterium, or the Catholic tradition, nor does he try to justify his arguments on their basis, although he will sometimes use an example or otherwise indicate some connection with an aspect of the faith or religious culture. He does this however, by way of emphasis or illustration, not as the basis for his philosophical argument. He distinguishes the two academic disciplines—philosophy and theology—and respects the epistemological status of each of these areas of knowledge. There exists a unity of thought and a coherent search whose final goal is to find the truth about the human being.[11]

9. See, for instance, his lectures on ethics presented at the Catholic University of Lublin in the mid-1950s: Karol Wojtyła, *Wykłady Lubelskie* [Lublin lectures] (Lublin: KUL, 2006); see as well the series of articles published in the weekly *Tygodnik powszechny*. Also see Karol Wojtyła, *Elementarz etyczny* [Elements of ethics], in *Aby Chrystus się nami posługiwał* [So that Christ will use us] (Kraków: Wydawnictwo Znak, 2009), 139–89.

10. The audiences on this theme were presented in the years 1979 to 1984. See John Paul II, *Man and Woman*. See also Emmanuel Buch Camí, Pilar Ferrer, and Ildefonso Murillo, *Personalismo teológico. Brunner, Wojtyła, von Balthasar* [Theological personalism. Brunner, Wojtyła, von Balthasar] (Madrid: Fundación Emmanuel Mounier, 2007), 106ff.

11. John Paul II explicitly develops the relationship between philosophy and theology in the encyclical *Fides et Ratio*.

Massimo Serretti[12] suggests a reading of Karol Wojtyła's philosophical thought, beginning with his principal publications, that has been generally accepted by various specialists: (1) those publications dating from the 1950s until 1970 include his first essays in moral philosophy and ethics, writings developed while he was professor at the Catholic University of Lublin (1954–58), his habilitation thesis on Max Scheler (1959), and the volume *Love and Responsibility* (1960), and then those writings whose attention centers on contemporarily influential ethical systems, writings whose emphasis is on Kant and Scheler; (2) this period is marked by the publication of *Osoba i czyn* [*Person and Act*], an eminently anthropological publication which proposes to be the standard of a "new ethics of a personalist cut";[13] (3) the final period includes those works after the publication of *Person and Act*, which complement some anthropological themes and intend to reflect on other aspects that are not found in that work—intersubjectivity-subjectivity, sociability, fatherhood, and the personal subject, among others.

What results is a good stimulus for the student of philosophy to know that for the future Pope John Paul II it took a great effort to enter into metaphysics in his youth, but that eventually his constancy made it worth the pain:

At the beginning it was a great obstacle. My literary formation, centered on the humane sciences, did not prepare me at all for the theses and Scholastic formulas that the manual [of metaphysics] proposed to me from the first to the last page. I had to open a road through a dense forest of concepts, analyses, and axioms, without even being able to identify the terrain that I was treading on. After two months of clearing the underbrush, the light broke through and I discovered the profound reasons for that which I had not yet experienced or intuited. When I passed the

12. See Massimo Serretti, "Invitation to Read" to *Perché l'uomo. Scritti inediti di antropologia e filosofia* [Why man. Unpublished writings of anthropology and philosophy], by Karol Wojtyła, 5–10 (Vatican City: Libreria Editrice Vaticana, 1995). In the next synthesis I especially follow Pilar Ferrer, introduction to *Mi visión del hombre. Hacia una nueva ética* [My vision of man: Toward a new ethics], by Karol Wojtyła, trans. Pilar Ferrer (Madrid: Ediciones Palabra, 2003), 8ff.

13. Ferrer, introduction to *Mi visión*, 9.

examination, I said to the examiner that, in my judgment, the new vision of the world which I had won in that hand-to-hand combat with my metaphysics manual was more precious than the grade I received. And I was not exaggerating. That which intuition and sensibility had taught me up to then about the world, had remained solidly corroborated.[14]

As was indicated earlier, what Karol Wojtyła always sought in philosophy was the understanding and rational corroboration of the vital proposals of human existence, so that he might better understand the distinct dimensions of the person. And this can be seen from his earliest publications; at the center of his philosophical thought were anthropology and ethics.[15]

He completed his formation in Thomistic philosophy in the Pontifical University of St. Thomas Aquinas (Rome's *Angelicum*), where he defended his doctoral thesis in theology, "The Doctrine of Faith according to St. John of the Cross," which was directed by Fr. Reginald Garrigou-Lagrange, OP. This work "allowed him to deepen his habits of interiority, gave him a knowledge of the depths of the human being, fostered an interest that he would never lose in the question of consciousness in the face of the truth, and also gave him an introspective method for studying the human spirit."[16] In his thesis there arose a point of difference between him and his direc-

14. Frossard, *Be Not Afraid*, 15–16. The text referred to was that of Professor Kazimierz Wais. Kazimierz Wais (1865–1934) studied in Innsbruck, Rome, Freiburg, Louvain, Fulda, and Breslau under C. Gutberlet and Cardinal Mercier. The book with which Karol Wojtyła was initiated into philosophy was Kazimierz Wais, *Ontologija czyli Metafizyca ogólna* [Ontology or universal metaphysics] (Lwów: Bibljoteka Religijna, 1926). See Rodrigo Guerra López, "El aporte filosófico de Juan Pablo II. Homenaje al Papa en el XXV aniversario de su pontificado" [The philosophical contribution of John Paul II. Tribute to the Pope at the XXV anniversary of his pontificate], *Boletín CELAM*, no. 302 (2003): 8n6.

15. See, for example, Karol Wojtyła, "In Search of the Basis of Perfectionism in Ethics," in *Person and Community: Selected Essays*, trans. Teresa Sandok (New York: Peter Lang, 1993), 45–56; Karol Wojtyła, "The Problem of the Will in the Analysis of the Ethical Act," in *Person and Community*, 3–22, as well as other essays that are cited in our bibliography.

16. Juan Luis Lorda, *Antropología. Del Concilio Vaticano II a Juan Pablo II* [Anthropology. From Vatican II to John Paul II] (Madrid: Palabra, 1996), 98–99 (passage here translated by Adrian Reimers).

tor, since he refused to use the term "object" in reference to God;[17] it seems that his treatment introduced an innovation with respect to theological form and language. He maintained that one cannot "objectivize" the knowledge of God. In effect, he was maintaining that reason can arrive at the existence of God but cannot know the attributes of God from faith; for this there is needed a personal encounter with him, that is to say, to know him as one knows another person.[18] Apparently, it is here where we begin to perceive that, although they offer a valuable method for an objective approach to the faith, the metaphysical categories of Aristotelian-Thomistic philosophy do not prove adequate for the "subjective" approach to the experience of faith[19]—and furthermore, not only with respect to faith but with respect to the interior world of every human being.

When he returned to Poland, after defending his dissertation, he was assigned to parochial duties as parish assistant in Niegowic, a town twenty-five kilometers from Kraków. In 1951, at the insistence of Cardinal Sapieha,[20] he was granted a two-year sabbatical and was asked to continue his studies for a university teaching position. In this time he began preparing his habilitation thesis—a requisite to pursue an academic career in Poland—and, motivated by the search for a philosophy that would permit a better approach to the interiority and experience of the person, he began to study the phenomenology of Max Scheler.

It is appropriate to indicate the great influence of Roman Ingarden, disciple of Edmund Husserl, in the Polish intellectual world during those years and specifically among Wojtyła's colleagues in the Catholic University of Lublin. Phenomenology was firmly spreading in Europe among intellectuals in a way outlined in different currents: Husserl (transcendental phenomenology), Heidegger (hermeneutic phenomenology), Scheler and Ingarden (realist phe-

17. See Buttiglione, *Karol Wojtyła: The Thought*, 35n7.
18. See Weigel, *Witness to Hope*, 86.
19. Merecki, "Las fuentes," 16.
20. See Buttiglione, *Karol Wojtyła: The Thought*, 36.

nomenology), etc. The phenomenology of Ingarden differed in several fundamental theses with respect to his teacher Husserl. Whereas Husserl placed the epistemological status of the phenomenological *epoché* on the subjective plane as a product of consciousness, and thus fell into transcendental idealism, Ingarden, and other phenomenologists such as Scheler, admitted a basis in ontological realism. Karol Wojtyła would follow this latter realist line.[21]

In 1954 he was granted his habilitation with his thesis "Evaluation of the Possibility of Constructing a Christian Ethics on the Basis of Max Scheler's System," which was not published until 1959. Although he disagreed with some of Scheler's theses, phenomenology appeared to him to provide rich resources for undertaking a new anthropology.[22] In the autumn of 1954 Wojtyła was presented as professor at the Catholic University of Lublin (KUL), and he joined a group of lecturers[23] who intended to realize a program of perfecting the methodology of Thomas Aquinas's philosophy, especially his

21. See Wojtyła, *Mi visión*, 120. Later, in part 3 of this book, we will see that from a "synthesis" between the philosophy of being (Aristotle, Thomas Aquinas) and the philosophy of consciousness (Scheler) arises Wojtyła's philosophical method.

22. Wojtyła's thesis, published in Spanish as *Max Scheler y la ética cristiana* [Max Scheler and Christian Ethics], trans. Gonzalo Haya (Madrid: BAC, 1982), was originally entitled *Ocena możliwości zbudowanie etyki chrześcijańskiej: przy założeniach systemu Maksa Schelera* [Evaluation of the possibility of constructing a Christian ethics on the basis of Max Scheler's system] (Vatican City: Librería Editrice Vaticana, 1980). In the conclusions of this work are synthesized two of the author's principal disagreements with Max Scheler. In general terms, the first has to do with the impossibility, owing to the phenomenological method, of attaining to ethical values in an objective way, and the second with the total closing in Scheler's system of the role of conscience in the person's moral life (see Wojtyła, *Max Scheler*, 206–14). He also recognizes that Scheler's work can serve as an aid for the scientific study of Christian ethics (see ibid., 214–19), and says that "to the investigations of Max Scheler's ethical system there is certainly owed the merit of having called attention to the undisputed role of phenomenological experience in ethical values." Ibid., 218 (trans. Adrian Reimers).

23. This group included J. Kalinowski (dean of the faculty of philosophy, specialist in logic and the philosophy of law), S. Swieżawski (historian of philosophy and exponent of Maritain's existential Thomism), M. A. Krąpiec (Dominican specialist in metaphysics), K. Wojtyła (specialist in ethics), M. Kurdziałek (specialist in ancient philosophy), S. Kamiński (specialist in epistemology or the theory of knowledge). See Weigel, *Witness to Hope*, 135.

ethics, based on the idea of the ultimate end of man.[24] They reflected that to confront Marxism it was necessary to deepen humanism more completely. Wojtyła was very interested in the KUL project and slowly he came to realize that a methodological modification would not suffice, but that it was necessary to develop new foundations for ethics.[25]

The KUL point of departure would be philosophical realism:

They began with an ancient conviction—they would be radically realistic about the world and about the human capacity to know it. If our thinking and choosing lacks a tether to reality, the KUL philosophers believed, raw force takes over the world and truth becomes a function of power, not an expression of things-as-they-are.[26]

The three central themes upon which they would focus were *metaphysics*, to explain the foundations of reality; *anthropology*, to ask about the nature and destiny of human beings; and *ethics*, to know the appropriate way to act.

This group, the "Lublin school of ethics," constituted an authentic philosophical "community." Its members were friends both personally and professionally and came to form a true "team." Logically, they had discussions and at times different points of view, especially when one of them, Wojtyła among others, presented some more adventurous proposal that went beyond the canons of the tradition, but without pausing long enough to provide a sufficient critical foundation with citations or different cross-references.[27] Not only did these open and very human discussions provide a new and adequate framework for conceiving ethics, but they also presented material to develop with the students in the lecture halls. Professor Wojtyła very much involved his students, with whom he held frequent debates and whom he encouraged to deepen their arguments. His doctoral students became a great support in his research, above

---

24. Tadeusz Styczeń, "Introduction" [in Spanish] to *Mi visión*, 117ff.
25. Later this group would come to call itself "The Lublin school of ethics."
26. Weigel, *Witness to Hope*, 133.
27. Ibid., 135.

all when his pastoral duties did not allow him time to keep up to date with the technical publications that were coming out. His relationship with his students was that of friends, although there was always a respectful distance from the mentor.

In 1957, the professor went on vacation with philosophy, psychology, and medical students in the Mazurian Lakes country of northeastern Poland. There he discussed with them the draft of a book he was writing on sexual and marital ethics, which, like his monographic lectures for the next two years, would be called *Love and Responsibility....* According to Wojtyła's student and friend Jerzy Gałkowski, Wojtyła was not only interested in his students' judgment on the book's theoretical soundness, but also wanted to know if what he had written made sense to them practically and humanly.[28]

During those years, around 1956, through Stefan Swieżawski,[29] he came into contact with the work of the philosophical Thomist Jacques Maritain, one of the representatives of the personalism that had begun to arise in the 1930s.[30] Maritain would contribute various ideas that further influenced the development of Wojtyła's personalist philosophy, including several propositions that Wojtyła presented during the Second Vatican Council, such as, for example, aspects of social ethics, human dignity, and democracy that were contained in Maritain's integral humanism.[31] In the encyclical *Fides et Ratio*, Maritain appears in the list of thinkers who have fruitfully entered into the dialogue of faith and reason.[32] Thus, besides scho-

28. Ibid., 139.
29. See Guerra, "El aporte filosófico," 8n7.
30. "Personalism is a philosophy that is fundamentally characterized by locating the person at the center of its reflection and its conceptual structure. It flows from several sources, but took precise form in France in the 1930s and later acquired notable importance throughout all Europe, influencing such relevant events as the UN's Declaration on human rights or those texts of the Vatican Council II which refer to the human being or to religious freedom." Juan Manuel Burgos, *El Personalismo* [Personalism] (Madrid: Palabra, 2000), 7–8 (trans. Adrian Reimers).
31. See Weigel, *Witness to Hope*, 139.
32. "Obviously other names could be cited: and in referring to these I intend not to endorse every aspect of their thought, but simply to offer significant examples of a process of philosophical enquiry which was enriched by engaging the data of faith. One thing is certain: attention to the spiritual journey of these masters can only give

lastic metaphysics and realist phenomenology, the third important influence on his philosophy would be personalism. Over the years, Karol Wojtyła/John Paul II also came to be considered a personalist philosopher.

In 1960 he published *Love and Responsibility*. According to Wojtyła, the book arose from the pastoral needs that led him to seek answers to a series of questions pertaining to the relationships of couples, to marriage and sexuality. The Communist government had encouraged a series of practices contrary to Christianity in the area of sexual morality, and this brought many young people, married couples, and parents to look for arguments and counsel that would help them to go against this current. As George Weigel states:

As payback for its 1956 concessions to the Church, the Gomułka regime instituted a permissive abortion law, a direct assault on classic Catholic morality. Youngsters on state-sponsored summer outings were encouraged to experiment with sex as another means to pry them away from the Church. The communist campaign against traditional family life had its own secondary effects on sexual morality, for the linkage the Church taught between marital love and procreation was broken if men and women came to think of children as problems to be solved rather than as gifts to be cherished. Communist materialism also contributed to a cultural climate in which sexuality became morally devalued.[33]

In his dealing with young people, Fr. Wojtyła saw that the theme arose naturally, because they were seeking for answers to legitimate questions about love, marriage, and sexuality. This theme could not be set aside, and he wanted to find a way to explain how love is an essential characteristic of the person, which is made manifest in the genuine act of giving to another person, and that incarnated human love includes sexuality. More than "to command or forbid [the task was] to justify, to interpret, and to explain."[34]

The generation of that time wanted explanations, not imposi-

---

greater momentum to both the search for truth and the effort to apply the results of that search to the service of humanity." *Fides et Ratio*, no. 74.

33. Weigel, *Witness to Hope*, 140–41.

34. LR, 16. See Weigel, *Witness to Hope*, 141.

tions. For this reason, Wojtyła's book begins with an anthropological analysis of two aspects that are inseparably linked in the personal realm: sex and love. Love brings with it an aspect of personal responsibility toward the other, as well as toward God. When that love is embodied and sexually manifest, there is encountered a very positive and at the same time responsible meaning of one person toward another. It is here where Wojtyła speaks of the "personalistic norm," a variation of Kant's second categorical imperative, which states that a person may never be treated as a means but only as an end in himself.[35] In its positive sense this norm reads: "The person is a good towards which the only proper and adequate attitude is love."[36] Applying this to the sexual aspect, it indicates that one is to love and not to use, and this happens only when two persons freely seek the best for each other, not the egoistic pleasure of just one.[37]

In developing this theme, Wojtyła employs his new philosophical methodology, making manifest some of the foundations and keys from Aristotelian-Thomistic philosophy and also the phenomenological approach that readily connects theory with experience. He distinguishes in the human being the aspect of his nature with its capacities to perceive the elements of the external world and to react to them spontaneously, as well also as his personal aspect, which renders him unique through his possession of an interior life, by which he is distinguished from every other species of animal and which also renders him unique within his own species.

Two years before the publication of *Love and Responsibility*, Karol Wojtyła was consecrated auxiliary bishop of the Archdiocese of Kraków and his pastoral duties were increased.[38] He continued to

35. Immanuel Kant, *Grounding of the Metaphysics of Morals* (Indianapolis, Ind.: Hackett Publishing, 1993), 429.

36. LR, 41; AR, 53.

37. A more complete explanation of this important topic will be found in chapter 3, "Experience and Knowledge."

38. "On July 4, 1958, he was appointed titular bishop of Ombi and auxiliary of Krakow by Pope Pius XII, and was consecrated September 28, 1958, in Wawel Cathedral, Krakow, by Archbishop Eugeniusz Baziak.

On January 13, 1964, he was appointed archbishop of Krakow by Pope Paul VI, who give classes in the university, but with less frequency. (Later, even as archbishop of Kraków, he did not lose contact with the KUL, and he presented seminars in ethics and held meetings with his colleagues.) In 1962 two decisive events occurred. Archbishop Eugeniusz Baziak died—although archbishop of Lwów, he was in fact the acting archbishop of Kraków—and Karol Wojtyła took his place as temporary administrator until January 13, 1964, when he was named his successor in office.

The Second Vatican Council began in October 1962 and ended in 1965. Karol Wojtyła participated in the preparations and took part in the four sessions, where he presented eight oral and fourteen written interventions.[39] In general, he intervened on subjects such as liturgy, revelation, social communication, the Church, ecumenism, religious freedom, the apostolate of the laity, the Church in the contemporary world, and the ministry and life of priests.[40] In the third session of the Council, Pope Paul VI named him Archbishop of Kraków and his interventions were intensified by his rank. "Above all he intervened in relation to Lumen Gentium, Gaudium et Spes, and Dignitatis Humanae. In those three documents one can hear his voice and his orientations had influence."[41]

With respect to Gaudium et Spes, he suggested the style that would be appropriate for that document, and in the name of the Polish bishops he even presented an alternative text worked out by a team of thinkers. For this he was later called to form part of the editorial commission for this Pastoral Constitution, among whose members were Gabriel-Marie Garrone, Yves Congar, Henri de Lubac, and Jean Daniélou. Concerning Dignitatis Humanae, the Declaration on Reli-

made him a cardinal June 26, 1967 with the title of S. Cesareo in Palatio of the order of deacons, later elevated pro illa vice to the order of priests." http://www.news.va/en/news/biography-of-pope-john-paul-ii

39. See Angelo Scola, "Gli interventi di Karol Wojtyła al Concilio Ecumenico Vaticano II. Esposizione ed interpretazione teologica," in Karol Wojtyła. Filosofo, Teologo, Poeta. [Karol Wojtyła. Philosopher, Theologian, Poet], ed. Rocco Buttiglione, Carlo Fedeli, and Angelo Scola (Vatican City: Librería Editrice Vaticana, 1984) , 290.

40. Ibid.

41. See Lorda, Antropología, 106.

gious Liberty, he had much to say because of what was happening at the time to the peoples of Eastern Europe under Communist persecution. Karol Wojtyła proposed to establish the very bases of his anthropological conception by emphasizing the strict relationship among human conscience, freedom, and truth.[42]

Religious freedom, [Wojtyła] began, touched the heart of the dialogue between the Church and the world, because religious freedom had to do with what the Church thought about the human person and the human condition. It was important, therefore, to understand freedom in all its complex richness, and not to reduce it to a neutral, indifferent faculty of choice. Freedom, the archbishop of Kraków argued, was freedom *for*, not simply freedom *against*. And what freedom was *for* was truth. It was only by living in the truth that the human person was set free.[43]

This freedom "for" shows that it is a matter of a freedom that goes beyond the mere capacity to choose as an act of the will; freedom is not an "end in itself" but is rather ordered to the good of the person. For this reason, if one chooses an evil it is distorted and becomes license.[44]

Karol Wojtyła's interventions and proposals were logically in accord with his pastoral and intellectual experience. The theses about personalism, thought through at length, openly posed a new way of approaching the reality of the human being. His philosophical anthropology would extend theological anthropology to affirm that "Christ reveals man to himself." This idea appears in section 22 of *Gaudium et Spes*, one of the most important documents of Vatican II, which also emphasizes the human person as its principal concern.

Wojtyła always considered it a grace from God to have participated in the Council, a moment of spiritual enrichment in which he could feel the universality of the Church. Without a doubt it was an important milestone in his life, one which later guided the steps of his pontificate. Furthermore, he assumed this as a public responsi-

---

42. Ibid., 108–10.
43. Weigel, *Witness to Hope*, 164.
44. I address this subject more extensively in chapter 9, "Transcendence."

bility, and for this reason he kept his archdiocese informed about what was happening. After every Council session—each one lasted approximately two months—he presented classes and conferences to priests, intellectuals, seminarians, and students. He also took part in various Radio Vatican broadcasts to Poland and sent letters to the editors of *Tygodnik Powszechny*, a Catholic newspaper.[45]

Wojtyła came to qualify the Council as "personalist,"[46] because of the centrality of its treatment of the person, something as evident in *Dignitatis Humanae* as in *Gaudium et Spes*, and this did nothing but conform the philosophical and theological framework within which he had been working and would continue to work until the end of his life. In its intellectual aspect, his aim was to foment Christian humanism.[47]

During moments when the work at the Council allowed, he would write poetry and even began to sketch his next book, the most important of his philosophical works, *Person and Act*. The suggestion came from a priest in Kraków, Stanisław Czartoryski, after he had read *Love and Responsibility*. He said that Wojtyła had to write one about the person. This was an idea that had been ripening in his mind for several years, inasmuch as its elaboration would require "putting the older Aristotelian-Thomistic 'philosophy of being' together with the 'philosophy of consciousness' he had analyzed in the Scheler dissertation (e.g., to work out the relationship between the objective truth of things-as-they-are and our subjective or personal experience of that truth)."[48] He was persuaded that the principal struggle of his time must consist in deepening the concept of the person in order to discover his most essential characteristics, such as his otherness and dignity. This intuition was increasingly

---

45. "By reason of its literary quality and intellectual dynamism, *Tygodnik Powszechny* was communist-run Poland's best newspaper, the most reliable source of unfiltered information, and the most open, interesting forum for social commentary.... [It] was constantly harassed by the state, its content censored and its circulation manipulated by the government's monopoly on newsprint." Weigel, *Witness to Hope*, 109.

46. See ibid., 170.   47. See ibid.

48. Ibid., 173.

confirmed during the unfolding of the Council, where he could listen and understand in a universal way the crisis of humanism through which humanity was passing. All the Council's documents and works were a response to these challenges of the modern world, and Wojtyła thought it appropriate to provide solid arguments from philosophy in a way that would reach even nonbelieving persons.

I devote my very rare free moments to a work that is close to my heart and devoted to the metaphysical sense and mystery of the PERSON. It seems to me that the debate today is being played out on that level. The evil of our times consists in the first place in a kind of degradation, indeed in a pulverization, of the fundamental uniqueness of each human person. This evil is even much more of the metaphysical order than of the moral order.[49]

Osoba i czyn (Person and Act) was published in 1969, and it is the work in which he presents his philosophy in its most complete form, centering his reflections on the human person. In this work he seeks to provide a solid basis for the idea of the person and his characteristics, using his own methodology to combine metaphysics and phenomenology: "it is not simply an original anthropological essay; it is a very powerful attempt to re-found the Thomistic anthropology in the light of phenomenology, the change of perspective being the instrument he utilized to achieve it."[50] Although Wojtyła's principal concerns were ethical, in this work he emphasized the anthropology on which ethics necessarily depends. The key to this work is that it is from the human act that we can comprehend the person. Of course, this has powerful ethical implications. His purpose is to put metaphysical reflection into dialogue with the person's interiority. It is dense work and hard to read, but most scholars regard it as Wojtyła's most finished and mature philosophical work.

In 1970 the Catholic University of Lublin organized a debate on Osoba i czyn, which was especially critical.[51] Several colleagues, es-

49. Citation taken from Weigel, Witness to Hope, 174.
50. Juan Manuel Burgos, "La antropología personalista de Persona y acción," in La filosofía personalista, 121.
51. See Weigel, Witness to Hope, 213.

pecially those who were the most "orthodox" Thomists, criticized the mixture between phenomenology and Thomism. Other and younger lecturers accepted it with interest and even enthusiasm.[52] In a subsequent publication, Wojtyła wrote about this debate, indicating that the central point did not refer to cosmology or philosophy of nature, but to philosophical anthropology and ethics, that is, reflection on the human being. In the period 1972–78, by interventions in congresses, and by articles published especially in *Analecta Husserliana*, Wojtyła clarified and sharpened the ideas expressed in *Person and Act*.[53]

Because of problems with the Communist government, Wojtyła could not be promoted to the next academic rank, since promotion would have required their approval. He continued teaching in the Chair of Ethics with the rank of docent (instructor), which was inferior on the academic scale, but in 1978 the rector of the university found a loophole and named him "honorary professor," a lifetime tenure that did not require the intervention of the government.[54] In any event, after his election as supreme pontiff, he left teaching and was replaced in the chair by Tadeusz Styczeń.[55]

After he was named a cardinal, his functions were not limited to Poland, but he had to accept duties relating to the Holy See and to participate in various synods of bishops, undertake pastoral jour-

52. See Buttiglione, *Karol Wojtyła: The Thought*, 40–41. In a clarifying note, referring to Thomism, Buttiglione remarks that in Wojtyła, "the diffidence about a modernizing interpretation is accompanied by an explicit conviction that it is necessary to integrate St. Thomas and to develop in an original way those facets of the Christian philosophy which he did not examine." Ibid., 40n33.

53. Buttiglione maintains that a new American edition of *Osoba i czyn* in 1979 allowed a worldwide diffusion of Wojtyła's thought, but the translation was very much criticized by scholars of this work, because at several points it was "excessively interpretative and unfaithful to the original" and because, the critics said, it tilted much of Wojtyła's thought and terminology toward the side of phenomenology. For example, not using the Aristotelian-Thomistic technical term *hypokeimenon* or *suppositum*, which is the metaphysical subject in which inhere all the attributes of the person, reduces the importance of one of the key concepts of the person. See ibid., 42n37; and 117n1.

54. See Weigel, *Witness to Hope*, 214.

55. See Buttiglione, *Karol Wojtyła: The Thought*, 38.

neys to different parts of the world, and prepare documents for the congregations of which he was a member. He always found time to continue writing poetry or some philosophical article and sometimes to take part in a philosophical conference, as was the case in 1974 when he participated in the International Thomistic Congress in Rome, Naples, and Fossanova, where he presented a paper on "The Personal Structure of Self-Determination."[56]

In 1976 he was called to Rome to preach the Lenten retreat for Pope Paul VI and the Roman Curia. There were in all twenty-two sermons which he had to prepare in Italian. These texts were subsequently published and contain many experiences from his life in Poland, as well as Wojtyła's spiritual vision.[57]

Beginning with his election as supreme pontiff of the Catholic Church, the thought of Karol Wojtyła merges with that of John Paul II, and his philosophical developments are often immersed in his allocutions, letters, encyclicals, and so on. This development is conducted from the same line of thought and especially from the foundations laid in *Person and Act*. "It was the final chapter of *Person and Act* ... which introduced [the concept of participation] into personalism strictly speaking and which was to be the theme developed in philosophical articles after *Person and Act*."[58] It is logical that his intellectual production during his pontificate should center on pastoral and theological matters, rather than on those that are technically philosophical, which in this way pass onto another level.

56. Karol Wojtyła, "The Personal Structure of Self-Determination," in *Person and Community*, 187–95. See Weigel, *Witness to Hope*, 236.
57. Karol Wojtyła, *Sign of Contradiction* (New York: Seabury Press, 1979).
58. Emmanuel Buch Camí et al., *Personalismo teológico*, 109.

2 ∽

WOJTYŁA'S METHOD

One of the most striking aspects of Karol Wojtyła's philosophical work is his method. One initial analysis comes from María José Franquet, who presents the elements of Wojtyła's methodology that can be observed in the book *Person and Act*; his analysis could also be applied in part to *Love and Responsibility*. It could not, however, be applied to his essays, since, being less extensive than a monograph, they adopt a more direct method to deepen themes of metaphysics or phenomenology. In his essays, Wojtyła develops a systematic method of analysis, which relies on arguments of ontological and phenomenological anthropology of a realist nature.[1]

Franquet's analysis is as follows:

Control over his own method of investigation allows Wojtyła to address personal subjectivity by taking as a starting point a phenomenology of action. However, phenomenology is an auxiliary [first methodological moment] and precedes a subsequent onto-phenomenological development [second methodological moment] and ontological [third methodological moment] that Wojtyła concentrates on in his notion of ontic support. Thereupon, the onto-psycho-phenomenological understanding of

---

1. The most complete collection of Karol Wojtyła's essays in English is found in Wojtyła, *Person and Community*. In the bibliography of the present work, the essays are listed in more detail. In general, the publications for these essays are *Tygodnik Powszechny*, *Esprit et vérité*, *Znak*, *Ateneum kapłańskie*, *Roczniki filozoficzne*, *Il Nuovo Areopago*, *The Review of Metaphysics*, *Analecta Husserliana*, *Asprenas*, *Rivista de Filosofia Neoscolastica*, *Colloquium Salutis*, and *Roczniki teologiczne-kanoniczne*.

the person is performed during the first two moments of understanding: a first phenomenological moment summed up in the analysis of experience; a second inductive moment, whose object is to achieve the semantic unit of what is given in experience [that is, the essential knowledge]; the onto-ontological understanding, in a third reductive moment that articulates the theme ascertained in previous moments with the ontology. It can be said that in the person's onto-ontology the third theme is focused in line with Wojtylian anthropology, although, as has been indicated, it is very tentative.[2]

Rodrigo Guerra López offers another approach, quoting authors who align Wojtyła's thought with certain philosophical currents; he orders those authors according to three kinds of methodological orientation,[3] which are:

1. Karol Wojtyła as a fundamentally Thomist philosopher: Although Wojtyła uses modern language, similar to that of the phenomenologist, in reality he reiterates Aquinas's classic theses, adapting them to the exigencies of the contemporary philosophical debate. Examples of thinkers who maintain this position include:

Mieczysław Albert Krąpiec, OP, ""Książka Kardynała Karola Wojtyła monografia osoby jako podmiot moralności" [Cardinal Karol Wojtyła's book: A monograph on the person as the subject of morality], Analecta Cracoviensia 5–6 (1973–74): 57–61.

Georges Kalinowski, Autour de "Personne et Acte" de Karol Cardinal Wojtyła. Articles et Conférences sur une rencontré du thomisme avec la phénoménologie [Concerning "Person and Act" of Cardinal Karol Wojtyła. Articles and Lectures on an encounter of Thomism with phenomenology] (Aix-en-Provence: Presses universitaires d'Aix-Marseille, 1987). Especially "La reforme du

---

2. María José Franquet, Persona, Acción y Libertad. Las claves de la antropología de Karol Wojtyla [Person, Action and Freedom. Keys to Karol Wojtyła's anthropology] (Pamplona: Eunsa, 1996), 139–40.

3. See Rodrigo Guerra López, Volver a la persona. El método filosófico de Karol Wojtyla [Turn to the person. The philosophical method of Karol Wojtyła] (Madrid: Caparrós Editores, 2002), 301–9. All the sources for the following paragraphs come from Guerra's book. I have repeated the full information and filled in some missing data to facilitate the research work of readers.

thomisme et de la phenomenologie chez Karol Wojtyła selon Rocco Buttiglione," 101–23.

Andrew N. Woznicki, *A Christian Humanism: Karol Wojtyła's Existential Personalism* (New Britain, Conn.: Mariel Publications, 1980), 9–11.

Jerzy W. Gałkowski, "The Place of Thomism in the Anthropology of K. Wojtyła," *Angelicum* 65 (1988): 181.

Kenneth L. Schmitz, *At the Center of the Human Drama: The Philosophical Anthropology of Karol Wojtyła/Pope John Paul II* (Washington, D.C.: The Catholic University of America Press, 1993), 36.

Jarosław Kupczak, *Destined for Liberty: The Human Person in the Thought of Karol Wojtyła/John Paul II* (Washington, D.C.: The Catholic University of America Press, 2000).

Abelardo Lobato, "La persona en el pensamiento de Karol Wojtyla" [The person in the thought of Karol Wojtyła], *Angelicum* 56 (1979): 208–9.

Adrian J. Reimers, *Truth about the Good: Moral Norms in the Thought of John Paul II* (Washington, D.C.: The Catholic University of America Press, 2011), xvi–xvii, 44–45.

2. Karol Wojtyła as a descriptive-phenomenologist: These authors admit that Wojtyła has received a Thomist training but hold that his intellectual evolution took him to a reformulated modality of phenomenology with metaphysical components. His work is a recasting of phenomenology, but it remains on the experiential-descriptive level and then draws on ontological explanations. In this group we may cite:

Philippe M. Jobert, "Jean-Paul II Philosophie de la transition de l'Antropologie classique a l'Antropologie moderne" [John Paul II: Philosophy of the transition from classical to modern anthropology], in *Karol Wojtyła. Filosofo, Teologo e Poeta. Atti del I Colloquio internazionale del Pensiero Cristiano organizzato da ISTRA - Istituto di Studi Per La Transizione: Roma, 23–25 settembre 1983* [Karol Wojtyła. Philosopher, theologian and poet. Proceedings of the 1st International Colloquium organized by the Christian thought ISTRA - Institute of Studies for Transition: Rome, September 23–25, 1983], ed. Rocco Buttiglione, Carlo Fedeli, and Angelo Scola, 47–52 (Vatican City: Libreria Editrice Vaticana, 1984).

Stephen Dinan, "The Phenomenological Anthropology of Karol Wojtyła," *The New Scholasticism* 55 (1988): 317–30.

Giovanni Reale, "Fondamenti e concetti-base di 'Persona e atto' di Karol Wojtyła" [Fundamentals and basic concepts of Karol Wojtyła's 'Person and act'], in Karol Wojtyła, *Persona e Atto. Testo polacco a fronte* [Person and Act. Polish-Italian bilingual edition] (Milan: Bompiani, 2001), 5–27.

María José Franquet, *Persona, Acción y Libertad. Las claves de la antropología en Karol Wojtyła* [Person, Action and Freedom. The keys of anthropology in Karol Wojtyła] (Pamplona: Eunsa. Ediciones Universidad de Navarra S.A., 1996), 47n55, 133n149, 139–40.

3. Karol Wojtyła as a realist phenomenologist is heir to, among others, traditional Thomism, the Louvain school's Thomism, Gilson and Maritain's existential Thomism, Mieczysław Kotlarczyk's theater, and Dietrich von Hildebrand's realist phenomenology, as well as his own research on Kant and Scheler. However his methodology is original and irreducible.

In fact, the key factor that defines Wojtyła is not his belonging to a particular school of thought … nor following some kind of canon of philosophical orthodoxy—whatever it is—but an intellectual disposition radically oriented *to return to the things themselves*. Even more, *to return to the human being as person*.[4]

Here the authors admit seeing in Wojtyła's work a phenomenology which covers the effort to arrive at ontological positions; it supposes the experiential-descriptive moment but also the inductive and reductive moments, which are expressed in a metaphysical way.

4. Guerra López, *Volver a la persona*, 307 (emphasis in the original).

"Metaphysics is not considered as an external, adjacent or subsequent reality of phenomenology but rather goes through and across transphenomenically."[5] The author cites as examples philosophers who think in this way:

> Emmanuel Levinas, "Notas sobre el pensamiento filosófico del cardenal Wojtyla" [Notes on the philosophical thought of Cardinal Wojtyła], *Communio. Revista Católica Internacional* 4, March–April (1982): 99–102.
> Hans Köchler, "The Phenomenology of Karol Wojtyła: On the Problem of the Phenomenological Foundation of Anthropology," *Philosophy and Phenomenological Research* 42 (1982): 327.
> Jean-Luc Marion, "L'Autotranscendance de l'homme signe de contradiction dans la pensée de Karol Wojtyła" [The self-transcendence of man as a sign of contradiction in the thought of Karol Wojtyła], in *Karol Wojtyła Filosofo, Teologo, Poeta*, 53–70.
> Rocco Buttiglione, *Karol Wojtyła: The Thought of the Man Who Became Pope John Paul II.*
> Josef Seifert, "Karol Cardinal Wojtyła (Pope John Paul II) as Philosopher and The Cracow/Lublin School of Philosophy," *Aletheia* 2 (1981): 133–45.
> Juan Miguel Palacios, "La Escuela ética de Lublin y Cracovia" [The Ethical School of Lublin and Krakow], *Sillar. Revista Católica de Cultura* 2, no. 5, January–March (1982): 65–66.
> Józef Tischner, "L'aspetto metodologico dell'opera 'Persona e Atto'" [The methodological aspect of the work 'Person and Act'], in *La filosofia di Karol Wojtyła: atti del Seminario di studi, Universita di Bari, 25–26 gennaio 1983* [The philosophy of Karol Wojtyła: proceedings of the seminar studies, University of Bari: January 25–26, 1983], ed. Rocco Buttiglione et al., 101–6 (Bologna: CSEO, 1983).

5. Ibid.

Massimo Serreti, "Invitation to Read" to *Perché l'uomo*, by Karol Wojtyła, 5–40.

John H. Nota, "Phenomenological Experience in Karol Wojtyła," in *The Thought of Pope John Paul II. A Collection of Essays and Studies*, ed. John M. McDermott (Rome: Editrice Pontificia Università Gregoriana, 1993), 197–203.

Robert F. Harvanek, "The Philosophical Foundations of the Thought of John Paul II," in *The Thought of Pope John Paul II: A Collection of Essays and Studies*, ed. John M. McDermott, 1–21.

Constantino Esposito, "Fenomenologia e ontologia" [Phenomenology and Ontology], in *Karol Wojtyła e il pensiero europeo contemporaneo* [Karol Wojtyła and contemporary European thought], ed. Constantino Esposito et al. (Bologna: CSEO, 1984), 26–33.

Peter Simpson, *On Karol Wojtyła*, 10–13.

The general conclusion reached by Guerra López's study about Wojtyła's philosophical method is summarized in the following text:

Karol Wojtyła's method is philosophical, phenomenologist and realist … it is not enough to assert that the scope of the method is metaphysical; it is, instead, more properly called metaphysical-personalistic. It is in the turn to the person where we seem to find a new opportunity to rethink metaphysics and philosophy in general after the crisis of Enlightenment and empiricist modernity. Likewise, it is in turning to the person where we seem to find encoded the fundamental grammar that eventually will enable us to rethink the methods of the human and social sciences and their interdisciplinary relations. In a word, the method proposed by Karol Wojtyła recaptures the significance of philosophy as knowledge constitutively open, participative and progressive, and thereby provides thought in general with an opportunity to legitimate itself in the truth, simultaneously recognizing the singularity of human beings and their essence without contradiction.[6]

---

6. Ibid., 311 (emphasis in the original).

On the other hand, this methodology also helps to situate the philosopher in a determinate current of thought. After what has been said so far, may it be said that Wojtyła is Thomist or phenomenologist? Adrian Reimers points out that Wojtyła, in the development of his philosophy, takes into account Thomist and realist phenomenology, but his main preoccupation is the person explained by an adequate anthropology and ethics coherent with this anthropology. "[I]n his philosophical *corpus* ... he never presents a totally developed anthropological theory comparable, for example, to that of Saint Thomas Aquinas or even of René Descartes."[7] As was already mentioned in Chapter 1, philosophy—metaphysics, ethics, and epistemology—is a means to better understand the person; the ends of research are not to compose a theoretical framework that will disassemble other theories and establish itself as a philosophical model. Its aim is better knowledge of the human being. Of course in the development of his work, he must stress the differences with other philosophies that oppose his approaches, such as empiricism, Kantianism, and even Schelerian ethics, but all of this points to what really matters to him: 'understanding man, the human person.'"[8] Ultimately, Reimers suggests that all Wojtyła's philosophical work is a "philosophical personalism" which has metaphysical roots.[9]

7. Adrian J. Reimers, "La antropología personalista de Karol Wojtyla" [The personalist anthropology of Karol Wojtyła], in *Propuestas antropológicas del siglo XX* [Anthropological proposals of the twentieth century], ed. Juan Fernando Sellés (Pamplona: Eunsa, 2007) (emphasis in the original), 2:309.

8. Adrian J. Reimers, "Karol Wojtyła's methodology. Thomism and phenomenology in the theology of the body," in *Colloquium on Karol Wojtyła/John Paul II University of St. Thomas* (unpublished manuscript, October 2012).

9. Adrian J. Reimers, *Truth about the Good: Moral Norms in the Thought of John Paul II* (Ave Maria, Fla.: Sapientia Press of Ave Maria University, 2011), xvi–xvii.

PART II ॐ

REASON AND FAITH IN
THE PHILOSOPHY OF KAROL
WOJTYŁA/JOHN PAUL II

ADRIAN J. REIMERS

3 ∿

EXPERIENCE AND KNOWLEDGE

A central theme of Karol Wojtyła's *Love and Responsibility* is that love can exist only in truth. Love, which so profoundly involves our feelings—our sentiment for beauty, the emotional longing for another, the physical desires arising from our sexual nature—love cannot truly be love unless it is founded on truth. A concatenation of emotional experiences does not suffice truly to constitute love. But love certainly depends on experience. Indeed, love arises from our experience.[1] Let us begin by reflecting on love, because not only does love depend on knowledge of the truth but also our knowledge of the truth depends in a way on love. We are persons, and as such we seek the truth. But even more, we seek love.

Our question in this chapter concerns the nature of experience and its relationship with truth, and we shall seek the answer to this question primarily (but not exclusively) in Wojtyła's study *Osoba i czyn* (*Person and Act*), where our author explores the foundations of human acting and its basis in truth.

This chapter and the two following are based on lectures of a seminar titled "The Anthropology of John Paul II" presented at the University CEU San Pablo of Madrid in April 2011.

1. See LR, 76; AR, 95.

Experience: The Problem of Reductionism

The project of *Person and Act* is to grasp the essence of the person by examining his acts, for the person can be known through his acts.[2] Therefore, starting from a phenomenological standpoint—that is, from disciplined analyses of the essences of certain experiences—Wojtyła's treatise attempts to arrive at the truth about the human person. In order to start with experience, he first questions precisely the nature of experience itself. For the ordinary person, the "man on the street," this is not the difficult question that it is for the philosopher. To understand experience, many philosophers have redefined it, reducing it to one of its components or conditions and thereby impoverishing it. And this impoverishment profoundly affects one's epistemology and the resulting account of knowable truth. The question of experience itself is central. At the beginning of *Person and Act*, Karol Wojtyła writes: "This study arises from the need to show the objective aspect of that great cognitive process that can be defined ... as the experience of the human being [*doświadczenie człowieka*]."[3] To identify more precisely his concerns, let us first consider some important reductionist approaches to experience, after which we will return to Wojtyła's text and analysis.

Karol Wojtyła himself indicates the most fundamental form of reductionism when he writes, "The object of experience is not only the momentary sensible phenomenon."[4] For David Hume and the empiricist tradition, all experience reduces to sense impressions and inner feelings, most of which derive from sense impressions.[5] Whatever ideas we may have of the world concerning the properties of water or lodestone, about gravity or God, or even regarding dragons and golden mountains, must derive from sense impressions.

---

2. See PEA, 839–41; PA 39–40; OC, 56–57; AP 9–10.
3. PEA, 831. See PA 31; OC, 51; AP 3.
4. PEA, 832. See PA 32; OC, 52; AP 4.
5. See David Hume, *An Inquiry concerning Human Understanding* (Indianapolis: Bobbs-Merrill, 1955), 30.

If they do not, then they are meaningless. They do not refer to authentic experience. There is a further kind of experience that Hume admits, specifically the moral sentiments.[6] When we contemplate certain kinds of events, perhaps the nobility of a gentleman defending his honor or the wickedness of a patricide son, we experience moral sentiments, in the one case admiration and in the other horror. These experiences found our capacity to form moral judgments, and hence, like our judgments about the world, moral judgments can be founded only on feelings.

Although much of Hume's theory has subsequently been found wanting, its structural principles persist today. This is perhaps most evident in sense-data theory and its intersection with contemporary cognitive sciences. Thanks to modern neuroscience we understand well how environmental factors stimulate the nerve endings in the skin, the retinal receptors, the inner ear, and so one, from which signals are transmitted by synapses in the nervous system to appropriate sections of the brain by means of weak electric signals. The argument can be made—an argument very much in accord with Hume's account—that what we call "experience" is a construct by the brain as it combines sensory inputs. Properly speaking, human experience would then be nothing more than the data provided by the senses and the brain's organization and storage of these sensory inputs from the environment. Therefore, what we call experience must ultimately be the purely physical result of the interaction of the organism with aspects of its environment.

Such an account finds strong support from current interpretations of evolutionary theory. According to Darwin, the human species is simply the product of the operation of the mechanism of natural selection operating on inherited variations.[7] In the course of

6. See David Hume, "An Enquiry concerning the Principles of Morals, Section I: Of the general Principles of Morals," in *Hume's Ethical Writings*, ed. Alasdair MacIntyre, 23–28 (New York: Collier Books, 1965); and "A Treatise of Human Nature, Book III, Section II: Moral Distinctions Derived from a Moral Sense," in ibid., 196–202.

7. See Charles Darwin, *The Descent of Man* (Chicago: Encyclopaedia Britannica, 1952), 590.

this evolution, intelligence proved to be a powerful survival mechanism:

No one doubts that [developed mental faculties] are of the utmost importance to animals in a state of nature. The same conclusion may be extended to man; the intellect must have been all-important to him, even at a very remote period, as enabling him to invent and use language, to make weapons, tools, traps, &c., whereby with the aid of his social habits, he long ago became the most dominant of all living creatures.[8]

This materialist account of the origin of the human species is reflected philosophically in the pragmatism of William James, who argues that truth is nothing other than whatever "works" to get us through life. "What is true is useful and what is useful true."[9] For James, true beliefs are simply states of mind that help us successfully get through life. He offers the example of a tired and hungry man lost in the woods who comes upon a cow path. He thinks to himself that a cow path will lead him to some human habitation where he will find shelter and food. He then proves the truth of this by following the path and coming to a farmhouse. He really cares nothing about having a correspondence of his mind with the reality of things. All that he cares about is to save himself. If his thought about the cow path is true, its only importance is that it has been useful. The contemporary American philosopher Daniel Dennett has put the matter more succinctly: "All brains are, in essence, *anticipation machines*."[10] Whether the organism at issue is a sea squirt or an associate professor, the brain serves the same basic function: to anticipate opportunities and dangers in the environment so that the organism may survive. The brain is not really concerned with knowing some sort of immaterial truth but only with providing the information necessary for the organism to make its way successfully through its world. Experience and the cognition consequent upon it

8. Ibid., 591–92.
9. William James, *Pragmatism* (Buffalo: Prometheus Books, 1991), 89–91.
10. Daniel Dennett, *Consciousness Explained* (Boston: Little, Brown & Co., 1991), 177 (emphasis in the original).

are nothing other than the complex of neural responses that enable us to meet our survival needs and forestall discomfort.

The contemporary materialist account of experience is compelling. As a classroom professor I can attest to the widespread, almost casual acceptance of it among undergraduates, who accept that this is what science has proved. But Karol Wojtyła argues that an accurate account of experience demands much more than a materialist or scientific reductionism. Experience is more than the reception and inner cataloging of sensations.

The Experience of the Human Being

Karol Wojtyła starts with the question of the human being's experience, and this starting point is especially important. Why? Far from being a kind of "side issue," a matter to be addressed once we have solved the more fundamental scientific questions, the question of the human being is central. If we start only with the data of sensation, as does Hume, or with the mechanisms of the organism, following modern scientism, then we inevitably fall into reductionism. If the starting point is sensation, then everything is to be explained in terms of sensation. So, for example, J. J. C. Smart states that the purpose of physics is to order and predict future sense experiences.[11] Of course, certain ontological presuppositions lie implicit in this. If reality is only and nothing more than an agglomeration of physical particles governed by strict mathematical laws (which may be statistical, such as those of quantum mechanics), then it is impossible for the human being to be anything other than a kind of derivative reality. To understand the constitutive parts would therefore be in principle to understand the whole. But we may—indeed, we must—ask whether such a starting point is required. Many argue today that metaphysics must strive to avoid anthropomorphism, by

11. See John J.C. Smart, *Philosophy and Scientific Realism* (London: Routledge & Kegan Paul, 1963), 2.

which is understood any grasp or conception of reality that refers to or derives from human interest, need, or conception.[12] This position rests upon distrust of the human and of human experience, because the very fact that something is experienced constitutes it a matter of human interest and therefore potentially a falsification. Furthermore, human experience is limited by the peculiar structure of our bodies, the cultures we live in, the planet we live on, and so forth. However, if truth is a matter of knowing reality and its characteristics, the only access we have to reality is through experience. If what we perceive with our senses, interact with by our bodies, and reconstruct intellectually with our minds is not real, then we may ask, what else could possibly constitute reality?

A Human Being Acts

Karol Wojtyła starts with the experience of the human being. The key that he uses to access this experience is the experience of the human act, which is a common experience that each of us has every day. His specific project is to investigate the content of this experience, "A human being acts,"[13] an experience that a person has of himself and of others, which therefore has a twofold aspect, the interior and the exterior. "I" can see that you are making an omelet and then "I" have the experience of eating it. Wojtyła insists here that if we attempt to reduce the act merely to the sensations that accompany it, then we inevitably falsify the experience and fall into contradictions and errors. Why? To account adequately for the human act, we must consider not only its subjective aspects but its efficacy as well. Let us consider this more closely.

An act that is not intentionally efficacious falls short of being an act. Efficient causality is intrinsic to human act, as is also human

12. See, for instance, John Hawthorne, "Three-dimensionalism," in *Metaphysical Essays* (Oxford: Oxford University Press, 2006), see esp. 108–9; also in Smart, *Philosophy*, 149ff. See esp. chap. 7. For a critique of this kind of position, see Christian Smith, *What Is a Person?* (Chicago: University of Chicago Press, 2010), 123–49. See esp. chap. 3.
13. PEA, 838. See PA 48; OC, 57; AP, 15.

subjectivity. The act arises within human consciousness from an experience of need or desire, in response to which the person envisions a a plan to meet that need. "I feel hungry, and I want something to eat." To fulfill that desire he undertakes certain actions. "I will cook an omelet." But this is precisely the point. In the experience of cooking the omelet, one feels the heat of the stove, hears the cracking of the eggs, smells the butter's aroma, and so on, but these are not the essential element. What is essential is that an omelet comes into being. The agent seeks effectively to change something in the world, to bring something new into being. Wojtyła calls this capacity to effect change, or effective causality, *operativity*. Without this element of operativity, the experiences involved in cooking would be pointless. We could not even speak of an act. Let us note in passing—but not irrelevantly—that in this requirement for operativity is a vital element that Kant misses in his ethics when he insists that the goodness of the will does not depend on the intended end of one's action.[14] Karol Wojtyła, by contrast, holds it to be important that whatever one's sense-experience may be and regardless of any other inner state, the acting person is trying to accomplish something. This necessarily implies that the person who acts consciously is also an object that has physical properties and capabilities by which he can change things in the world. Of course, it can happen that an act may fail of its intended operativity, because of the resistance of material things or because of the person's own bodily deficiencies.[15] Nevertheless, that the end is intended is constitutive of the act as act.

Therefore, because the act has a twofold character as subjective and objective, so too is the person both subject and object.[16] By his subjectivity he is conscious of the world and consciously present to

14. In the original source: "*Der gute Wille ist nicht durch das, was er bewirkt oder ausrichtet, nicht durch seine Tauglichkeit zur Erreichung irgend eines vorgesetzten Zweckes, sondern allein durch das Wollen, d. i. an sich, gut.*" Immanuel Kant, *Grundlegung zur Metaphysik der Sitten* [Groundwork of the Metaphysics of Morals], in *Kant's gesammelte Schriften* [Kant's Collected Writings], 4:394 (Berlin: Druck und Verlag von George Reimer, 1911).
15. See PEA, 1104–1105; PA, 310–11; OC, 250–51; AP, 214–15.
16. See LR, 21; AR, 27

himself. Karol Wojtyła's account differs significantly and importantly from that of most philosophers of consciousness. Instead of giving epistemological primacy to consciousness, Wojtyła maintains that one's consciousness of himself arises from his conscious experience as a willing agent in the world. Perhaps because of Descartes's overly sharp distinction between himself as a "thinking subject" and his bodily existence in the world, or perhaps because of the empiricist presuppositions of Hume, many philosophers today—and here we may include many phenomenologists—regard consciousness as a kind of "given," as a peculiar property upon which human personhood and rationality are founded. According to such a view, the person is constituted, as it were, simply by the totality of his conscious experiences. For instance, Scheler writes that "the person may *never* be conceived as a *thing* or as a *substance* that has these or those faculties and powers, including a 'faculty' or a 'power' of reason, etc. Rather the person is the immediately co-experienced *unity* of experience."[17]

Precisely at this point, Karol Wojtyła's analysis becomes metaphysical. If the person is both subject and object, that is, if he is both a self-aware center of consciousness and an agent of change within the nexus of physical bodies in the world, then he cannot simply be reduced either to the one or to the other. He is not simply a center of consciousness.[18] Neither is he merely one object among many in the world, a "something" that is not "someone." The human person exists as a *suppositum*, by which is expressed "the being as subjective foundation of existence and action."[19] The *suppositum* or "metaphysical subjectivity"[20] is not directly accessible to experience; it is

17. Max Scheler, *Der Formalismus in der Ethik und die materiale Wertethik: Neuer Versuch der Grundlegung eines ethischen Personalismus* [Formalism in Ethics and Non-Formal Ethics of Values: A new attempt toward the foundation of an ethical personalism] (Franke Verlag: Bern und München, 1966), 371 (emphasis in the original).

18. See PEA, 852; OC, 68; LR, 21–22; AR, 27–28; Karol Wojtyła, "Person: Subject and Community," in *Person and Community*, 219–20.

19. PEA, 888. See OC, 93; Wojtyła, "Person: Subject and Community," 221–23; Wojtyła, "La persona: sujeto y comunidad," in *El hombre y su destino*, 50.

20. Wojtyła, "Person: Subject and Community," 223. See Wojtyła, "La persona: sujeto y comunidad," 49.

"transphenomenal," by which Wojtyła means that, although it is not itself phenomenal, it is grasped through phenomena and therefore must be known only by reason. Hence, metaphysical analysis is necessary adequately to comprehend the human person. If we exclude the metaphysical analysis, then we are forced to reduce our comprehension of what the human being is either to the material or to the purely phenomenal or sensational. As we shall see, this metaphysical comprehension—or more properly, metaphysical aspect of our comprehension—plays an essential role in forming human experience.

Horizontal Transcendence

In the experience of operativity, the acting person's effective causality in the world, Wojtyła discovers "horizontal transcendence," which is simply the subject's surpassing his subjective limits toward an object. It is the directing of oneself toward a value.[21] This transcendence has two aspects, which we may identify as the "appetitive" and the "efficacious." The experience of a value ordinarily takes the form of a desire, characteristically the desire for what one does not have. In such a case, the object of desire constitutes a "value." The person is motivated by values to undertake actions. The connection with operativity is evident, for one must act effectively to attain what he wants. The desire for a value by its very nature points to the non-self, because the appetite is a desire for what one lacks. Thus, Wojtyła coins the expression "horizontal transcendence" to describe the "going out of oneself" characteristic of desire and the attempt to fulfill it.

An important and (especially among analytic philosophers) often neglected aspect of experience is the distinction between appetite and sensation, which is fundamental to human experience of ourselves and of the world. The experience of appetite is not found in sensation as such, even if sensation may be a component of it.

21. PEA, 982, 988. See OC, 164, 168–69; PA, 185, 216; AP, 119, 142; Wojtyła, "Personal structure," 191.

An appetite is different from a cognition, and it is directed toward a good or a value that exists independently of one's consciousness. The hungry man is not simply enduring unpleasant sensations in his stomach; he is also experiencing the urge to act in certain specific ways, specifically to eat, and his attention is drawn to opportunities to satisfy this desire. This example demonstrates how the experience of values directly manifests the reality of the person's directedness to the world outside his consciousness, the reality of "horizontal transcendence."[22] And, *pace* Descartes, we cannot make sense of our consciousness of values without reference to the body, the unique means by which one interacts with the world. In virtue of this "horizontal transcendence," experience shows the existence of the objectively existing world outside the subjectivity of consciousness.

We see, thus, that experience cannot reduce to the operation of the senses alone, because appetites direct us not to sensations but to things. A hungry smoker may notice that he is smoking more to alleviate his craving for food, but as soon as he realizes this, he sees that he has made a mistake. Ingesting cigarette smoke will not satisfy his appetite. An important subtheme of Steinbeck's novel *The Grapes of Wrath* is the inadequacy of a diet deficient in protein, which is absent from the diet of the poor migrants. They can eat but cannot get what their bodies need. An appetite is for a "kind of thing." Because we have appetites to satisfy, we need knowledge of the world about us, and we need to do science in order to gain this knowledge about ourselves and the world about us. Because horizontal transcendence requires knowledge of the world, human experience is by its very essence cognitive. We experience "things" in the world, and not simply a plenum of raw data.

In *Love and Responsibility*, Karol Wojtyła develops this analysis of appetite and value in depth. In the second section of chapter 1 of that work, titled "The Person and the Sexual Impulse," our author

---

22. PEA, 982. See OC, 164–65; PA, 185; AP, 119.

raises the question whether the sexual urge can be reduced to an instinct, which he defines as a "reflex mode of action, which is not dependent on conscious thought."[23] If it could be, then sexual behavior would inevitably and necessarily be triggered by certain sensual stimuli. But, he writes, since the sexual urge has an existential and biological significance that the human being can understand, "[t]he proper end of the [sexual] urge, the end *per se*, is something suprapersonal, the existence of the species *Homo*, the constant prolongation of its existence."[24] Properly speaking, the object of the urge is not simply a source of sensual stimuli but a person of the other sex. Wojtyła's point here is that the sexual appetite is not directed simply toward an image present to the senses nor toward some source of sense stimulation, but that it is to be understood in terms of its biological significance. What is desired is not simply a bearer of sexual characteristics but another being, a human being.

He carries this line of thinking further in the next chapter of *Love and Responsibility* in the section intriguingly titled "A Metaphysical Analysis of Love." There he considers various components or manifestations of love—attraction, sexual desire, goodwill, sympathy, and so on. Here we may restrict our considerations to the issue of "desire," which arises from the organism and from the animal appetite to reproduce. The person experiences a desire to unite sexually with another person, but that desire never remains only at the physical level. Karol Wojtyła writes: "Love as desire cannot be reduced to desire itself. It is simply the crystallization of the objective need of one being directed towards another being which is for it a good and an object of longing. *In the mind of the subject, love-as-desire is not felt as mere desire.*"[25] Even a minimum of reflection on human experience will reveal the truth of this. One of the important challenges of adolescence is to sort out the differences among sexual desire, the attraction to beauty, the satisfactions of friendship, and so on. In

---

23. See LR, 45; AR, 58.   24. LR, 51. See AR, 65.
25. LR, 81 (emphasis in the original). See AR, 101.

human beings sexual desire, which arises from within the organism whose reproductive structures are very similar to those of other primates, becomes very complex, precisely because "it is experienced" not as a purely physical craving, but as an aspect of a complex desire for a being, specifically for another person.

There is, of course, much more that we could say concerning the relationship that arises between persons because of sexual desire, but for our present purposes we simply cite this as a particularly important manifestation of the horizontal transcendence of the person toward experienced values. Horizontal transcendence is "essential" to human experience; without such transcendence we cannot speak of human experience. But human experience is necessarily formed by knowledge, by the person's understanding of the world and the things around him. It is not essential that this understanding be infallibly accurate—indeed, in cannot be—but it must be the work of reason as it interprets and attempts to comprehend the world.

It follows, therefore, that not only does experience form comprehension but also comprehension forms experiences. Wojtyła writes, "To comprehend is nothing else than to grasp intellectually the meaning of things or the relations between things. All this is extraneous to consciousness."[26] In virtue of his comprehension of things, the person lives in a world that is structured by their meaning. Mark Twain writes of the "the romance and the beauty" of the Mississippi River in the eyes of the tourist,[27] but then he relates how the experienced pilot recognizes the dangers concealed in these beauties. We can almost say that, because of his greater and more thorough understanding of the river and its characteristics, the pilot sails on a different river than does the tourist. Structured by his superior comprehension, the pilot's consciousness of the river is different from the tourist's.

---

26. PEA, 875. See OC, 84; PA, 76; AP, 36.
27. Mark Twain, *Life on the Mississippi* (Chapel Hill: University of North Carolina at Chapel Hill, 1999), 188–21. http://docsouth.unc.edu/southlit/twainlife/twain.html.

Vertical Transcendence

If horizontal transcendence is the transcendence of the person toward values outside himself, the analysis thus far has indicated, albeit indirectly, that such transcendence does not suffice to account for human experience. In virtue of his freedom, the human person is capable also of "vertical transcendence."[28] This transcendence "is inherent to self-dominion and self-possession as specific structural properties of the person."[29] Vertical transcendence is that in terms of which self-determination is made possible by the subject's directing himself toward the truth about the good. It is a consequence of the spiritual nature of the person, by which he is centered or focused on goodness and truth. As such, the person can, as it were, "stand above" the realm of his experiences and evaluate them according to their truth, especially the truth of the values represented by them. This is a particularly serious and important claim, because in arguing that vertical transcendence is intrinsic to the person in act, Karol Wojtyła challenges materialism at its root. Before we explore the concept of vertical transcendence itself, we do well to examine some allied and perhaps controversial concepts, specifically, Karol Wojtyła's understanding of "freedom" and of the "spiritual nature" of the person.

Freedom

In the contemporary American philosophical environment, it is difficult to talk about freedom because of the widespread assumption that the experience of freedom is an illusion, that the notion of personal freedom contradicts well-established facts about the world. Consider Peter Van Inwagen's comments:

Here is what I mean by saying that free will is a mystery: Anyone who has though carefully about the problem of free will and who has come to a

---

28. See PEA, 982; OC, 164–65; PA, 185; AP, 119.
29. PEA, 998. See OC, 176; PA, 188; AP, 121–22.

conclusion about free will that is detailed and systematic enough to be called a theory of free will must accept *some* proposition that seems self-evidently false. To choose what theory of free will to accept is to choose *which* seemingly self-evidently false proposition one accepts.[30]

Which self-evident propositions would one have to accept to defend free will? According to John Searle, we would have to repudiate science, which is solidly founded on the premise that every change in the world has a cause.[31] But we cannot reject science, which has proven its value for attaining important knowledge. Therefore, we must acknowledge that our sense of having free will is an illusion. Van Inwagen, for his part, acknowledges that denying free will must result in also denying self-evident propositions, which are precisely propositions that arise from ordinary human experience. We all experience ourselves as being free. For Searle and many of his materialist colleagues, this experience must ultimately be an illusion. For Van Inwagen it is a mystery that we may never resolve. But what is the experience of freedom, of free will?

David Hume, in accord with his sensationalist premises, finds this experience in a "feeling."[32] The experience of freedom is an interior feeling that one had caused an event and could have caused another. This "feeling," however, is not a perception; it does not show the causal connection between the agent and the effect he is supposed to have brought about. This position is not far from the position of thinkers such as John Searle, who argues, "The characteristic experience that gives us the conviction of human freedom ... is the experience of engaging in voluntary, intentional human actions," and further on, "for reasons I don't really understand, evolution has given us a form of experience of voluntary action where the experience of freedom ... is built into the very structure of

---

30. Peter van Inwagen, *The Problem of Evil: The Gifford Lectures Delivered in the University of St Andrews in 2003* (Oxford: Clarendon Press, 2006), 70 (emphasis in original).

31. See John R. Searle, *The Rediscovery of the Mind* (Cambridge, Mass.: MIT Press, 1992), 4, 10–11.

32. See Hume, *Inquiry*, 80.

conscious, voluntary, intentional human behaviour."[33] But this is not the only way to look at the experience of freedom. In fact, it is a deceptive way to frame the issue.

This entire discussion of the opposition of freedom to determinism is wrongly framed, because the framers ignore the "perspective of the acting person."[34] According to Karol Wojtyła, freedom is the power of self-determination.[35] The evidence of freedom is neither the feeling "I did it myself" nor the judgment "he [or I] could have done otherwise," but rather the experience "I can, but I do not have to."[36] The difference is quite simple. The "perspective of the acting person" is not that of the observer but of the agent in the state of dynamizing himself (or not). When playing chess, my bishop does not move until I decide to reach out and take it in my hand. I can move the piece to the long diagonal, but I do not have to. I may choose to move the rook instead. But I can neither simply predict nor observe. As the acting person, I must move my piece. After murdering his wife, Othello could excuse himself and blame Iago. He could have regretted the life-choices that led to this tragic marriage. But as he entered the bedroom, it was up to him to kill Desdemona. "She will not die unless I, Othello, kill her." To be sure, both Othello and the chess player are subject to outside forces. A third party—or even the acting person himself—may consider the event after the fact and search for the factors influencing the agent. Mikhail Botvinnik was very successful with his bishops on the long diagonals. Perhaps hero-worship has clouded my own chessic judgment, inducing me

33. John R. Searle, *Minds, Brains and Science* (Cambridge, Mass.: Harvard University Press, 1984), 95, 98. See Peter van Inwagen, *Metaphysics* (Boulder, Colo.: Westview Press, 1993), 192–96.

34. See John Paul II, Encyclical *Veritatis Splendor* (Vatican City: Libreria Editrice Vaticana, 1993), no. 78 (henceforth *Veritatis Splendor*).

35. See LR, 47; Wojtyła, "Personal structure," 190; Karol Wojtyła, "Participation or Alienation," in *Person and Community*, 199; PEA, 1026, 1063; OC, 197–98; PA, 180; AP, 115–16; AR, 59.

36. See in Polish, "*Mogę—nie muszę,*" OC, 162, 166; in Italian, "*Posso ma non sono costretto,*" PEA, 978, 984ff.; in Spanish, "*Puedo, pero no tengo que,*" PA, 167; in English, "*I may but I need not,*" AP, 105.

to place my own bishops on the long diagonal without sufficient thought. But external factors notwithstanding, the acting person himself cannot escape his freedom. The act does not take place until he performs it, and hence freedom is intrinsic to the experience of the person in act.

Because the person is free, his life is in his own hand. He has the power of self-determination. Indeed, the evidence for freedom as self-determination is more compelling than that for the free choice of the will. Even if the alcoholic feels himself compelled to drink—if in an honest moment he must admit, "Tonight I will be drunk again"—he can nevertheless plan his future and attempt to take control by looking for a rehabilitation center, by joining a twelve-step program, or by taking other steps that may lead to his liberation from his addiction. Self-determination is an everyday experience for young people as they decide whether to enter the university or to learn a trade, whether to study business or the arts, and so on. Because we are rational beings, we can sketch out a future and take steps to realize this future. We are free to reshape our lives. Of course, this freedom is not absolute. A heavyset young person is probably foolish to plan a career in tennis. Nevertheless, freedom is real and inescapable.

Spiritual Nature

Because we are rational beings, we are spiritual beings. Karol Wojtyła writes, "*Inner life means spiritual life. It revolves around truth and goodness.*"[37] This is a direct consequence of the person's rationality. He has his own desires—"No one else can want for me."[38] Here again we are speaking on the level of experience. Others may well seek to influence what I want, by argument, seduction, or force, but they cannot "want" for me. We need only think of the mother insisting that the boy eat his spinach and then asking him, "See! Wasn't that good?" Her little son, of course, thinks it is not and wants no

37. LR, 23 (emphasis in the original). See AR, 29.
38. LR, 24. See AR, 31.

more. Of course, much more is at stake than the taste of vegetables, because the range of good is infinite, and this is precisely the point.

That we are spiritual beings is, for Karol Wojtyła, a matter of experience and not an ontological claim that there exists within us a non-material part called a spirit. Nor does he appeal to his own (and presumably his reader's) power of introspection. Rather his appeal is to the ordinary experience of every person that our lives do "in fact" revolve around truth and goodness. Later, he will write, "Within visible creation, man is the only creature who knows that he knows, and is therefore interested in the real truth of what he perceives. People cannot be genuinely indifferent to the question of whether what they know is true or not."[39] Similarly, human beings are universally concerned with what is genuinely good and not only with what is "good" but with what is "best." As Plato observed, "Nobody is satisfied to acquire things that are merely believed to be good, however, but everyone wants things that really *are* good and disdains mere belief here."[40] Whether the issue at hand is the quality of the meat in the refrigerator, the government's tax policies, the choice of a spouse, or the direction of one's life, human beings want what is genuinely good. *"Inner life means spiritual life. It revolves around truth and goodness."* Each human being knows by experience that he has an inner life and therefore that he is a spiritual being. Of course, this experience has important metaphysical consequences, but for now we simply note that this experience of the inner life is an ordinary, irreducible aspect of human experience.

This spiritual aspect of the human being, an aspect consequent upon our rationality and freedom, entails that the human person is capable not only of horizontal but also of vertical transcendence. Indeed, this vertical transcendence is a sign of the spirituality of the human person.[41] In a way, horizontal transcendence corresponds with the operations of the human appetites in the world, as the or-

---

39. *Fides et Ratio*, no. 25.
40. Plato, *Republic* 505d.
41. PEA, 1060. See *OC*, 223; PA, 255–67; AP, 174–83.

ganism is directed toward those things in its environment by which these appetites can be satisfied. Indeed, scientific reductionism can, by analyzing various appetites and their sources within the organism, attempt to account for all human experiences. Therefore they argue that traits that we regard as characteristically human, such as language and certain emotions, can be reduced to the functioning of biological mechanisms by which we are adapted to survive in a hostile world.[42] Hence, biologist Craig Stanford succinctly reduces language thus: "Language is a social behavior. It evolved in a context in which getting points across had some survival and reproductive value."[43] Just as beavers slap their tails on the water to warn others of impending danger, human beings have evolved with the ability to construct complex signals for the same purpose: "'Fear not, till Birnam Wood / Do come to Dunsinane': and now a wood / Comes toward Dunsinane. Arm, arm, and out!"[44] So does Macbeth warn of impending attack. Perhaps it may appear unfair to compare the beaver's warning with Shakespeare's dramatic poetry, but precisely here do we discover vertical transcendence. To be sure, like the beaver, Macbeth intends simply to warn his soldiers of danger, but what are Shakespeare's intentions? And what are our intentions as we read or watch this play? Our interest is not simply in the fictional death of one obscure monarch. Many kings have been killed in battle, but we are concerned with the wickedness of "this" Scottish king. Our minds are captivated by the contradictions in Macbeth's values and the degradation of his virtues. Much more is happening in this play than occurs in an educational film about beavers and their predatory neighbors. Shakespeare's play directs our attention to the implicit standards and norms by which values are to be judged.

42. See Ian Tattersall, "How We Came to Be Human," *Scientific American* 16, no. 2 (2006): 71; Joseph LeDoux, *Synaptic Self: How Our Brains Become Who We Are* (New York: Viking, 2002), 21.

43. Craig B. Stanford, *Significant Others: The Ape-Human Continuum and the Quest for Human Nature* (New York: Basic Books, 2001), 152 (emphasis in the original).

44. *Macbeth*, ed. W. J. Craig (New York: Oxford University Press, 1919), 5.5.44–46. References are to act, scene, and line.

This is precisely what vertical transcendence concerns. As a spiritual being—as one who lives from an interior life—the human being can question his values and integrate them according to some higher standard of goodness. This is precisely the direction of Karol Wojtyła's argument in the second chapter of *Love and Responsibility*, where he identifies, describes, and analyzes the various aspects of the human experience of love. Commonly—and we read this even in the popular press—the reductionist account will reduce human love to the sexual impulse, explaining the desire of one person for another in terms of evolutionarily based mating strategies, based on indicators of female fertility, masculine strength, and so on. Recognizing that in fact purely biological factors do not entirely suffice for an account of human sexual behavior, many scientists will also factor in the need, common to human beings and the higher apes, for companionship and stable community life. (Of course these cultural factors too must ultimately find their roots in biology.) When we look at human experience, however, we see a rather confusing aggregation of factors—confusing not primarily to scientists and philosophers, but to everyone and especially to the young. Love begins with attraction, and attraction is toward beauty. "O she teaches the torches to burn bright!"[45] exclaims Romeo upon seeing Juliet. Furthermore, attraction may be triggered not so much by physical features as by other qualities, such as intelligence, nobility, sense of humor, athletic prowess, and so on. Somewhat separate from this is sexual desire itself, which is not (and is, for that matter, seldom experienced as) the simple admiration of beauty. In Bizet's *Carmen*, Don José's fiancée, Micaëla, is beautiful, but the opera's eponymous heroine is sexually desirable, and every man in the town square wants her. Micaëla's beauty and virtue are attractive indeed, but Carmen's potent sexuality works differently and more compellingly upon Don José's soul. A further factor helping to constitute love is sympathy, the natural attunement one feels with a person

45. *Romeo and Juliet* (Craig), 1.5.48.

who shares one's own interests, loves, and hates. Sympathy is the natural door to friendship, which may itself open the door to erotic love. Now the point is simply that these experiential factors may well conflict with each other in a given person's life. The task then is to sort them out.

A researcher in cultural evolution theory may offer hypotheses that integrate the operation of the urge to procreate with social behavior and aesthetic responses and use these hypotheses to explain the sublimation of the sexual desire in certain personality types. If we consider these apparent conflicts between material factors and transcendent values from the point of view of the acting person, however, the problem is quite different. The girl of eighteen may be in love with a very handsome but unemployed young man of whom her parents disapprove. They find his character to be lacking, but she must decide what to do, how to proceed, and in doing so, she implicitly chooses her standards of judgment. She may choose charm and physical appearance or, respecting her parent's judgment, she may consider his character more closely and critically. *The factors and the values that the lover experiences do not present themselves in experience as integrated.* Karol Wojtyła writes: "The integration of love requires the individual consciously and by acts of the will to impose a shape on all the material that sensual and emotional reactions provide."[46] This integration can be accomplished only in terms of some governing principle.

In his analysis of sensuality, Karol Wojtyła indicates the reason this integration is needed and the direction it must take.

The promptings of sensuality would give a man all the guidance he needs in his sexual life if, in the first place, his sexual reactions were infallibly guided by instinct, and if in the second place the object of those reactions—a person of the opposite sex—did not demand a different attitude from that which is proper to sensuality.[47]

---

46. LR, 153. See AR, 187.
47. LR, 107. See AR, 132.

We have observed already why human sexual reactions are not infallibly guided by instinct. Let us consider here the objection in the "second place" that Wojtyła presents, that a person of the opposite sex demands "a different attitude from that which is proper to sensuality." The person given in experience is not merely a bearer of desirable sexual characteristics and indeed is given to experience as more than simply a phenomenal event. The beloved is desirable for a variety of reasons, which is to say that the beloved represents a variety of values. She is physically beautiful and at times sexually desirable. He is funny and makes her laugh. He admires her deep convictions and her willingness to stand up for them. She appreciates his temperance when his acquaintances become crude. All these values stir emotions and reactions within the lover. But how should he respond? Neither admiration for beauty nor desire, neither delight in the other's masculinity or feminity nor the joy of laughter of itself, adequately and fully provides the lover with the guidance he needs for his actions. He needs an overarching principle, a truth about the good.

Experience of the Person

In different ways, attraction to a person's beauty, sensual desires, sympathy, and so on all constitute aspects of the experience of the person, but they are incomplete. Taken alone, none of them suffices if we are to make sense of our experience. Reductionism does not make sense. Let me qualify this. Of course, a philosopher can become a reductionist. More important, anyone can become reductionist in his attitude toward others, reducing them to values that concern only himself. We need only consider Helen Gurley Brown's *Sex and the Single Girl*, which teaches young women how to use men sexually to get the finer things in life, or any man who builds his life on the principle that "everyone has his price."[48] Furthermore, it is

48. Helen G. Brown, *Sex and the Single Girl* (Fort Lee, New Jersey: Barricade Books, 2003).

indeed true that one can direct his life according to such principles and in such a way that he will never experience counterexamples to them, simply because his principles of interpretation do eventually limit his range of experience. If one's guiding principle is that "it's a dog-eat-dog world" and that everyone is an adversary, then he cannot even recognize someone who is not trying to outdo him. Existentially, reductionism is possible. However, it is not necessarily entailed by experience.

Emotion and the Person

One of the most refreshing and challenging aspects of Karol Wojtyła's thought is his account of emotion, a theme from which many philosophers shy away. It is tempting and easy to regard emotion as an inexplicable surd in human experience, an inexplicable sort of feeling that is either superfluous to rationality or foundational to a romantic conception of human life. Emotion is supposed to be either the subjective baggage attendant upon our evolutionary heritage or the basis for everything worthwhile in human life. Indeed, an important theme in *Love and Responsibility* is the difference between love and the emotions with which it is so often identified, and a careful reading shows Karol Wojtyła to have developed a compelling and satisfying account of human emotion and its roots in the human intellect and will. If we understand this account of emotion, we will be rewarded with a deep insight into the inadequacy of reductionist accounts of experience.

As we examine the experience of emotion carefully we discover its two aspects. First, emotions arise from the encounter with values and not simply from the information provided by the senses.[49] The senses provide data but do not of themselves inspire emotions. This is clear from any number of experiences of sense-deception. If I see someone from behind who might be my friend, I experience a

49. See PEA, 1148–49; OC, 288–91; LR, 102; AR, 126–27; PA, 330; AP, 228.

momentary joy, until the person turns around and, upon my seeing that he is someone else, my emotion of joy vanishes. Similarly,
fear disappears when the snake in the garden is discovered to be a
piece of garden hose. The object of emotion is an "object of value"
and not simply a stimulus of the senses. Our emotional responses
therefore constitute an experience not only of "values" but also of
"things." Second, we find that although emotions may have physical effects (tingling skin, heart palpitations, and the like) they are
not constituted by these things. Rather, emotion is experienced as
involving the whole person. If I burn my hand on the stove, the pain
is localized, but the resultant fear remains in my being long after
the pain is gone. We may say that the feet of the burn victim will not
approach the stove that burned his hand. It is the whole person who
experiences the emotion, because it is the person whose values are
reflected by the emotion. Through our emotions, our experience of
values we become aware of good and evil.[50]

In *Person and Act* Wojtyła first addresses emotions negatively, in
an analysis of the emotionalization of consciousness.[51] This emotionalization begins "when, in their reflection [in consciousness],
the meaning of single emotive facts vanishes as well as the objects
related to them, when in a way the sensations overcome the human
being's comprehension of them. In practice it is a surrender of self-
knowledge."[52] The problem of emotionalization, therefore, is that
the self becomes submerged, as it were, in the emotions that over-
whelm it; the self thus ceases accurately to reflect the reality of the
situation with which the person is confronted. In this submersion,
the self is obscured and ceases to govern its own life and behavior.
At this point in his argument, Karol Wojtyła argues that, although
emotions are states that "happen to" a human being, they can—and
should—be governed by the knowledge of the world and of self.

Let us notice, however, what this implies about emotion. Emo-

---

50. See PEA, 1151–53; OC, 291–94; PA, 360–62; AP, 250–51.
51. See PEA, 896–904; OC, 99–105; PA, 97–105; AP, 50–56.
52. PEA, 900. See OC, 101; PA, 101; AP, 52–53.

tion is an engagement of the entire person by some value, which for its part is not "known" by emotion. The emotion properly attaches to some particular thing, some valuable reality in the world. The emotionalized person has, as we often observe, "lost touch" with reality and needs to get a more realistic perspective on the situation. (Think of the young adolescent whose "life will be ruined" by failure to make the basketball team or the cast of the senior play. Teenagers live much of their lives in an emotionalized state. Learning how to control and manage emotions is one of the challenges of growing up.) On the other hand, as emotion arises from the apprehension of some value, it has the effect of energizing the person for action with respect to that value. The soldier motivated by patriotism and love for his companions will fight more energetically. The young man in love is constantly attentive to the desires of his beloved and is more ardent in his pursuit of her.

Wojtyła's perspective on emotion is instructive. On the one hand, he does not reduce it to an irrational happening that overwhelms consciousness, in the manner of the love potion in the legend of Tristan and Iseult. Emotion does happen to a person, sometimes unexpectedly but not irrationally (think of the camper's sudden fear when a bear appears). And furthermore, emotion can be mastered. On the other hand, emotion does not reduce to a concatenation of sensations and actions, as though sadness, for example, were nothing other than the experience of a certain lethargy accompanied by the impulse to weep, or anger simply the experience of accelerated heart rate and heightened attentiveness and readiness to fight. Antonio, the eponymous merchant of Venice in Shakespeare's play, complains, "In sooth, I know not why I am so sad."[53] The merchant is struck with inexplicable sadness, to be sure, but he believes that it has a reason, a cause which his friends, Salarino and Salanio, propose to be anxiety about his ships. We know that Shakespeare is foreshadowing the troubles that Antonio will soon face, but we

---

53. *Merchant of Venice* (Craig), 1.1.1.

also know that Salarino and Salanio are right, that uncertainty and the possibility (even remote) of financial ruin can cast an investor into a melancholic mood. We are emotional beings because things are important to us. The analytic reductionism that would reduce emotion to its manifestations and symptoms fails to come to grips with the experience itself, as does the irrational romanticism that reduces emotion to the mysterious inner engine by which our lives are directed—especially in matters of love.

Conclusion

For Karol Wojtyła the question of man is the central issue of our time. We need to understand what the human being is. There is needed an "adequate anthropology," an anthropology that relies on the "experience of man."[54] The question, however, is controverted. On the basis of well-developed scientific theories, philosophers and scientists today argue that the human being is nothing other than an accident of nature, the accidental outcome of the random interactions of material particles derived from the primordial Big Bang. In much of the literature on human nature by both scientists and philosophers, we find a persistent rejection of human subjectivity. We read, for instance: "The common, naïve impression that we use the mind to initiate and control our physical actions has long been rejected almost universally in science, following the doctrine of scientific materialism, which predicates that a full account of brain behavior and reality is possible in terms purely physical."[55] And "the choice we are tacitly presented with is between a 'scientific' approach, as represented by one or another of the current versions of 'materialism', and an 'antiscientific' approach, as represented by Cartesianism or some other traditional religious conception of the

54. See John Paul II, *Man and Woman*, 13:1–2, 178–79; John Paul II, *Mężczyzną i niewiastą*, 44.
55. Roger W. Sperry, "Consciousness and Causality," in *The Oxford Companion to the Mind*, ed. Richard L. Gregory, 164 (Oxford: Oxford University Press, 1987).

mind."[56] It is very easy to find many texts arguing that any perspective that attributes significance to the human mind, to human subjectivity, is fundamentally flawed. It is assumed that those who do not accept scientific materialism are simply blind to the facts, or, as Searle puts it, "in the grip of faith."[57] To believe that there is something special about human beings—that they enjoy personal freedom, that they have any kind of higher destiny, that they are capable of sacrificial love—is to move into a sentimental realm of religion and myth and to leave the real world of fact and science.

The strength of Karol Wojtyła's argument is that he appeals precisely to experience. To be sure, the question of the relationship between human experience and scientific method is complex, but it is hard (and not a little strange) to maintain that experience is irrelevant to knowledge. Wojtyła's project is to sketch out the contours of human experience itself and to take that experience as fundamental for the knowledge of the human person. If we want to give an adequate account of the human being—and we must keep in mind that this is something that pertains deeply to us all—then we cannot ignore or explain away certain central aspects of our experience. Although it may be possible to isolate different *loci* in the brain as the centers for different kinds of experience, our experience of ourselves as acting persons who feel emotion and respond to things in the world, responding as integrated wholes, is genuine and irreducible. Karol Wojtyła's challenge, then, is that with a sufficiently rich understanding of experience, we can know the truth about the person—a very important truth.

56. Searle, Rediscovery, 4.
57. Ibid., 90.

4 ∾

TRUTH ABOUT THE HUMAN PERSON

The Meaning of "Truth"

Karol Wojtyła/John Paul II clearly accepts the Aristotelian-Thomistic concept of truth as the correspondence of intellect and thing—*adequatio intelletus et rei*.[1] Because truth is this correspondence, it can neither be reduced to nor be founded exclusively upon consciousness. The reality of operativity (or efficacy—*sprawcość*) or the efficient causality of the human act, upon which Karol Wojtyła had insisted in his *Person and Act*,[2] demands that the person attain to the truth concerning those things which he intends to affect in the world, concerning his actions and their consequences. Without truth, properly understood as the correspondence between the mind and the object of its thought, he cannot act effectively in the real world. The intention to act effectively, that is, to complete a human act, implies an understanding of reality. In this way, Karol Wojtyła/John Paul II shows himself to be a philosophical realist.

Philosophical realism implies not only that we can acquire knowledge of facts and individual things but also that we can comprehend the structures of reality as a whole. The world, as world,

---

1. Karol Wojtyła, "The Problem of Experience in Ethics," in *Person and Community,* 116–17; *Fides et Ratio,* no. 44, 56. Also Aquinas, *De Veritate* 1, 1.

2. See PEA, 909–24; PA, 111–26; OC, 109–20; AP, 60–71.

is not a simple collection of things or of facts—in Wittgenstein's words: "1. The world is all that is the case. 1.1. The world is the totality of facts, not of things."[3] Rather it is precisely because the world has a structure "as a world" that the human being can comprehend it intellectually. We are not like the lions, who cannot survive anywhere except Africa (or someplace similar); on the contrary, thanks to human understanding of different environments, we can invent clothing, weapons for hunting and other tools, and adapt to European and American forests, and even to the extreme conditions of the Arctic. Because the soul, as Aristotle says, is in some way all things,[4] we can know the world "as a world" and hence develop sciences and technology. The human person is capable of conforming himself and adapting his actions to the world—to all reality—in order to act effectively. It is important to emphasize that knowledge, and ultimately understanding, does not consist simply in an assembly of facts, a catalogue of ideas based on sense-data. On the contrary, understanding implies and consists in the formation, the "informing," of the mind. In a way, what the person knows "exists" in his mind. The mind of the chemist is "chemistry"; he thinks "chemically." Sherlock Holmes[5] laments to Watson that, because of his peculiar mentality he cannot enjoy the beauty of the English countryside. Where Watson sees lovely gardens and byways lined with shrubs, he (Sherlock) can see only opportunities for criminals. But this, of course, is precisely the secret to his success in solving crimes that leave Watson baffled. Holmes's mind is criminological; it is formed by crime.

Of particular importance to John Paul II is the knowledge of the person. In his *Love and Responsibility*, Karol Wojtyła insists on the necessity of truth in order to attain to genuine love.[6] Therefore we

3. Ludwig Wittgenstein, *Tractatus Logico-Philosophicus*, 1, 1.1, trans. David Pears and Brian McGuinness (London: Routledge & Kegan Paul, 1961), 6–7.

4. Aristotle, *On The Soul* Bk. 3, Ch 8 431 b21.

5. Arthur Conan Doyle, "The Adventure of the Copper Beeches," in *The Complete Adventures and Memoirs of Sherlock Holmes* (New York: Bramhall House, 1975), 161.

6. See LR, 119–20; AR, 147–48.

need to understand how we can know the human person. What is the truth concerning the person?

The Truth about the Person

We begin this section with an especially important text from the Second Vatican Council, which John Paul II cites frequently in his papal writings:

Indeed, the Lord Jesus ... implied a certain likeness between the union of the divine Persons, and the unity of God's sons in truth and charity. This likeness reveals that man, who is the only creature on earth which God willed for itself, cannot fully find himself except through a sincere gift of himself.[7]

This text is important not only theologically and ecclesiastically but philosophically as well. There are two aspects of this text to which we should devote our attention. First, man is a creature desired or willed for himself, that is, not for the use of any other creature nor even for God himself. Second, man—the human person—can find his complete realization only in the sincere gift of self for others.

The first aspect reflects an important principle, which Karol Wojtyła develops in *Love and Responsibility*, namely, that the person cannot be used as someone else's instrument, as merely a means for the other to attain his own ends.[8] The person lives according to his own reason and freedom, from his interior.[9] He is *sui juris*. For a person to be utilized by another for ends with which he may not agree constitutes an alienation of self, because his self-possession is a condition of his capacity to act, to be an agent. In *Love and Responsibility*, Wojtyła insists that not even God himself can use the person.[10] Thanks to his rationality and freedom, by his interiority, the person is master of himself and enjoys self-possession and self-

---

7. Vatican Council II, *Pastoral Constitution Gaudium et Spes* (Vatican City: Librería Editrice Vaticana, 1965), no. 24 (henceforth *Gaudium et Spes*).

8. See LR, 26–27; AR, 34–35. 9. See LR, 22–23; AR, 28–29.

10. See LR, 27; AR, 35.

determination. Precisely from this results the "personalist principle," which, in its negative form, states: the person cannot be instrumentalized, that is, treated as an object for use. In its positive form it states: the only appropriate attitude toward the person is love.[11]

And let us recall that love demands truth. However, if it is necessary to treat the person according to the truth, we must ask what the truth is. How can we know the truth concerning the person? Let us begin with an example. From the zoological sciences the horseman knows horses, that they are a kind of mammal, herbivorous, strong, social. Furthermore, he knows much about "this" horse, which is his own—when it likes to race, its tendency to nervousness, its habits during competition, and so on. A good horseman knows horses and knows his own horse well. Because of this, he can use it to win a race, work on his ranch, or pull a cart.

Similarly, we can speak of the knowledge of the human being. Like the horse, the human being is a mammal and social, but also an omnivore and not very strong. Existing in space and time among other physical objects and animals, he has many limitations. Ludwig van Beethoven was born in Bonn in 1770—not in Athens in 428 BC, as Plato was—and he spoke German (and not Greek). His father was an alcoholic. In spite of these limitations, Beethoven achieved something supra-temporal; although he died in 1827, his music is still heard today. How is it that a young man from an unknown family and without the advantages enjoyed by many other young men of his era came to write such great musical works? It is a mystery. We cannot enter into his mind, into his soul, to know what inspired him. How can we understand Beethoven? And furthermore, how can I come to know the truth about my friend, my children, my wife?

11. See LR, 41; AR, 51.

Original Solitude

In his audiences on the theology of the body,[12] John Paul II analyzes the account in Genesis concerning the creation of the human race. There we read the words of the Lord, "It is not good that the man should be alone; I want to make him a help similar to himself" (Gen. 2:18).[13] John Paul II continues:

The analysis of the pertinent passages of Genesis [see Gen. 2] has brought us to surprising conclusions with regard to anthropology, that is the fundamental science about man, contained in this book. In fact, in relatively few sentences, the ancient text sketches man as a *person with the subjectivity characterizing the person.*[14]

What John Paul II discovers in this account is the solitude of the human being. In order to find a suitable help for the man, God presents him with all the animals so that he might examine and name them. However, among the animals the man found no adequate help. Why? He recognized immediately that he was superior to the animals. It was "he" who named "them." He had rationality and they did not. Certainly in one sense he had a body similar to those of the animals, and for this reason he too was an animal—but a different kind of animal. The man is "rational animal." In other words, the man is distinguished from the animals by his "subjectivity."

We can say that his solitude arose from two different factors. The first was his subjectivity itself. Adam was not a mere thing but a subject capable of thinking about his actions and decisions; he was the "author" of what he did. Furthermore, having received from the Lord the commandment not to eat of the tree of the knowledge of good and evil, he was "responsible" for his actions, for his behavior. His life did not pertain only to the order limited to Eden and its environs, but was open to the Infinite. His task, which he had received

---

12. John Paul II, *Man and Woman.*

13. Unless otherwise noted, translations of Scripture are drawn directly from *Man and Woman He Created Them.*

14. John Paul II, *Man and Woman,* 6:1, 150–51.

from God the Creator, was not limited to the satisfaction of vital necessities, but he was to exercise dominion over the earth as God's "viceroy." In virtue of his relationship with God, the Covenant, he became a "Partner with the Absolute."[15] To this profound experience of one's own subjectivity, John Paul II gives the name "solitude," and in this sense solitude is an essential property of the human being, something that pertains to his spiritual character, without which he would not be a person. The second factor from which the man's solitude arose was that he was the only human being in the garden. He had no one with whom to talk, work, or play—to share his life. To solve this problem—"It is not good for the man to be alone"—God created the woman.

Just here we should pause briefly to reflect on John Paul II's method. Clearly, the account of creation in Genesis 2 has a mythical character.[16] That the human race appeared in southern Africa between 50,000 and 100,000 years ago does not constitute a problem for his analysis. His interest is not in reconstructing the history of the human race—this is a task for sciences such as anthropology and paleontology—but to "reconstruct the constitutive elements of man's original experience."[17] The text from Genesis presents us in mythical form an account of the primordial experiences that lie at the root of all human experience, in which we can "discover the extraordinary nature of what is ordinary."[18] We can say that these scriptural texts offer John Paul II a theme for a phenomenological analysis. That is to say, not only do the texts from Genesis present supernatural truths, authentic revelations of the interior life of God himself, but they also reveal primordial perspectives on our own nature and being. For this reason, John Paul II's analysis has a character as much philosophical as theological.

15. See ibid., 6:2, 151.
17. Ibid., 11:1, 169.
16. See ibid., 3:1, 138, note.
18. Ibid., 11:1, 170.

Encounter with the Woman

When the man awoke and met the woman he said, "This time she is flesh from my flesh and bones from my bones" (Gen. 2:23). Although many writers focus on this passage as the discovery of someone of the opposite sex, as the moment at which a man rejoices at seeing a woman for the first time, what John Paul II finds to be of primary significance is that the man rejoices to find a person like himself. With his exclamation, Adam expresses his joy in meeting a "help similar to himself." This similarity is not to be found only or even primarily in the physical. By its power and speed, the horse can, of course, serve as a help. The dog is clever and can help to herd cattle and sheep. The woman, however, is "flesh from my flesh," which is to say, "a person like me." She is a person with her own subjectivity, founded in her intelligence and freedom. The woman enjoys her own interior solitude, because she too is a "partner with the Absolute," before Whom she is responsible. She is a fitting help to Adam because she is equal to him. John Paul II comments thus on the words of Genesis 2:23:

The man speaks these words as if it were only at the sight of the woman that he could identify and call by name *that which makes them in a visible way similar, the one to the other,* and at the same time *that in which humanity is manifested.* In the light of the earlier analysis of all the 'bodies' man came in contact with and conceptually defined, giving them their names [*animalia*], the expression 'flesh from my flesh' takes on precisely this meaning: the body reveals man. This concise formula already contains all that human science will ever be able to say about the structure of the body as an organism, about its vitality, about its particular sexual physiology, etc. In this first expression of the man, 'flesh from my flesh' contains also a reference to that by which that body is authentically human.[19]

"The body reveals man." This carries us beyond Hume's position and past all reductionism. Strictly speaking, Hume is capable of experiencing little more than shapes and colors.[20] In his imagina-

---

19. Ibid., 9:4, 164 (emphasis in the original).
20. See also Jarosław Kupczak, *Destined for Liberty: The Human Person in the Philosophy*

tion, at least, Descartes could see the figures walking outside his window, wearing their hats and coats, and question whether these were truly men or perhaps automatons.[21] However, what the author of Genesis wrote, which John Paul II affirms, is that the man could see immediately that "this . . . is flesh of my flesh," a person like me.

So how do we respond to reductionism? If we turn to ordinary human experience, we are not surprised that Adam recognized Eve as a person. If, as a person makes his way through life, he is unable to recognize another human being as a person—that is to say, as a being with an interior life, with sentiments, thoughts, desires, and emotions—we recognize that he is abnormal. It may be that he has autism, which prevents one from recognizing the motions and intentions of other persons. However, autism is not paradigmatic but abnormal. Normal, in the sense of "ordinary," experience is precisely "normal."

In his introduction to *Person and Act*, Karol Wojtyła directs us toward the totality of our experience as human beings, experience that has two aspects, the interior and the exterior. To pretend that these aspects may be irreconcilable, that what we experience physically is, as Descartes supposes, absolutely distinct and separate from what goes on in our minds, is false and badly misleading. That is to say, the "I" whose hand picks up the physical volume of *Meditations* is the same "I" that thinks about Descartes. "Therefore for myself I am not only 'interiority,' but also 'exteriority,' an object of both experiences, interior and exterior."[22] But if we regard it as a fiction to separate the interior from the exterior of the "I" who I am, it is likewise a fiction to separate the interior from the exterior of another human being.[23] I do not experience simply a flux of shapes and colors in my visual

of *Karol Wojtyła/John Paul II* (Washington, D.C.: The Catholic University of America Press, 2000), 62.

21. René Descartes, "Meditation II," in *Meditations on First Philosophy*, trans. Donald. A. Cress (Indianapolis: Hackett Publishing Company, 1993), 13.

22. PEA, 836. See PA, 37; OC, 55–56; AP, 7.

23. See the excellent article by Krzysztof Guzowski, "El personalismo de comunión en Karol Wojtyła," in Burgos, *La filosofía personalista*, esp. 196–97.

consciousness, nor a series of images of a body in different positions and places. I see a person dancing or playing football. Even if he is deceiving us, we know that a conscious agent intends to accomplish something, an intention that we may perhaps eventually discover. Police detectives do this every day, recognizing that the casual pedestrian stumbling amiably in a crowd is in fact picking pockets. This expression from the theology of the body—"the body reveals man"—is a logical consequence of the principle in *Person and Act*, "the act reveals the person."

After presenting this principle in the theology of the body, John Paul II continues: "This concise formula already contains all that human science will ever be able to say about the structure of the body as an organism, about its vitality, about its particular sexual physiology, etc."[24] Of course, neither this phrase, "the body reveals man," nor its scriptural inspiration, "this is flesh of my flesh," tells us anything about the human body's respiration or its omnivorous diet, about either the woman's monthly cycle or the man's sexual impulses. Why, then, does John Paul II say that this formula contains "everything" that science can say about the human organism? The answer is that this information about the body's organic structure and its physiology must be situated within the more fundamental understanding of the human being as an integrated whole. The structure and physiology of the human organism serve the personal—and hence the spiritual—life of the person. Just as St. Thomas Aquinas teaches that the body exists for the good of the soul, so does John Paul II insist that the body manifests the person.[25]

Besides being a person, the woman is also a feminine being who can unite with the man so that the two become "one flesh," and from this union there may result a new person. The "spousal" meaning of the body arises from the capacity of these persons, man and woman, to give themselves freely in love.[26] This means that the body

24. John Paul II, *Man and Woman*, 9:4, 164.
25. See Aquinas, ST I-II, q. 2, a. 5.
26. See John Paul II, *Man and Woman*, 14:5, 184.

has its own significance, which surpasses that of a merely material thing, that of a kind of amalgamated material thing with which intelligence can do what it wishes. And this significance is its spousal meaning,[27] which signifies the *"power to express love: precisely that love in which the human person becomes a gift and—through this gift—fulfils the very meaning of his being and existence."*[28] This means that not only do the man and the woman mutually complement each other, but furthermore that they can make of themselves each a gift for the other. This mutual donation constitutes a *communio personarum*, a communion of persons. Here we find the heart, the core of John Paul II's teaching on human love and, in reality, not only on the love between man and woman but on every human love: the communion of persons.

Truth about "This" Person

Our theme is the truth—the truth about the person—and our reflections thus far do not suffice for a response concerning the truth about the person, because the person is—precisely in virtue of being a person—unrepeatable. Thanks to his individuality, his unrepeatability, we can speak of the truth about "this" person, and of course when we treat of love, this truth becomes very important. The young man may be handsome and charming, but she needs to know if he is honorable. Don José loved Carmen greatly for her beauty and sex appeal, but he should have known too that she was unfaithful to her lovers and a smuggler. By ignoring these important truths, Don José fell into a life of crime and eventually murdered Carmen. Every father and mother tries to teach their children to fix their attention not only on appearances but on the deeper reality about a girlfriend or boyfriend.

Concerning every person we can speak of his "facticity," of his physical and psychological characteristics. This person is not simply

27. In Italian, "*sponsale*"; in Polish, "*oblubieńczym*."
28. John Paul II, *Man and Woman*, 15:1, 185–86 (emphasis in the original).

a person, but is a man or a woman, tall or short, intelligent, or athletic, speaks Spanish, Polish, Chinese, or some other language. And beyond these qualities, an expert (e.g., a physician) could say much more even than someone who already knows this person. However, we know well that to know much about a person does not constitute knowledge of his personality, of "who he is." That she was a Gypsy did not imply that Carmen had to be a criminal. When we speak of the truth about the person, we are thinking of something more than his "facticity." We are thinking of the mystery that this person is. When we speak of the knowledge of a person, of knowing the truth about this person, we are thinking of his spiritual character. To be spiritual means to live from an interior life, a life centered on truth and goodness.[29] It means, in fact, to be constantly in search of the truth about the perfect good, which is necessarily to be found only in God the Creator. But can one know a spiritual being? To pose the problem more sharply: If truth is the correspondence between intellect and thing (adequatio intellectus et rei), what sense can we make of the correspondence between an intellect and something that is not fixed, between the mind and a being whose identity is based on his self-determination and his transcendence toward the good in general?

"The Man Knew His Wife"

The Scriptures mention the man's knowledge of his wife in Genesis 4, where we read: "Now Adam knew Eve his wife and she conceived and bore Cain" (Gen. 4:1). The scriptural sense of this word "knew" here is "had sexual relations with."[30] In the New Testament, we again see this usage, when Mary expresses puzzlement over how she can be the mother of the Messiah: "How can this be since I do not know a man?" (Luke 1:34). John Paul II analyzes this sense, so

29. See LR, 22–23; AR, 28–29.
30. John Paul II, Man and Woman, 205. John Paul II initially cites a modern translation which reads, "Adam united himself with his wife."

strange to our modern ears, of "knowledge as sexual union," something that is certainly not a mental action but a very physical one.[31] How can we consider this action, in which rationality seems to play so small a role, to be a form of knowledge?

To begin with, John Paul II notes that the ancient sense of "to know" implied not so much a mental process, a fact about the mind, as the experience of something in its totality. And in the sexual union, in the mutual union of their bodies, man and woman experience each other in their emotions, sentiments, and intentions. However, especially in our era, we tend toward a vision of this union that is too limited, regarding it in terms of pleasure, emotional satisfaction, and mutual diversion or "fun."

The reality of this union, nevertheless, is more complex. As the scriptural text notes, this knowledge can result in the conception of a new life. The sexual union serves the biological continuation of the human species and therefore has an important natural significance. Furthermore, it also plays a metaphysical role, because that which this union procreates is not only an animal but also a person—that is, a spiritual being. Karol Wojtyła writes: "The parents know that they participate in the genesis of a person. We know that the person is not only an organism. The human body is the body of a person, because it forms a substantial unity with the human spirit."[32] Therefore, according to John Paul II, this knowledge is realized completely in paternity and maternity.[33] The "thou" with which "I" am united can become a mother or father by this union. Wojtyła writes: "Procreation brings it about that 'the man and the woman (his wife)' *know each other reciprocally in the 'third,' originated by both*. For this reason, the 'knowledge' becomes in some way a revelation of the new man, in whom both, the man and the woman, again recognize each other, their humanity, their living image."[34] Furthermore,

31. See ibid., 20:22, 204–18.
32. LR, 55. See AR, 69.
33. John Paul II, *Man and Woman*, 21:2, 210–11.
34. Ibid., 21:4, 211–12 (emphasis in the original).

because this physical union does not suffice to create a spiritual being, the action of God the Creator is needed as the cause with which the parents procreate a spiritual being. Such a union, this union of the two, is the mutual experience of each one in his totality. But what is it that this knowledge knows?

"Communio personarum"

The Scriptures reveal that man is created by God in His own image (Gen. 1:27). He is *imago Dei*. Furthermore, although it is a datum of Revelation, that man is an image of the divine is also reflected in ancient myths and in ancient philosophy. Plato, for example, speaks of finding a glimpse of the divine in the human soul.[35] And in *Love and Responsibility*, our author explains that this image is philosophically almost identical with the notion of person that he had developed.[36] From the most ancient days in the history of Christianity, the image of God was understood as situated in the immortal soul, in the rationality of the human being. John Paul II affirms that this identification is correct and constitutes "*the immutable basis of all Christian anthropology.*"[37] Later on, however, in *Mulieris Dignitatem* he adds that the person cannot live alone, but

... he can exist only as a "unity of the two," and therefore *in relation to another human person*. It is a question here of a mutual relationship: man to woman and woman to man. Being a person in the image and likeness of God thus also involves existing in a relationship, in relation to the other "I." ... The fact that man "created as man and woman" is the image of God means not only that each of them individually is like God, as a rational and free being. It also means that man and woman, created as a "unity of the two" in their common humanity, are called to live in a communion of love, and in this way to mirror in the world the communion of love that is in God.[38]

35. See Plato, *Republic* 518b.
36. See LR, 40–41; AR, 50–51.
37. John Paul II, Apostolic *Letter Mulieris Dignitatem* (Vatican City: Librería Editrice Vaticana, 1988) no. 6 (henceforth *Mulieris Dignitatem*) (emphasis in the original).
38. *Mulieris Dignitatem*, no. 7. See also John Paul II, *Man and Woman*, 9:2–3, 162–63.

That God is communion of love means that persons in his image are also to live in community of love, in communion. As a datum of Revelation, the mystery of the Trinity surpasses the powers of human understanding and hence of philosophy, but it does shed light on the nature of the human person, a light to which the text of *Gaudium et Spes* refers: "man ... cannot fully find himself except through a sincere gift of himself."[39]

In his encyclical *Fides et Ratio*, John Paul II discusses the question of faith in relation to human knowledge.[40] The act of thinking is profoundly personal, to the point that we hold it as a uniquely human privilege that "my" thoughts belong to "me." Modern philosophy bases the autonomy of the person on this ability to think, this capacity for reasoning. On the other hand, we have to admit that most of our knowledge originates not within our own experience but in that of others. We receive knowledge from parents, teachers, friends, journalists, scientists and many others, and this is not merely the knowledge of facts but also our understanding of various aspects of the world. In 2003 the majority of Americans "knew" that the invasion of Iraq was necessary for peace and freedom in that region, as well as for the security of the United States. At that same time the majority of French people "knew" that the invasion was a horrible mistake, which could lead only to instability and suffering for the Iraqis and greater dangers for other countries. Now we may consider that Americans are intelligent, and that many of them have the opportunity to read the international press. But the French are also intelligent and many could have read the American press. If we ask how it is possible that two nations of intelligent people could disagree so profoundly, the answer is simple. Americans trust their leaders and discussed these matters among themselves. By the same token, the French trusted their leaders and discussed these matters with other French people. To a very great extent we learn

---

39. *Gaudium et Spes*, no. 24.
40. See *Fides et Ratio*, no. 31 and 32.

what and how to think from those around us. This fact gives rise to questions and problems, of course. A situation like this does not mean that we must accept relativism, for instance, that there cannot be a truth about the war in Iraq. Indeed, each of us is responsible to try to discern to what extent he may have uncritically accepted his beliefs from others.

John Paul II argues that because it is not possible for a single person to know all the facts about the world or for him to attain complete comprehension of the physical and social sciences, we need to entrust ourselves to the testimony of other persons. "This means that the human being—the one who seeks the truth—is also *the one who lives by belief*,"[41] and furthermore, "In believing, we entrust ourselves to the knowledge acquired by other people."[42] This trust establishes a relationship between the two persons, the one who entrusts and the one who confidently receives. This necessity for entrusting ourselves to others implies not only that the person enjoys access to more facts and theories, although this is true, but also that he becomes enriched by his trust in other persons. In this way he can "enter into a relationship with them which is intimate and enduring."[43] John Paul II continues: "At the same time, however, knowledge through belief, grounded as it is on trust between persons, is linked to truth: in the act of believing, men and women entrust themselves to the truth which the other declares to them."[44] Precisely because of this, the need to trust in the knowledge and understanding of others does not constitute a weakness. On the contrary, it strengthens us. One who knows—whether this be you or I or René Descartes—is not merely an autonomous center of reason and knowledge. The sharing of knowledge creates a community. Indeed, do we not speak of the scientific or the philosophical community? In this mutual entrusting with other persons we can realize the truth and arrive at secure knowledge.

41. Ibid., no. 31 (emphasis in the original).
42. Ibid., no. 32.
43. Ibid.
44. Ibid.

"Now Adam knew Eve his wife and she conceived and bore Cain." In this "knowing" the man and the woman were each mutually entrusted to the other. And—note well!—the woman conceived, which means that "she had a conception." Let us notice this language, the language of "knowledge" and "conception." This term "conception" is not only biological but also intellectual. In an intellectual encounter—whether this be between teacher and students or in any honest discussion—one encounters the truth, not only the truth about things and theories, but also the truth of the person who shares his understanding and knowledge. I encounter the truth through the person who loves me and to whom I can entrust myself.[45] It is the same dynamism that one finds in the sexual union, in which the man entrusts himself to the woman and she to him. Together they attain an understanding of self, an understanding that is manifest in the being of a new person.

Conclusion

Arguing from the Aristotelian principle that the soul is, in some way, all things, St. Thomas Aquinas maintains that the vision of the divine essence, in which vision consists the happiness of the human being, is nothing other than the conformation of the soul with the Divine Essence itself.[46] The human being in his ultimate happiness must become "deiform,"[47] which is to say, the human intellect, by the action of God himself, is conformed to the Divine Essence. This Essence itself becomes the form by which the beatified intellect understands what it understands. Therefore we can say that the beatified person participates in God's own life and thought. Because by his intelligence God is Creator of all things, he is the truth of all truths. Therefore, to know God is to know the perfect truth. Such a

---

45. See Stanisław Grygiel, Preface to L'amore e la sua regola: Karol Wojtyła e l'esperienza dell' "Ambiente" di Cracovia (Siena: Edizione Cantagalli, 2009), 1–12.

46. Aquinas, ST I-II, q. 3, a. 8.

47. Aquinas, ST I, q. 12, a. 5.

relationship is possible only with God, of course, but the relationship of knowledge with another person shares a participated, albeit distant, likeness with knowledge of God.

In this chapter we have spoken of the truth about the person, understanding by this the "human person." In his writings Karol Wojtyła/John Paul II has given us the key to understand what it means to know a person. To know the truth is to be conformed to the essence of that which is known. The mind of the chemist is "chemistry." Where the truth of the person is concerned, it is a question of con-forming oneself to what the person truly is. However, the person, as a spiritual being, is not something determinate like a tree or a cat. He is a living mystery. This mystery notwithstanding, John Paul II offers us a key to understand the truth about the person. Two persons can know each other—know the truth of the other as a person—only insofar as they share a common life ordered to the transcendent and authentic common good. To have a true mental image of the person one must conform his soul to what the other person is. This conformation is realized not in thought alone, but it requires the sharing of life. Just as the student entrusts himself to the expert and his teaching, those who love each other—be they members of a family, friends, or spouses (the paradigmatic case)— mutually entrust themselves to each other and by this come to know each other in truth. Because a spiritual being is oriented toward the true and the good, his destiny cannot be other than the Absolute True and Good. The knowledge of that person can be realized only in terms of that relationship with the absolute Good. In this way, knowledge depends on love.

5 ∾

THE CHALLENGE OF NIHILISM

Our Home

In 1990 as the spacecraft Voyager was about to pass the limits of
our solar system into deep space, the astronomer Carl Sagan asked
that the craft's camera be turned back to take a picture of our planet. In this photograph, the earth appears as a pale blue dot. Commenting on the photo, Sagan wrote:

Look again at that dot. That's here. That's home. That's us. On it everyone
you love, everyone you know, everyone you ever heard of, every human
being who ever was, lived out their lives. The aggregate of our joy and
suffering, thousands of confident religions, ideologies, and economic
doctrines ... every hero and coward, every creator and destroyer of civilization, every king and peasant, every young couple in love, every mother
and father, hopeful child, inventor and explorer, every teacher of morals,
every corrupt politician, every 'superstar,' every 'supreme leader,' every
saint and sinner in the history of our species lived there—on a mote of
dust suspended in a sunbeam....

There is perhaps no better demonstration of the folly of human con-
ceits than this distant image of our tiny world. To me, it underscores our
responsibility to deal more kindly with one another, and to preserve and
cherish the pale blue dot, the only home we've ever known.[1]

1. Carl Sagan and Ann Druyan, *Pale Blue Dot: A Vision of the Human Future in Space*
(New York: Random House, 1994), 8–9.

84

Everything that we think is important—our loves, our ambitions, projects, and conquests—is to be found on this pale blue dot, this "mote of dust," in the isolation of one small planet in one galaxy among millions of galaxies, and from this the astronomer draws a moral lesson. Sagan calls on us to be more humble, to recognize how very tiny we are in the immensity of the universe. Our pride is "folly." We have only one home, this earth, and it is "our responsibility to deal more kindly with one another, and to preserve and cherish the pale blue dot." Many have found Sagan's reflections on the "pale blue dot" to be moving and inspiring. The scientist, drawing upon scientific truths, teaches us how to live, how to transcend our petty rivalries, our political, cultural, and religious ideologies. The photograph of that pale blue dot shows us how to live.

Or does it? In reality, Sagan's scientific data offer no moral principle, because they lack any essential reference to good or evil. Rather, he presents an aesthetic vision that is attractive and compelling to the sensitive and contemplative mind of a scientist. But can Sagan's argumentation convince someone who is not fascinated by the mysteries of the cosmos, who does not delight in the beauty of the night sky? In particular, can it convince a "destroyer of civilization?" Genghis Khan once said, "The greatest happiness is to vanquish your enemies, to chase them before you, to rob them of their wealth, to see those dear to them bathed in tears, to clasp to your bosom their wives and daughters."[2] Such a conqueror was doubtless able to recognize that in comparison to the vastness of the night sky and the size of the earth, men are very little things. He might even grant that the universe beyond this earth could be much greater than he imagined. But to his mind such reflections are doubtless irrelevant to "real life." Sagan's inspiring remarks will not emotionally, aesthetically, or intellectually move a man who finds his life's happiness in rape and plunder. It is true, perhaps, that no moral principle

2. Henry H. Howorth, *History of the Mongols from the 9th to the 19th Century* (New York: Cosimo, 2008), 1:110.

was important to the Khan, but *we* are able to judge between him and King David, who sang the praises of God and humbled himself when convicted by the prophet of murder (see 2 Sam. 12:7–13). We believe we can identify an important difference between the proud destroyer of civilizations and the humble ruler of a just kingdom. We should explore this thought further.

Sagan argues that because our planet is so tiny we are not important, and this is nihilism. The conqueror, the superstar, but also every father and mother, is engaged in activity so minuscule in its physical scope as to be meaningless. Sagan maintains—and for this we could cite many other scientists—that we are nothing more than an accident of chance, with no natural end, no purpose, desired by neither the universe nor by any higher intelligence. We are, simply, just here.

But on this pale blue dot are places where the gentle azure has become smudged. Consider the concentration camp at Auschwitz. What can we say about this smudge on our dot? or about Hiroshima or the Gulag? By contrast, what might we say about the vision of the Second Vatican Council: "all things on earth should be related to man as their center and crown?"[3]

Christ Reveals Man to Himself

Let us turn now to another text from the Council, a text frequently cited by John Paul II.

The truth is that only in the mystery of the incarnate Word does the mystery of man take on light. For Adam, the first man, was a figure of Him Who was to come, namely Christ the Lord. Christ, the final Adam, by the revelation of the mystery of the Father and His love, fully reveals man to man himself and makes his supreme calling clear.... By suffering for us He not only provided us with an example for our imitation, He blazed a trail, and if we follow it, life and death are made holy and take on a new meaning.[4]

3. *Gaudium et Spes*, no. 12.
4. Ibid., no. 22.

Although this is a theological and ecclesial text, based on Revelation, on the mysteries of the Incarnation and Redemption, it also has a philosophical sense from which we may derive some important principles. Let us consider.

The Incarnate Word "fully reveals man to man himself." That is, if God himself, the Supreme Being, purely spiritual, is incarnate as man, then our human nature is capable of expressing—and not only of expressing but indeed of assuming—divinity. The human being is not simply an organism subject to biological laws, but is capable of far surpassing every material thing. Furthermore, in teaching that Christ "makes his supreme calling clear," the Council implies that the human being has a vocation, a transcendent destiny, which is the reason for his dignity.[5] And finally the Council writes that in his "suffering for us [Christ] not only provided us with an example for our imitation, He blazed a trail, and if we follow it, life and death are made holy and take on a new meaning."[6] This is to say not only that the sufferings of Christ had value, but that therefore our own sufferings can also be of value. In fact, the text calls on us to imitate Christ precisely in his suffering.

Thus it is that we have two alternative focal points of morality: One presents a frigid vision of man, alone and lost in an immense universe, a fact which the astronomer hopes will induce him to humility—that is to say, to recognize his unimportance—and to respect for the earth and for others. And the other presents man as a being who, although not very big or powerful, has a nature that God himself can share, who has a vocation that transcends earthly conditions, and who can be saved by his sufferings. At this point we may turn to the thought of Karol Wojtyła/John Paul II on transcendence and the challenge of nihilism.

5. See ibid., no. 19.
6. Ibid., no. 22.

Nihilism

John Paul II characterizes nihilism philosophically as the stance "which is at once the denial of all foundations and the negation of all objective truth."[7] This characterization appears in the chapter of *Fides et Ratio* entitled "Current Requirements and Tasks," in which the pope insisted upon the importance of a philosophy adequate to the Word of God and open to the transcendent. When we hear this word, "nihilism," we tend to think of great, "heroic" nihilists such as Nietzsche or Sartre, who so proudly affirmed their own dignity with a "no" to the Almighty. However, the most common and dangerous nihilism is that ordinary, everyday nihilism of the empiricism and utilitarianism of our era.[8] It is to this nihilism that we devote our attention now.

In *Fides et Ratio* John Paul II warns against four errors of contemporary philosophy and their consequences.[9] These are (1) eclecticism, (2) historicism, (3) scientism, and (4) pragmatism. The first is the incoherent combination of ideas from many philosophies, while the second relativizes every idea by maintaining that any given idea pertains only to its own epoch. Important as these errors are, in this essay we will focus our attention on the third and fourth errors.

Scientism

Science and the scientific method are different from scientism, which is a philosophy that "refuses to admit the validity of forms of knowledge other than those of the positive sciences; and it relegates religious, theological, ethical and aesthetic knowledge to the realm of mere fantasy."[10] Of course, since the sixteenth century the sciences have proven marvelously successful in discovering the secrets of the natural world. Mathematical abstraction, together with controlled experimentation, has provided modern scientists with the

---

7. *Fides et Ratio*, no. 90.   8. LR, 57. See AR, 72.
9. *Fides et Ratio*, no. 86–89.   10. Ibid., no. 88.

power to solve problems that baffled Aristotelian science. A good example is that of the trajectory of a projectile such as a cannonball. What kind of curve does it trace? Aristotelian science could not answer this question, but every physics student, by applying differential calculus to two simple formulas, can determine that the curve is a parabola. By mathematical abstraction, the scientist reduces a physical object to a certain mathematical entity, treating a planet or a cannonball as a point-mass, represented by a certain number, moving with a certain velocity in a specific direction, represented by a vector. Modern biology is constructed on the basis of the DNA molecule with its four constituent nucleotides arranged in a double-helix structure. The process of the inheritance of physical characteristics is explained by the mechanical interactions of DNA and RNA. To test and validate a scientific theory the scientist needs to perform controlled experiments, designed precisely to answer a single question. Such experiments must exclude all the factors that can affect the result with the exception of the unique factor concerning which the scientist seeks a result. This concept of science, founded on the bases of mathematics and controlled experimentation, opened for us the doors to understand physics, biology, chemistry and their respective sub-fields, so that today we can travel into space, diagnose and cure illnesses, predict storms, and invent marvelous machines of every kind. Without doubt, the sciences are as valuable for acquiring technology to improve the conditions of our lives as for attaining to truths about the natural world. It is folly to reject modern science.

Science, though, is not—and does not imply—the same thing as scientism. The foundational principles of the sciences imply that all modern sciences must be abstractions from reality. Here let us turn to *Love and Responsibility*, where we read:

This habit of confusing the order of existence with the biological order, or rather of allowing the second to obscure the first, is part of that generalized empiricism which seems to weigh so heavily on the mind of ... modern intellectuals.... The "biological order," as a product of the human intellect which abstracts its elements from a larger reality, has man for its immediate author. The claim to autonomy in one's ethical views is a short jump from this. It is otherwise with the "order of nature," which means the totality of the cosmic relationships that arise among really existing entities. It is therefore the order of existence, and the laws which govern it have their foundation in Him, Who is the unfailing source of that existence, in God the Creator.[11]

In this text Wojtyła denies neither the authentic intellectual value nor the achievements of the biological sciences. What he does say is that this order is an abstraction, which, by its very nature as an abstraction, does not take into account those aspects that are not accessible to the canons of the science. For example, according to these canons we cannot account for the fact that the communicative signals of a human being can be regulated by the laws of logic, that is, the laws that govern the meanings of words and inferences of propositions. Biology can say nothing about the fact that this sound "cat" is related to this sound "lion," even though this science can tell us much about the relationship between house cats and lions.

The error of scientism consists in reducing all knowledge to only that which the empirical sciences can know. But this reduction necessarily implies that there is not—nor can there be—any knowledge of the good, nor of being. As St. Thomas Aquinas observes,[12] the notion of good plays no role in mathematics, because every mathematical being—whether number or figure—regarded mathematically, is nothing more than an abstraction. This implies that the notion of good can find no place in mathematical science, because every object that this science studies is, in principle, mathematical in type. And in reality, scientists insist precisely on this point, that the concepts of end, good, or purpose can find no place in their science.

So, even though we may speak of evolution as a process the result of which is our own species, the human race, if we wish to speak precisely we ought not to refer to this as a process in such a way as

11. LR, 57. See AR, 72.
12. Aquinas, ST I, q. 5, a. 3, ad 4.

to imply that nature and its evolutionary mechanisms "intend" or "are directed" to the existence of human beings.[13] If these events had taken a different path, which had not resulted in our species, it would not have committed an error; nothing would have "gone wrong." And if this applies to the truth about the species, so much more does it apply to the truth about an individual member of the species. Although we speak of a man's death as a shame or even a tragedy, this perspective is merely subjective. And so, John Paul II writes that scientism "dismisses values as mere products of the emotions and rejects the notion of being in order to clear the way for pure and simple facticity."[14]

It is important that scientism does not even permit knowledge of being. Of course, we can speak of "human being" or of "being happy," but of this reality "being" there can be no science. The empirical sciences do not need this concept. The sciences treat of entities that behave according to invariant natural laws, which determine their movements and the effects of their interactions with other entities. In the world known only to the sciences there occurs neither generation nor corruption but only change. A new thing is nothing more than a new arrangement of matter. If we ask why our planet exists, the response will take the form of an analysis of the effects of gravity acting upon particles of interstellar dust. And if we ask why Socrates existed . . . well, we all know the processes by which a man and woman become parents, a process that includes interactions of cells and DNA. The biological material grows under nature's conditions and according to nature's laws, so that the resulting Athenian is nothing more than an arrangement of organic matter. Therefore, there is no need for a concept of "being," because the concepts of physics (and perhaps also of chemistry or some other science) suffice.

Wojtyła maintains that the result of this empiricism is "autonomy in ethical opinions," an autonomy that is manifest principally in the

13. Indeed, it is incorrect even to refer to evolution as a "process" in the ordinary understanding of that term.
14. *Fides et Ratio*, no. 88.

ethics of utilitarianism. This autonomy may be found dramatically presented in Nietzsche's concept of the *Übermensch*, but much more influential are the principles of Jeremy Bentham—the "greatest happiness of the greatest number"—and of John Stuart Mill—the "greatest happiness principle." In his Lublin Lectures Karol Wojtyła observes that Bentham explicitly and forcefully repudiates every metaphysical concept and insists that what the human being seeks can be nothing other than pleasure and the avoidance of pain.[15] In his development of Bentham's ideas, John Stuart Mill affirms that happiness consists in pleasure and the absence of pain, and that even though happiness can take many different forms, including intellectual pleasures and delight in the virtues, nevertheless what everyone desires is pleasure. Mill clearly believes that the best pleasures are those of the English gentleman of the Victorian era and that, adequately educated, everyone would aspire to this happiness. In fact, we can say that Mill foresaw a prosperous industrialized democratic society very much like that of the contemporary United Kingdom—or of the United States and the European Union. It is an attractive vision. Nevertheless, such a vision lacks fundamental values. It does not suffice to give meaning to human life.

Pragmatism

Utilitarianism is founded on happiness, but on happiness understood as "pleasure." And as a kind of feeling, pleasure is necessarily subjective. Certainly, most human persons enjoy good food, friendship and love, social safety and peace. For this reason we see how utilitarianism is the practical philosophy of our leaders for many spheres of social life. What is it that we expect from a leader in a contemporary democracy? That he be pragmatic. And certainly within limits he should be so. However, we should not forget the danger that "pragmatism" represents, about which John Paul II

15. Karol Wojtyła, *Lubliner Vorlesungen* [Lublin Lectures], trans. Anneliese D. Spranger and Edda Wiener (Stuttgart-Degerloch: Seewald Verlag, 1981), 342–43.

warns in his encyclical, where he defines it as the "attitude of mind which, in making its choices, precludes theoretical considerations or judgments based on ethical principles."[16]

In our times we place much confidence in the knowledge of experts, in those who know the laws of economics and development, of the social sciences such as psychology and criminology, and of the education of children and young people. In a world so confusing and in a society so complex that we do not know what to do, there exists the temptation to place our confidence in experts, in those who know what we do not. However, writes John Paul II,

> The consequences of this are clear: in practice, the great moral decisions of humanity are subordinated to decisions taken one after another by institutional agencies. Moreover, anthropology itself is severely compromised by a one-dimensional vision of the human being, a vision which excludes the great ethical dilemmas and the existential analyses of the meaning of suffering and sacrifice, of life and death.[17]

In other words, the knowledge of the experts becomes systematized and institutionalized, and for our part we entrust ourselves not to wisdom but to technical knowledge. This lack of wisdom is manifest as one of the central themes of *The Best and the Brightest*,[18] David Halberstam's history of the administrative inner circle of the American presidents Kennedy and Johnson. These men, drawn from the most prestigious universities and foundations in the United States, had much knowledge, but their *hubris* led these two presidential administrations into the Vietnam War. They thought that they could manage the complexities of the political and military situation of an insurgency in Southeast Asia the same way one can manage an automobile manufacturing company.

However, the true danger of utilitarian pragmatism is worse yet. John Paul II speaks of a "one-dimensional vision of the human being, a vision which excludes the great ethical dilemmas and the

16. *Fides et Ratio*, no. 89.
17. Ibid.
18. David Halberstam, *The Best and the Brightest* (New York: Random House, 1972).

existential analyses of the meaning of suffering and sacrifice, of life and death."[19] On the personal level, it is necessary to find an answer to the question of the meaning of life—and not in the abstract. "I" need to know the meaning of "my" life. "You" need to know the meaning of "your" own life. The Polish pope reminds us of the exhortation engraved over the entrance of the temple at Delphi: "Know thyself,"[20] and he adds that the human being is "the one who knows himself." We may also recall Socrates, who exhorted the Athenians to care for their souls instead of looking out only for their investments and social ambitions, and he warned them that "the unexamined life is not worth living."[21] John Paul II himself reminds us that all men and women are philosophers precisely because we all want to know the truth about the meaning our own lives.[22] Not to seek this meaning or not to try to know oneself means to live only in horizontal transcendence, responding only to the different stimuli of the environment but without understanding why. It is to remain a victim of the forces about one, enjoying the agreeable, yes, but suffering the disagreeable without any possibility of understanding. And, according to utilitarian principles, a life without pleasures is not worthwhile.

South African philosopher David Benatar maintains, on the basis of utilitarian principles, that to conceive and bear children is a moral evil, because if the good consists in pleasure without suffering and the evil of pain, then parents mistreat their children precisely in giving them life.[23] No matter how wealthy they may be, no matter what advantages they may offer them . . . they can never protect their children from pain. To give birth is to condemn a baby to certain suffering. When the *New York Times* ran a column by Peter Singer on Benatar, many readers responded in the newspaper's "blog" saying that Benatar is right, that although they do not intend suicide they

19. *Fides et Ratio*, no. 89   20. Ibid., no. 2.
21. Plato, *Apology of Socrates* 38a5–6.   22. *Fides et Ratio*, no. 5, and esp. no. 30.
23. David Benatar, *Better Never to Have Been: The Harm of Coming into Existence* (Oxford: Oxford University Press, 2006).

would prefer not to have been born.[24] It is well worth our noting that the readers of the *New York Times* are cultured, educated people. This newspaper plays an important role in the cultural life of the United States and reflects the country's higher culture.

Isn't this curious? Since the beginnings of the human race, the birth of a baby has been an occasion of joy. When couples marry they hope to form a family with their own children. To be pregnant has been something good and natural. Contemporary utilitarianism, however, teaches us not only that these sentiments are wrong, but—on one interpretation—that these actions are morally evil. Popular periodicals now assure us that married couples enjoy greater life-satisfaction if they avoid parenthood. Thus has the utilitarian attitude become manifest in the most prosperous and comfortable societies in the history of the world. But we may well suspect that if suffering and death have no meaning, then neither has life itself.

Not far from the lovely city of Kraków, Poland, is the town of Auschwitz, where the Nazis murdered a million Jews. What can we say about this? If the life of a prosperous and educated American has no meaning, what meaning can possibly be found in the sufferings that occurred in this concentration camp? But if the sufferings of those million Jews have no meaning, then it is not worth the trouble to visit the concentration camp. Their sufferings are not worth remembering but simply constitute a fact from the past that means nothing to you or me. However, when my wife and I visited the camp in 2011, we saw a group of Israelis wearing white mantles and walking among the ruins of the barracks and ovens of Birkenau, praying for the dead. The presence of these Jews, members of the people who had been especially targeted in this camp, is a sign of hope in a hopeless place. The sufferings and deaths of the million Jews in that place were profoundly meaningful, a reality to which the visiting Israelis bore testimony.

24. Peter Singer, "Should This Be the Last Generation?" *New York Times*, June 6, 2010, New York edition. http://opinionator.blogs.nytimes.com/2010/06/06/should-this-be-the-last-generation.

Transcendence and the Meaning of Life

In the preceding chapter, we considered the first encounter of the man with the woman, where Adam recognized, "This one at last is bone of my bones and flesh of my flesh" (Gen. 2:23). She was a help similar to him, another person with whom he could enter into communion. And she was not only another person. She was also a woman, a female person, a person of the opposite sex. She and the man could unite so as to become "one flesh" (Gen. 2:24), and by this conceive another person, their son or daughter. Because they are both persons (and not brute animals) their union has to come about not by mere instinct but by a free decision of both. Their union results from the free mutual gift of self. The man surrenders himself to the woman and she herself to him. Of course, this union is possible because of the biological structures of their respective bodies as male and female, but it is not the result of those structures alone. John Paul II writes:

According to Genesis 2:25, the man and the woman "did not feel shame"; seeing and knowing each other in all the peace and tranquility of the interior gaze, they "communicate" in the fullness of humanity, which shows itself in them as reciprocal complementarity precisely because they are "male" and "female." At the same time, they "communicate" based on the communion of persons in which they become a mutual gift for each other, through masculinity and femininity.[25]

John Paul II finds it very significant that although the man and woman were naked, they "felt no shame" (Gen. 2:24). This absence of shame does not indicate a kind of naïveté or immaturity typical of small children, but instead it manifests the "transparency" and innocence of those who do not yet suffer the effects of concupiscence. Their union can be realized only through the exercise of freedom on the part of both. Because of this, John Paul II discovers here the "spousal meaning" of the body. In this state of "original innocence" Adam and Eve could respond totally according to this meaning,

25. John Paul II, *Man and Woman*, 13:1, 177. General audience, January 2, 1980.

each seeing the other not as an object to be used or enjoyed but as a person to love. In fact, the structure of this relation is almost totally opposed to our contemporary understanding of erotic love, which centers so much on the acquisition and possession of the beloved. John Paul II compares this relationship of human love with that which exists between the Creator and his creation, in particular with human beings. This relation introduces *"a new dimension, a new criterion of understanding and interpretation that we will call 'hermeneutics of the gift.'"*[26] Because the human being is a person—a rational being—who can receive a gift, creation itself has the character of a gift. John Paul II notes that the story of creation culminates with the judgment "God saw everything that he had made, and indeed, it was very good" (Gen. 1:31). Through these words we are led to glimpse in love the divine motive for creation, the source, as it were, from which it springs: *"only love, in fact, gives rise to the good and is well pleased with the good."*[27]

Here we find an indication of the authentic nature of love, a nature whose paradigm is found in matrimonial love, which consists in the mutual total gift of self. How is such a love realized? What is its structure? The seat of an authentic love cannot be in the inclinations, nor can it be in sensual desires, nor even in the emotions, but it must be in the spiritual powers of the person, that is to say, in his will and rationality. To love is to give oneself for the good of the beloved, and furthermore, this cannot be for any good but for the transcendental good, a good which is desired not only for the beloved but also for the lover himself. What joins the two together is the common good, which is a common end.[28] In other words, if I love you, I want for you what is genuinely good, your self-realization according to the truth, while at the same time you want to same for me. Wojtyła writes, *"When two different people consciously choose a common aim this puts them on a footing of equality and precludes the*

26. Ibid., 13:2, 179 (emphasis in the original).
27. Ibid. See 1 Cor. 13 (emphasis in the original).
28. See LR, 29; AR, 37.

possibility that one of them might be subordinated to the other."[29] The result is a mutual love, the communion of persons, in which neither the man nor the woman is used by the other. Wojtyła adds, *"Marriage is one of the most important areas where this principle is put into practice."*[30]

Among the common goods of marriage are temporal objectives such as mutual friendship, the establishment of a home, and the bearing of children. "He" recognizes that for "her" the good includes being a mother, and "she" recognizes that it is good for "him" to be a father, and together they realize a domestic community (which is a cell of the society). However, "he" and "she" are also persons, each of whom lives from his own subjectivity and is a "partner of the Absolute." Therefore their ultimate destiny cannot be limited to the terrestrial, to the temporal. And because the ultimate good of the person cannot be less than God himself,[31] to love another person means to desire that person to attain to God. Hence, marital love requires the total commitment to the eternal good of the beloved.

Our theme here, however, is not marriage but nihilism and the meaning of life. Let us consider John Paul II's words: "In the nihilist interpretation, life is no more than an occasion for sensations and experiences in which the ephemeral has pride of place. Nihilism is at the root of the widespread mentality which claims that a definitive commitment should no longer be made, because everything is fleeting and provisional."[32]

That there is no possibility of an authentic and strong love without intelligent and voluntary commitment is a principle that pertains not only to matrimonial love, but within appropriate limits, to every type of love. In this way, love constitutes a response to nihilism, and it is worthwhile to explore this response.

"Nihilism," writes John Paul II, "is a denial of the humanity and

29. LR, 28–29 (emphasis in the original). See AR, 37.
30. LR, 30 (emphasis in the original). See AR, 37.
31. *Fides et Ratio*, nos. 13, 15; *Veritatis Splendor*, nos. 12, 13. See also LR, 23; AR, 30.
32. *Fides et Ratio*, no. 46.

of the very identity of the human being,"[33] and by this negation denies also the dignity of the human being. As we have seen, it denies human dignity by denying being and good. To affirm the humanity of the person and his identity means to affirm the truth about him, about the person. Of course the person is limited by space and time, by his corporeality, and in this way is a finite being. Furthermore, the person is vulnerable to evil, to error and pain, and finally to death. However, because the person is also, as the earlier paper argued, infinite—he is a mystery—our knowledge of him is always partial and fallible. For this reason, every interpretation of the human being, every theory, fails to attain to the complete truth about the person. Human thought does not suffice to capture the human being in his totality. Precisely in this consists the grave danger of reductionism, whether materialist or utilitarian. We can say that the full knowledge of the person belongs only to God.

The person—"I" am a person, and "you" are, too—can surrender himself to another person even to the point of the total gift of self that is realized between husband and wife, in the sacrifice of the martyrs, and in the vows of consecrated religious. Let us recall here the fundamental principle of *Person and Act* that the person is revealed in the act.[34] By their very nature, our thoughts and linguistic expressions are variable and fallible. However, over the extent of his life the person can (and should) grow. The commitment to the good of the other, which constitutes genuine love, by its essence constitutes also an affirmation of the value of the person. It is to say that "you"—my beloved, my friend, my son or daughter, my wife or husband—have value and that this value is not the limited value of a tool or a thing but is rather an absolute value. I surrender myself to you for your good, and with this surrender, I affirm your value. But furthermore, in this affirmation is implicit not only what is affirmed of "you" (your value) but also that which is said of "me," because total commitment confirms the complete possession of oneself. It

33. Ibid., no. 90.
34. See PEA, 840–43; PA, 40–45; OC, 58–59; AP, 10–13.

matters not what may happen—I am yours. The commitment of the will which love represents is also an affirmation of the transcendence of the agent-person himself.

Conclusion

Early in this chapter I cited a text from the Second Vatican Council, a text of great importance to John Paul II, in which the council fathers affirmed that "only in the mystery of the incarnate Word does the mystery of man take on light." In this text we can discover three philosophically important themes: (1) the capacity of our human body to express the divine, even to the point that Christ is God Incarnate, (2) the transcendental vocation of the human person, and (3) the value of human sufferings, even to the point of attaining the realization of our ultimate vocation. Let us consider these three themes.

First is the meaning of the human body. According to scientism nothing—including the human body—has any meaning; things merely have properties or physical characteristics that determine the course of its interactions with other things. This concept, "meaning," plays no role in the sciences. In a certain way we can say that in the exact sciences "meaning" has no meaning. However, this lack of meaning is a fiction. The argument that John Paul II develops on the basis of Genesis 2 is not theological but phenomenological. That one person can recognize immediately that another human being is a person is a fact of experience. Adam's exclamation, "This one at last is bone of my bones and flesh of my flesh" (Gen. 2:23), does not require divine Revelation but is a truth that human reason can discover. And furthermore, even though much more rare in our experience, the mutual recognition of the meaning of the body in its masculinity and femininity as gift is real and accessible to reason. I would argue that this experience is discovered precisely in the delightful experience of falling in love. "Is it possible that such a lovely person could love me?"

The human body is not as strong or as fast as the bodies of the animals, but it is marvelously adapted to the spiritual being, to intelligence. Not only do we have a large brain, but we have also marvelously well articulated hands, flexible tongues, and erect posture—even the absence of body hair may serve our rationality. In virtue of our intellectual and corporeal abilities we can act as co-creators of the world. As such, the human being is a sign in the world of its Creator. He is *imago Dei*.

Perhaps the most dangerous and destructive error of nihilism is the denial of the human being's transcendental vocation, because this denial renders impossible an authentic love between persons. Without a common transcendent good, lovers cannot escape the problem of "using" each other. If I act only on the earthly level, with no transcendence other than the horizontal, then the other person can be nothing else than something to stimulate my senses and satisfy my desires—or an enemy to frustrate my intentions. Love, if it is to be genuine love, must proceed from the one person to the other as a gift of self for the good of the other. The nihilistic vision of love is either one of lonely persons seeking relief from their internal pain or simply of the seekers of sexual experiences and superficial emotions. We can recall—to take just one example—the middle-aged man in the film *Lost in Translation*,[35] estranged from his wife and alone on business in Tokyo, leading an aimless life, not knowing what he really wants. There he makes a new young friend, a newly-wed neglected by her ambitious husband. Both are existentially lost, unable to speak the Japanese language, but, more seriously, unable to articulate their need for authentic communion.

Finally there is the question of suffering. Let us think again of those Israeli Jews, walking around Birkenau and praying. Why should they pray? They could neither alleviate the sufferings nor restore the lives of the million Jewish prisoners who had died there. What they could do was to bear witness that God knows, that those lives so hor-

---

35. See film *Lost in Translation*, director Sofia Coppola, 2003.

ribly degraded in that place were of value in God's eyes. John Paul II knew the value of suffering, about which he wrote in *Salvifici Doloris*. Love as the total gift of self implies that a love without suffering is banal; because of its very nature, the gift of self requires the sacrifice of one's own desires and freedom. It is precisely in suffering that authentic love is manifest. In *Fides et Ratio* he wrote: "the prime commitment of theology is seen to be the understanding of God's kenosis, a grand and mysterious truth for the human mind, which finds it inconceivable that suffering and death can express a love which gives itself and seeks nothing in return."[36] The value of suffering finds its ultimate instance in the mystery of the Redemption, but this total love of Jesus Christ can be reflected in the love between a man and a woman.

"Look again at that dot. That's here. That's home." Yes, it is our home but it is not us. "On it everyone you love, everyone you know, everyone you ever heard of, every human being who ever was, lived out their lives." True enough. On this pale blue dot, so small as to be hard to find on the Voyager photograph, on this mote of galactic dust there live beings who know this galaxy and its structure, who know what a black hole is and how it works, and, what is more, who know something of the Being that created this galaxy and the entire universe. By their intelligence and freedom these human beings can surpass the behavior of every other object in the universe. They can give of themselves in friendship and love for others, sharing in the love and intelligence of the Creator of all things.

36. *Fides et Ratio*, no. 93.

PART III ∾

THE ANTHROPOLOGY OF
PERSON AND ACT

MIGUEL ACOSTA

6 ∾

INTRODUCTION TO WOJTYŁA'S PHILOSOPHICAL ANTHROPOLOGY

After spending years teaching ethics, and from his own pastoral experience, Karol Wojtyła recognized the need to present his own thorough account of the concept "person," one that did not follow the classical explanations that described the human being by beginning with the powers or faculties in order to analyze its objects and operations. With this focus is emphasized the idea of "human nature," that is, those essential aspects which differentiate the human being from other natural beings. However, Wojtyła saw that the distinguishing feature comes more clearly from subjectivity, from the side of the person. Although the study of our nature manifests to us qualitative characteristics unique to our species, the concept "person" goes further; it considers not only the exceptionality of the human species but the exceptionality of "each" human being with his individual characteristics and his unique interior world. So, how can we explain this personal activity without confusing it with the operations of human nature but without excluding either? For our author, the classical anthropological focal points were not appropriate to give such an explanation; it was necessary to find another way to "reinterpret" the classical concepts in order better to discover the richness of the person. With this objective he began his project of an anthropology of the person from the point of view of action. The result was *Person and Act*.

Person and Act is an original work;[1] its focus is distinct from what we are used to seeing concerning the philosophy of human nature or philosophical anthropology. At the same time it is Wojtyła's principal philosophical work. Its originality is due to the new methodology that he employs to explain the "man-person." He believes that the adequate starting point for the inquiry of this theme is the living experience of the human being. The way to access the interiority of the person cannot be the analysis of faculties but human action itself. This new focus requires him to make use of a conceptual repertoire that does not confuse his exposition with the classical categories of the philosophy of the human being. Wojtyła starts with the human act, from his living experience and piece by piece discovers the capacities and dynamisms that have their origin in the person. In other words, he does not directly assume the human faculties in order to show their effects; he proceeds in the opposite direction. It is the lived experience itself that brings me to understand what there is in me and who I am. It is a matter of starting from an existential phenomenology that proceeds to enter into the psychology and metaphysics of the human person.

When it was published, *Person and Act* was accepted by his Polish colleagues with great interest, and it generated an intense debate in the Catholic University of Lublin. He received very positive comments, but not without criticism. Weigel's qualification, "extraordinarily dense,"[2] reflects the views of many readers. In jest and irony, Tadeusz Styczeń noted to his friend John Paul II, "Perhaps it could be translated from Polish into Polish, to make it easier to un-

---

1. Wojtyła himself comments on this novelty in the Preface of *Person and Act* in "Analecta Husserliana": "This presentation of the problem, completely new in relation to traditional philosophy [and by traditional philosophy we understand here the pre-Cartesian philosophy and above all the heritage of Aristotle, and, among Catholic schools of thought, of St. Thomas Aquinas], has provoked me to undertake an attempt at reinterpreting certain formulations proper to this whole philosophy." AP, 13.

2. Weigel, *Witness to Hope*, 174.

derstand for the reader—including me."[3] In turn, some students of Wojtyła's work took note of various deficiencies in translations of this work, especially of the English in 1979 and the Spanish in 1982. In my view, the task of translating it is not easy, owing to the specific meanings that some words and expressions have which cannot be taken literally and which have to be contextualized according to the meaning that the author imposes according to his methodology. All this has not facilitated Karol Wojtyła's anthropology, but thanks to doctoral theses and articles in specialized journals, as well as to the institutes that are dedicated to reflection on his philosophical and theological writings, the very rich content of *Person and Act* is slowly being discovered.

In my opinion, the genuine difficulty consists in "putting on his way of thinking." His work is based on "the systems of metaphysics, of anthropology, and of Aristotelian-Thomistic ethics on one hand, and to phenomenology, above all in Scheler's interpretation, and through Scheler's critique also to Kant,"[4] and, as we have said, Wojtyła introduces new conceptual categories that help him to explain his philosophical itinerary. This does not mean that he takes no account of the tradition; quite to the contrary, the contributions of the philosophies mentioned above always underlie his thought. In any event, it is necessary to take care, because in some cases the terms have different connotations in Thomistic philosophy than in phenomenology, and Wojtyła utilizes both. Which one to choose? It depends on the context in which he is using a particular term and the tradition that most adequately yields the idea the he intends to express. For example, the term "sensation" in Thomistic philosophy is situated in the ambit of sense cognition depending on the intellective power. In Scheler's phenomenology, "sensation" is a type of affect that is neither emotion and nor cognition. We will see this further on, in chapter 8, "Consciousness and Operativity," which concerns the integration of the psyche.

3. Ibid.
4. AP, xiv. See PA (1982), xii.

To offer a comparison that expresses most graphically what I am trying to explain, when the infinitesimal calculus appeared, the mathematicians who were accustomed to the algebraic method had to adapt to a new way of approaching the techniques that involved the calculus. It was a matter of a new kind of approximation, in which they tried to emulate the change and the treatment of quantities that were difficult to measure. Until this point, algebra had studied a static and immobile reality. Leibniz and Newton invented a new methodology to solve these problems, using an idea that had already originated with the Greeks Eudoxus of Cnidus and Archimedes of Syracuse. They had to change their manner of thinking, beginning with the common bases of algebra, trigonometry, and analytic geometry (just recently developed by Descartes). They were obliged to "invent" a new methodology and even a new symbolism to represent their ideas, such as for example, the well-known integral symbol, "$\int$." Once understood, however, the method's valuable utility became manifest. Something similar is happening here.

One of the objectives of this work is simply to facilitate the comprehension of Wojtyła's new methodology so that his philosophical anthropology may be better understood. How can we do this? There are many studies and commentaries on *Person and Act* written by experts on our author's work in which the ideas about the different themes in our author's work are presented. Perhaps the best known is the work of Rocco Buttiglione, who in the 1980s completed a highly praised approach to Karol Wojtyła's thought.[5] So, what is new in this present study?

The objective of studying philosophical anthropology starting from *Person and Act*, such as is conceived here, involves following along the development of the original work, bringing out the central ideas, but without straying far from the author's style or terminology. The idea is to "put ourselves in his shoes" and to walk in them, trying to remain as faithful as possible to his thought, but at the

5. See Buttiglione, *Karol Wojtyła: The Thought.*

same time clarifying those concepts or ways of speaking that may prove difficult. For this reason the route we traverse will have the same order as his work, with numerous direct citations from the author and continual references to the original text, in such a way that the reader can confront both and by this comprehend the meaning of what Wojtyła is explaining. I will for the most part follow the principal points of *Person and Act*, commenting on the author's own words in order to respect his ideas with the greatest possible fidelity. I have preferred to be very zealous in this and have kept the critical commentaries to the minimum.

Another objective is to facilitate the understanding of anyone who approaches our author's work in order then to "venture" to plunge more deeply into the original sources of Wojtyła's magnificent work—that is, I aim to carry out a propaedeutic task. This work is not only for undergraduates or graduates in philosophy; there are many students of Wojtyła's or John Paul II's work who are philosophically trained but for whom a "softer" initiation to *Person and Act* would be helpful. In this sense, the responsibility is great because I intend that, in my work here, the comprehension of the person on the basis of action will not require as much effort as it does in the original work. It must be said nevertheless that the philosophical themes are of themselves often difficult, and we may not give up the effort of entering into the comprehension of a theme simply because we want to undertake what is "more agreeable and less difficult." *Person and Act* is a work of great philosophical density, because it delves into characteristics that require abstraction and some initial philosophical flexibility, but truly the effort is worth the pain, and one finds great satisfaction in better understanding who the human person is. I said that is it a great responsibility, because this study aspires to be a help and an invitation to examine Wojtyła's philosophy more deeply, not a reason to turn away.

Study of the human being has continued for as long as there has been philosophy. According to the different kinds of philosophy, there have been developed different conceptions of the human being. Who are we? Where do we come from? Why are we partially alike and partly different? Why am I a thinking being? What is going on inside me? What will happen when I die? These are questions that every human being poses to himself throughout his life. Depending on the responses that one gives to these questions, he will configure his way of life and his future, and so we could say that his responses determine the end and meaning of his life.

It is curious that many people say that they do not want to know anything about philosophy because it is now out of style and allegedly does no good. Since we naturally pose the questions formulated above, it is impossible to avoid philosophy, and even if we do not wish it, each of us has a way of facing his life and of understanding the world and existence. Philosophy is nothing else than explaining in a more academic form that model of life which each one of us has and transmits to others by his works or his ideas.

From antiquity reflection on the human being in western culture has been carried out from religion or from philosophy. It should be remembered that in antiquity science was situated within the heart of philosophy and at times was confused with it. Later, science began to separate itself methodologically from philosophy, and it sought to explain the world and human beings from the standpoint of its own methodology. In the nineteenth century, the developing sciences of paleoanthropology, experimental psychology, and sociology began to discover much that was previously not known concerning the biological origin and the socio-cultural development of human beings; and for its part, psychology also began to discover new aspects of human interiority, especially at the end of the nineteenth century, when Brentano and Husserl refuted some theses of psychologism and rediscovered the idea of intentionality—today very important for the study of the mind. In 1927 Max Scheler presented a lecture, which was published a year later under the title "The Human Place in the Cosmos." His proposal was to resort to the natural and the human sciences in order to situate the human species within the natural world. With this idea he coined a term that he began to use in his works and which spread among other German philosophers: "Philosophical anthropology" (*philosophische Antropologie*). In 1929 his book was published posthumously.[6] Beginning then, this term began to spread through Europe and the rest of the world.

Philosophical anthropology is the philosophical reflection concerning the human being, which considers the greatest number possible of characteristics, scientific, cultural, and even theological, and on their basis seeks to respond to the great questions, including those indicated above. Logically there are distinct methodologies, some of which recapture the traditions of the history of thought. Philosophical anthropology is a "philosophy of the human being" with a broader focus which, besides treating essential and at times metaphysical characteristics of the human being, also pauses to analyze the existential. When we use the word "personalist" it is because the center of the philosophical perspective takes as its point of departure the concept of person. As Wojtyła says:

The term "person" has been coined to signify that a man cannot be wholly contained within the concept "individual member of the species," but that there is something more to him, a particular richness and perfection in the manner of his being, which can only be brought out by the use of the word "person."[7]

Because of this, the title of the book put a very special stress in two words: person and act. And this is why we emphasize the expression "Personalist Philosophical Anthropology."

Person and Act is an "attempt at reinterpreting certain formulations proper to this whole (traditional) philosophy," starting from the question: "What is the relationship between action as interpreted by the traditional ethic as *actus humanus*, and the action as experience?"[8] Thus, beginning with ethical investigations, Karol

---

6. English edition: Max Scheler, *The Human Place in the Cosmos* (Evanston, Ill.: Northwestern University Press, 2008).

7. See LR, 22.

8. AP, xiii–xiv. See PA (1982), xii.

Wojtyła ends with a new form of development for philosophical anthropology.

The work is divided into four parts in logical sequence, and for this reason it is best for us not to step out of this order of development, since we will see presented concepts that will later serve to explain others. These concepts are sometimes neologisms, while others are terms known in the above-mentioned philosophical traditions, but with a special connotation which can differ from the characteristic use in one of those philosophical systems among those that the author bases his thought on.

Now let us review for a moment the sequence of our exposition of *Person and Act*. The entry door for the study of the person in act is "experience," and by way of introduction, before even beginning with the first part of the work, he explains his methodology, synthesizing the plan of the entire book. In the Introduction, he stops to consider in what way experience is the basis of knowledge of the person who is acting, and how this experience is interiorized, being converted into something objective which uncovers the subjective in man, thanks to consciousness.

Chapter 7, "Main Principles of *Person and Act*" is a synthesis of the main ideas of each part of Wojtyła's book. Here the reader can see the "big picture" of his anthropology and use these ideas as a compass in order to establish the relation between the other chapters.

Chapter 8, "Consciousness and Operativity" refers to the cognitive processes that objectivize the human act. Philosophy is a kind of knowledge, and the mode of understanding presupposes a theory of knowledge that explains how we know and what are the faculties and acts in this knowledge. As Wojtyła's methodology begins with the act, that is, with the experience of the man who acts consciously, it is first necessary to explain how this experience can be converted into objective knowledge. Here we are in the realm of the intelligence and why the human act, which is called "efficacious," is related to consciousness, where the personal "self" is made present.

Chapter 9, "Transcendence" refers to the voluntary processes that manifest human self-determination. Through human acts, several characteristics of subjectivity begin to be newly discovered, which lead to another and more profound interior dimension. Here are studied the foundations of personal freedom, which he calls "self-determination," and which is based on two anthropological structures "self-governance" and "self-possession." Here too are examined the inclination of the will to the truth, human responsibility, and happiness.

Chapter 10, "Integration," studies the psychosomatic unity of the human being in the person. Wojtyła uses the expression "man-person" to emphasize that the human being has an aspect of "somatic dynamism," which has its biological laws that develop and respond according to the innate mechanisms deriving from his genetic composition. And there is another aspect which transcends the "psychosomatic," since its effects not only do not reduce to the former but interact with it and greatly outweigh it, showing that they depend on a new dimension, unique in each human being, which is the personal dimension. Here there is developed an anthropology of the body with its distinct "potentialities" (somato-vegetative and psycho-emotive), and it also studies the integration of the entire human affective realm where the emotions and sentiments are activated.

The final chapter, "Participation," is a kind of complement—"comment" says Wojtyła[9]—to all the preceding development. In this chapter, the condition of the openness of the person and the social nature of the human being are put into relief, a theme that cannot be excluded in an anthropology as it considers man as an intersubjective being. Intersubjectivity is the note that founds the social relationships of the human being and affects his way of living and developing. This part is an as-yet unfinished "introduction," treating of the participation of the person when he acts "together with others." It is probable that Karol Wojtyła had wanted to complete this

9. See PA, 375; OC, 301; AP, 315.

part, as his subsequent essay, "Person: Subject and Community" strongly suggests, but then he was called to be Pope John Paul II and his activities were oriented in other directions. In any case, many of the ideas relating to this theme are expounded in his pastoral writings as pope of the Catholic Church. We can find such arguments in his social encyclicals, pastoral letters, and other documents of his pontifical magisterium.

Finally in this study we have chosen core concepts from each chapter that have a different significance from that in classical philosophy or which are fundamental for better understanding a chapter of *Person and Act* and other works of Wojtyła. More than a terminological dictionary, this purports to explain the concepts important for the thread of philosophical development in *Person and Act* as a didactic way of approaching the anthropology of Karol Wojtyła.

7 ∾

MAIN PRINCIPLES OF PERSON AND ACT

Although Karol Wojtyła's philosophical anthropology has been deepened in other works, its principles are contained in *Osoba i czyn* (*Person and Act*). To synthesize the philosophical journey that we are undertaking, it is necessary to summarize and list the central points of this anthropology. In the following pages, we will follow the order of *Osoba i czyn* to lay out Wojtyła's thoughts and to gain a broad view of them. The numbers in brackets indicate the corresponding Part in *Osoba i czyn* to which each key pertains. Under each subheading, I have referenced my subsequent chapter where the key point is enlarged. It may be useful to the reader, after reading each of the later chapters, to return to this present chapter, in order to fix the main ideas in his mind.

Experience as a Method ∾ See First Part of *Person and Act*, Consciousness and Operativity

The starting point of Karol Wojtyła's anthropology is the human action that can be verified through the experience that is objectified by consciousness.

This chapter has been translated from the Spanish by Ángela Gimeno Nogués and Paul Gordon.

Philosophy is a kind of knowledge that requires the elaboration of a logical discourse based on true premises. Nevertheless, there are aspects of life that elude this logical rigor—for example, affective experience or creative intuitions. These experiences do not thereby cease to be real or authentic. To better understand the human being, we have to make room for those kinds of experiences that are not learned as *logos*. Wojtyła believes it essential to take experience into account, and moreover, he is convinced that this is the most appropriate way to be able to unveil who the human person is. His philosophical method consists in the phenomenological and ontological analysis that starts with the acting person's experience.

Since experience includes different subjective forms of encounter with reality, to do philosophy it is necessary that our intelligence understand those forms objectively. Only then will it be able to develop logical arguments. In addition to the primary illuminating and reflective functions of consciousness, Wojtyła points out that this (consciousness) has another main function: "to form experience," which enables the human being to take particular note of his own subjectivity. This is the "reflexivity" of consciousness. This reflexivity is not the knowledge of self-consciousness, but it takes note of the experience lived in a particular way in the subjectivity of the person. The different acts of consciousness not only enable objectification (illuminating and reflective functions), but also capture objectively (reflexively) the subjectivity of experience. So experience is introduced as a fundamental focal point for knowing human subjectivity and the person.

Substantial Unity ∾ See First Part of *Person and Act*,
Consciousness and Operativity

All experiences that are retained in subjectivity and constitute man's internal world require a "metaphysical assumption," which is called *suppositum* and forms part of human nature.

The anthropology of the person posits that human nature is a substantial unity in which the material and the spiritual converge. Such unity presupposes a metaphysical conception that enables us to individualize the human being's potentialities and operations. From the point of view of action, we can distinguish an aspect of nature that is common to every human being and, at the same time, another exceptional aspect, metaphysically incommunicable, in each individual that constitutes his own identity, his personal "I."

Human nature is the principle of acts that gives the human species its particular "way of being." Hence, in its potentialities there is a natural orientation even prior to voluntariness. This orientation of the operation of its potentialities is not closed, but to a certain point open to the person's action. This enables great individual diversity. But there are aspects of the human being that escape his voluntary act and are common to everybody, namely, those that are located on a basic and independent (natural) level. It is on this level where unconscious, vegetative, and instinctive operations are situated. The aspect of nature and that of the person reciprocally overlap in a substantial unity.

Operativity ⟳ See First Part of *Person and Act,*
Consciousness and Operativity

Operativity is a particular moment of the person's experience, because it reveals the person and allows him to observe himself in his acting.

Concerning the double aspect of nature and person, the former can be identified with the structure "something happens in man," where the conscious "I" does not intervene. The latter is the full conscious manifestation of the human being and is identified with the structure "the human being acts." It is the most characteristic of the person.

When the human being acts he has the experience of himself as an agent of his own experience; he is a conscious cause of his causing. While accomplishing his act, he also realizes that he performs it; this is called "operativity." If there is not a conscious act, there is no operativity, but just an impersonal act of the subjectivity of "I." The experience "something happens in man" manifests "human subjectivity"; and in the structure "the human being acts" is discovered his "operativity." In other words, it is in the operativity where the person is fully manifested. But both structures form a unity in which one cannot be without the other. Both combine in the same subject and have the same *suppositum*, which assures the person's unity in his human nature.

Transcendence ∾ See Second Part of *Person and Act*, Transcendence

The analysis of operativity manifests a number of intrinsically personal aspects, the most important of which is transcendence, in which the capacity of self-possession and that for self-dominion converge; in turn, this convergence enables self-determination.

The will is not only a "capacity of nature" but also a "property of the person." The moment of "I want" suggests a personal structure that includes "I can, but I am not compelled," an expression of fundamental freedom. When analyzing the will from the act, one encounters two elements that constitute self-determination: self-possession and self-dominion. Through them, the human being can determine his operativity and develop himself throughout his life.

The will, in its character as a faculty, provides the control of the dynamizations of the human being, and its intentionality points to the values that the intelligence objectively presents *ad extra* (horizontal transcendence). But in its character of self-determination, the will refers to the "I" that has "self-possession" and "self-dominion"; then there is no talk of directing outward, but an orientation *ad intra*, toward the "I" (vertical transcendence). This reference to the "I" must also be accompanied by horizontal transcendence's reference to the truth; otherwise the "I" would fall into an autonomous subjectivism.

To the extent that the human being possesses consciousness of his own subjectivity—because one function of consciousness is the objectification of subjectivity—he has experience of his volitions and realizes his self-determination. Then the human being lives "in a different way" and understands the scope of his actions and his own self-development.

Truth and Morality ∽ See Second Part of *Person and Act*, Transcendence

The will is dependent with respect to the truth, and this helps the acting person's decision and choice. Thereby, truth constitutes the basis of the person's transcendence. Human action is never separate from morality.

In his self-development the human being can make mistakes. The way to recognize these is through the truth—for example, the knowledge of reality about the good objects toward which the will is directed, in which is included the experience of value in his search for personal fulfillment. Having knowledge means standing before the truth.

The truth about the moral good makes the act authentic for the self-realization of the person. To realize oneself is to bring to fullness the structure of the human being, which is characteristic of him by his personality and by his being someone who exercises his self-determination. Just as the will is subordinated to the truth, so too is freedom, since to choose moral evil is to determine oneself toward non-realization.

Just as intellectual consciousness can recognize the truth, moral conscience can perceive the veracity that awakens in the person the consciousness of obligation and at the same time the sense of responsibility for his acts. The human being is responsible for his behavior and for what happens to himself as a consequence of his behavior.

Integration ∽ See Third Part of *Person and Act*, Integration

The dynamism of the person presumes the underlying potentiality of his nature. When we observe that "something happens in the human being," we find two levels of potentiality, the somato-vegetative and the psycho-emotive levels. The human person has a corporeal component and another that is spiritual; these need to be integrated to achieve their plenitude.

The somato-vegetative dynamism refers to the physiological aspects of the human body as a real organism. The psycho-emotive dynamism is where is displayed the affectivity that is the result of the perception of the different experiences of which the human being is conscious.

There is a unity of the person with his psycho-somatic character. We cannot believe that the individual is a kind of "inhabitant" inside the body. For this reason, the natural dynamisms are part of the action of the person and they affect him as such. They cannot be treated independently from the whole that is the human being.

Corporeality ∽ See Third Part of *Person and Act*, Integration

The human body has great importance, and its care contributes to the realization of the person. The metaphysical consideration of the substantial unity recognizes that the human being has a material corporeal aspect and another aspect that is incorporeal; lacking either of these aspects, one is neither a human being nor a human person.

The human body has an external, visible aspect as well as an internal aspect that is usually not seen (where the organs are found that permit vitality). The body can also carry out certain operations on the margins of the individual's voluntariness. What is proper to the body is reactivity, since its order responds to natural ends. The individual cannot ignore such ends; for this reason we admit two kinds of subjectivity: one of the body—vegetative, reactive, and external to the consciousness—which follows the biological order, and another which corresponds to the integral subjectivity of the person. In the somatic potentiality there is a sphere that we can access voluntarily and another that acts on the margin of the will.

In human beings we can observe the presence of instincts, which are automatic reactions to external stimuli. These instincts can be directed by operativity, giving rise to abilities that permit the more skillful carrying out of certain activities. When the instincts are oriented by human voluntariness, they can lead to the integration or the disintegration of the person.

Almost the same as an instinct is an urge, which, more than a response, is a radical and deep natural yearning. It too is considered as "something that happens in the human being," and the person can bring it to the level of the person. An example is the sexual urge, which transcends the biological level to be integrated in the level of existence with personal love.

Affectivity ❧ See Third Part of *Person and Act*, Integration

The integration of the psycho-emotive dynamism is called emotion and covers the entire affective sphere of the human being. Although this dynamism acts at the natural level, it does not show itself like the somato-vegetative because it is not a reactive response, although it is rooted in and conditioned by the body. It is also affected by spiritual movements.

The psycho-emotive dynamism possesses different levels of operation because it mediates between the corporeal and the spiritual. Thus there are affective responses, such as the sensations which are linked to the corporeal, as well the emotions of desire or aversion linked to the inclinations of the will, and the even deeper movements of the person such as radical feelings of love or hate.

Emotivity together with veracity is the necessary condition for a good experience of values. Emotivity alone, acting outside of veracity, could have negative effects on the person. For this reason, the cognitive aspect is important, although not unique, in the integration of the person in action.

There can be tension between the spontaneity of the affective sphere and the operativity of the person; there can even be an emotionalization of consciousness, where the emotions are so strong that they impede an adequate integration. But such a radical opposition occurs only under extraordinary circumstances; we cannot believe that there is a clean and direct opposition between emotivity and operativity.

The education of affectivity and its adequate orientation toward values—toward those to which emotivity leads—facilitates integration. This is achieved by means of that habitual facility which, from the point of view of ethics, is called virtue.

Participation ∾ See Fourth Part of *Person and Act*, Participation

When the person performs an action (operativity), the values that emerge are related to transcendence and integration. All of them are synthesized in the concept "personalistic value." These values are prior to axiological or moral values, although they are related to them, because the values are analyzed at an ontological level. The personalistic value gives particular importance to participation.

The personalistic value makes clear the value that human action has. Beyond its classic consideration circumscribed around the will, "personalistic value" makes reference to the structures of self-possession and self-dominion, which permit horizontal and vertical transcendence. The person in action manifests an intrinsic value and thereby reveals the incommunicability of every human being; for this reason this intrinsic value is prior to any ethical value.

When a person's personalistic value enters into relation with others, participation arises; participation is an intrinsic property of the person when he acts "together with others." The participation of the person influences the realization and results of action in the community, and it has a close relationship with transcendence and integration themselves. An individual needs to exercise his actions "together with others" to be able to develop himself. This is a fundamental natural right.

Individualism and totalitarianism are two possible obstacles to the participation of the person. In the first, the individual is the supreme good to which all other interests in society should be subordinated. This leads to an isolation of the person that limits participation, and at times impedes it, because he sees others as obstacles to his ends. In totalitarianism, society purports to "protect itself" from the individual because it considers him to be a selfish being, which seeks only his own ends. Therefore it limits his freedom, generally by coercion.

Neighbor ᑴ See Fourth Part of *Person and Act*, Participation

An adequate participation requires living in community and attending to the common good. For this it is necessary to distinguish the type of community to which one belongs and to have authentic attitudes to cooperate with others in it. The consideration of the person as a "neighbor" stresses participation not only in the community but in humanity; in this way is "participation" given a universal sense.

Not all communities are the same. Some last a longer time, such as the community of existence (family, nation); others are temporary, such as a community of action (work, circles of friends). A person's participation should be adapted to the kind of community in which he acts. That participation could be authentic (solidarity, appropriate opposition, dialogue) if it contributed to the community's common aims; or inauthentic (conformism, escape) if it lacked intrinsic principles and personalistic value.

Even taking into account participation as a member of communities, the personalistic value highlights another aspect of participation that is even more absolute. This is the person's participation with some other person in their humanity. This means universally accepting the other who is denominated "neighbor."

The concept of neighbor erases all borders that can be established in communities and creates a common bond with another member of mankind. Being a "neighbor" is prior to being a "member" of the community. There is no opposition between them, but each is placed in a hierarchy of values according to the principle of humanity. The content of the commandment "love your neighbor as yourself" is clearly communitarian and shows properly the type of relationship that the personalistic value of the person deserves, which in turns allows the community to be kept alive and united. "The person is a good towards which the only proper and adequate attitude is love."[1]

1. LR, 41. See AR, 51.

8 ஓ

CONSCIOUSNESS AND OPERATIVITY

Experience

Wojtyła's starting point in philosophy in general is reality. So, like Aristotle, he begins from experience, but what does Wojtyła understand by "experience"?[1] In the introduction to *Person and Act*, this is the first concept that he explains, because it is presupposed as the basis of his methodology. "The present study emerges from the need for objectivization in the realm of that great cognitive process that can be defined at its basis as the experience of man."[2]

Wojtyła says that experience is the starting point of science because it permits a kind of first verification of the realism adopted in the practice of a science and a global verification that its methods are realist. The conscious identification of experience as the first requisite for knowledge determines a certain passage from prescientific to scientific thought.[3]

The most fundamental sense of experience is related to anthro-

---

1. Wojtyła explains that the full meaning of "experience" is found in the phenomenological perspective. "From the phenomenological point of view, experience is that source and basis of any knowledge of the object; this does not mean that there is only one kind of experience.... There are many kinds of experience in which the data are individual objects; for example, the experience of psychical acts of other individual, so also aesthetic experience, in which there are given to us works of art, and so on." PA, 39n1. See OC, 57n1; AP, 301n1.

2. PA, 31. See OC, 51; AP, 3.

3. See Wojtyła, "The Problem of Experience," 114, 125n3.

pology. In effect, there are two aspects that compose experience. These are like two meanings that are presented to the human being who is experiencing. The first is a "sense of reality": this is a matter of grasping the existence of something real, independent of the knower and of his cognitive act, which also exists as object of this cognitive act. The second aspect would be the "sense of knowing," in which is established a particular relationship between the knower and that which exists really and objectively. In the conjunction of these two senses "of reality and of knowing," the sense of knowing is manifest as a tendency toward that which is real and which exists objectively as true. Addressing the sense of knowing in relation to the sense of reality, Wojtyła writes: "The latter is a sense of reality in and through knowing—and the former is a sense of knowing through reality."[4] In his encounter with reality, the knower makes a particular contact or merging with that which exists, and which exists precisely in this way. In his aspiration to the truth, *adequatio rei et intellectus*,[5] his cognitive act surpasses the order of sensation. The same happens with experience: "there can be no purely sensory experience because we are not 'purely sensory' beings."[6] Because we cannot limit our speaking about the human being only to the sensory plane, it is necessary to acknowledge a meta-sensory dimension, which for the Greek tradition was "rationality" and for the medieval tradition, "spirituality." This affirmation is not an initial postulate, but rather it is deduced from the analysis of the effects of human action which are verified in experience, effects that demand an adequate or sufficient cause. One of Wojtyła's objectives is to manifest the complexity of the "structure" of the man-person.

On the other hand, the experience of man discloses two realms of reality, one which is exterior and the other, always accompanying the first, which is interior. The experience of reality is linked to an experience of one's own "self," and this double consciousness oc-

---

4. Ibid., 115. See PA, 336; OC, 274
5. "The correspondence between intellect and thing." Aquinas, *De Veritate* 1, 1.
6. Wojtyła, "The Problem of Experience," 116. See PA, 337; OC, 274.

curs in a continual manner, even though it is interrupted from time to time, for instance in sleep. But it always returns and continues the lived experience of the "self." "The object of such experience is not merely a transitory sensible phenomenon, but also the man himself who is revealed on the basis of all his experiences and who is simultaneously in each one of them [at this point we disregard other objects]."[7]

Experience as "sense of reality" and the experience of man (which includes experience as "sense of knowing") are united in such a way that in the very dynamism "reality-knowledge of reality," the human being structures his knowledge. This means that human knowledge possesses an essential tendency toward truth, which is brought about by means of continually more penetrating understandings, which pass through experience and depend on it.

This is Wojtyła's basic discovery, and therefore his entire philosophy is founded on the reality that comes through experience. This method serves also as the basis for his ethics, which is sustained in his anthropology. Experience is not simply the memory of having lived through a situation, nor is it the act of entering into contact with the reality that is impressed in certain of my reactions; rather, experience manifests a special form of entering into contact with reality. Let us analyze this more slowly.

The experience of a human being does not result from the apprehension of sensations that will then be integrated by the intelligence (Hume's empiricism), nor does it result from phenomena captured by the *apriori* forms of sensibility, but without having attained to the noumenon or reality in itself (Kant's phenomenalism), but rather it results in knowing—with the apprehension of sensations—there is an immaterial contact with the real thing (entity) from the very beginning. This is possible by means of "cognitive intentionality" in the Thomistic sense, which gives the human intellect the possibility of entering into "direct" contact with the ideal or real ob-

7. PA, 32. See OC, 52; AP, 4.

ject, which can be abstract or concrete,[8] without becoming trapped in subjective consciousness, as is characteristic of epistemological immanentism.[9] Experience indicates the direct character of knowing—intentionality—and establishes a strict relationship with it. In opposition to Hume, Wojtyła maintains that there is no reason to say that these objects or facts can be directly captured "only" through sensible acts. "It seems, rather, that the understanding is engaged already in experience itself, and thanks to it establishes a relationship with the object, a relationship that is also direct, albeit in a different way."[10]

This text is key, because it positions Wojtyła's philosophy clearly within the realist ambit, overcoming the subjectivist frameworks such as we encounter, for example, in Scheler's phenomenology.[11] Wojtyła says that Scheler divests experience of its essential content,

8. See Karol Wojtyła, *Lecciones de Lublin*, trans. Rafael Mora (Madrid: Ediciones Palabra, 2014), 37. *Wykłady Lubelskie* (Lublin: Towarzystwo Naukowe KUL, 2006), 25.

9. Intentionality is a medieval concept recovered by Brentano which passed into phenomenology in the twentieth century. Wojtyła could have had knowledge from both sources, but from phenomenology more probably through Brentano and Max Scheler, because Husserl did not understand intentionality in the classical sense. "A characteristic proper to the Aristotelian-Thomistic realism consists in admitting that knowledge is the immaterial appropriation of the forms of things. When Thomas Aquinas speaks of how the *anima est quodammodo omnia* ('the soul is in certain aspect every thing,' Aquinas, *De Veritate* 1, 1, ad 2), he connects with Aristotle's sentence which admits the immateriality of the soul and the possibility of its appropriating the forms of things. Since things are outside of us, we need to reach to them, to possess them in some way in order to know them. In realism, human knowledge is 'transobjective'; it is not confined in consciousness, as occurs in immanentism." Miguel Acosta, "La *intentio* como clave de la transobjetividad de la inteligencia en la filosofía realista" [The *intentio* as key to the transobjetivity of intelligence in the realist philosophy], in *Filosofía de la Inteligencia* [Philosophy of Intelligence], ed. Manuel Oriol, 93 (Madrid: Ediciones CEU, 2011).

10. PA, 40. See *OC*, 58; *AP*, 11.

11. "[Scheler] used the theoretical-cognitive premises of phenomenology in such a way that values are manifest, in particular moral values, only as the contents of an affective-cognitive perception.... This essentialism runs hand in hand with the lack of appreciation for the causal relationship of the person with respect to ethical values.... Scheler denies the being of the person as a substantial being who acts and substitutes being through a series of acts, that is, of experiences that are co-experienced in the experience of personal unity." Wojtyła, *Max Scheler*, 208.

which shows itself in its natural foundation given by experience itself—the fact that the work is linked to the subject of work—that
is, Scheler separates the action from the agent of the act, who is a
person.[12] "The language which Wojtyła uses is that of phenomenology, but what he intends also has to do with Thomistic metaphysical
knowledge."[13] Even so, Wojtyła finds some points of coincidence between realism and phenomenology: (1) in human experience there
is a degree of comprehension of that which is experienced, and
(2) there exists a unity of the acts of human cognition.[14]

What does Wojtyła intend, trying to bring together the Aristotelian-Thomistic position (metaphysics) and that of Scheler (phenomenology)? Why does he underscore the realism of experience and of
the cognition of experience? The answer is found in an essay published in 1978 under the title "Subjectivity and the Irreducible in the
Human Being."[15] There Wojtyła comments that, owing to the antino-
mies arising within the theory of knowledge, a line of division and
opposition has been traced between the "objective" and the "subjective." The "objective" was at the same time an ontological approach,
real (the human being as being), and the "subjective" appeared to
lead the human being away from the real, above all by the subjectivist tone of some idealist analyses based on pure consciousness.

I am convinced that *the line of demarcation between the subjectivistic* [idealis-
tic] *and objectivistic* [realistic] *views in anthropology and ethics must break down
and is in fact breaking down on the basis of the experience of the human being.* This
experience automatically frees us from pure consciousness as the subject
conceived and assumed *a priori* and leads us to the full concrete existence
of the human being, to the reality of the conscious subject.[16]

12. Styczeń, "Introduction" [in Spanish] to *Mi visión*, 121.
13. Buttiglione, *Karol Wojtyła: The Thought*, 124.
14. PA, 40. See OC, 58; AP, 10.
15. See Karol Wojtyła, "Subjectivity and the Irreducible in the Human Being," in
Person and Community, 209–17. I also suggest the article by Andrzej Poltawski, "The
Epistemological Basis of Karol Wojtyła's Philosophy," in *Karol Wojtyła. Filosofo*, ed.
Buttiglione, 79–91.
16. Wojtyła, "Subjectivity and the Irreducible," 210 (emphasis in the original). We

For this reason, Wojtyła locates the complementarity of the two philosophical methodologies in their common basis in the realism of experience. However, the question that always arises among Aristotelian-Thomistic philosophers is this: why does metaphysics prove to be insufficient to explain the human reality if anthropology can be studied under the structures of being and action? To this, Wojtyła responds that we can indeed come to a satisfactory explanation, because, in fact, the human being "acts" (*agere*) and "something happens in him" (*pati*), but if we desire to understand the human being as a person—unique in himself and unrepeatable—"it is experience that best manifests this characteristic."[17] "For then the issue is not just the metaphysical objectification of the human being as an acting subject, as the agent of acts, but the revelation of the person as a subject *experiencing* its acts and inner happenings, and with them its own subjectivity."[18]

When one tries to interpret the human being as agent (in action), the category "experience" will encounter a preponderant place in anthropology and ethics, because it will be situated on a certain point in the center of distinct interpretations. Realist phenomenology is a good help to develop this vital characteristic of the human being.

Wojtyła knows that the connection between objective reality and the subjective world passes through experience. Experience makes possible the objectification of the human dynamism [*operari*].[19]

---

agree with Rafael Mora's analysis in his Spanish translation of the Polish and adopt the same criteria for this study: "We translate *świadomość* by consciousness, to stress the dimension of self-referential subjectivity.... In addition, we use the word *operativity* to translate the Polish word *sprawczość*, which would be defined as the capacity for someone to be author or a cause of an effect." PA, 59. In Tymieniecka's English edition, *The Acting Person*, this Polish word [*sprawczość*] is rendered "efficacy."

17. About the specific characteristics of the concept "person," see LR, 22–23.

18. Wojtyła, "Subjectivity and the Irreducible," 213. See PA, 32; OC, 52 (emphasis in the original).

19. Wojtyla uses this term that comes from Aristotle (*dunamei*) and is used by the scholastics (*operari*) to stress the act or operation in humans' activity. See PA, 142n48: "the dynamism that may properly be called the activity of the human being as a person: that is, the act."

Therefore, the appeal to experience as the way to come to consciousness is the method that is to explain the person from his "action." He makes this strong claim: "*Today more than ever before we feel the need—and also see the greater possibility—of objectifying the problem of the subjectivity of the human being.*"[20] For this reason it is not enough to be concerned with the human being only as an objective being, "but we must also somehow treat the human being as a subject in which the specifically human subjectivity of the human being is determined by consciousness. And that dimension would seem to be none other than *personal* subjectivity."[21] Here we see what is the manner of attaining that "objectivizing of subjectivity" where consciousness plays a relevant role.

Consciousness and the *suppositum*

"Experience" does indicate something experienced by the human being, but beyond that it indicates a certain cognition. The human being knows himself in his experiences, but at the moment of interpreting himself to himself he must count on another fundamental element: consciousness. "Consciousness reveals the reality of the concrete human being as subject who has experience of himself."[22] This would make experience a "content of consciousness," since it is constituted not "in consciousness" but "through consciousness."[23] First let us clarify how consciousness is to be understood.

The concept of consciousness in Wojtyła does not follow Husserl's line of phenomenology but follows instead the realist tradition (Aristotle-Aquinas). The classical consciousness of realism is a "type" of cognitive act by which one adverts to his own act. Con-

20. Wojtyła, "Subjectivity and the Irreducible, 209. See PA, 25 (emphasis in the original).

21. Ibid., 210. See PA, 27 (emphasis in the original).

22. This footnote is lacking in the English translation in *Person and Community*: See Karol Wojtyla, "La subjetividad y lo irreductible en el hombre," in *El hombre y su destino*, 33n7.

23. See ibid.

sciousness is the reference "in the present" to the knowledge which is had of the real.[24] By contrast, Husserl's phenomenology admits that the object "is constituted" by means of consciousness. Wojtyła rejects this active function, the constitution of the object—and elaboration of cognition—on the part of consciousness, just as he also does not admit that consciousness is a faculty or an independent and self-sufficient reality, the unique subject of its contents. Were it so, we would be faced with immanentism.

Wojtyła believes that consciousness has a cognitive function that acts in a mirroring manner,[25] as a reflection that accompanies the act of knowing. "[T]he cognitive reason for the existence of consciousness and its acts does not consist in the penetration of the object, in objectivization, oriented to a comprehension that constitutes the object."[26] This is the task of the cognitive operation through the understanding.[27] Although he does not deny that consciousness is always consciousness of something, he rejects the intentional character of consciousness and of its acts, saying that it acts in a reflective manner. "Being aware implies further reflection on something which has already been worked out in the cognitive faculties."[28] As in a mirror, in consciousness is reproduced everything with which the human being has entered into contact exteriorly, through what he does and all the things that happen in him. In it are "contained" the entire "human being" as well as the world of this human being,[29] the concrete elements of reality and its interrelationships.

Consciousness provides some illumination that permits one to

24. Jacinto Choza, *Conciencia y afectividad (Aristóteles, Nietzsche, Freud)* [Consciousness and affectivity (Aristotle, Nietzsche, Freud)] (Pamplona: Eunsa, 1991), 156.

25. PA, 72. See OC, 81; AP, 33.

26. PA, 71. See OC, 80; AP, 32.

27. In a subjective act there is a double presence, that of the object and that of the subject himself. This means that not only do "I know," but also "I know that I know." Millán-Puelles says that they are "[t]wo different dimensions, even if so united to each other, that they constitute one indivisible act." Antonio Millán-Puelles, *La estructura de la subjetividad* [The Structure of Subjectivity] (Madrid: Rialp, 1967), 187.

28. Buttiglione, *Karol Wojtyła: The Thought*, 130.

29. PA, 82–83. See OC, 88–89; AP, 39–40.

see objects and their meanings thanks to that capacity to reflect knowledge and to contain the human being's experiences. In this sense it is inappropriately said that consciousness "knows." Often in the history of thought the image of light has been used in relation to consciousness. Consciousness "illuminates" the interior, the thoughts, the desires, the interior acts, and also exterior ones. Consciousness illuminates that which is reflected in it. Its privileged position as "companion" to knowledge permits it to bear within itself a faithful image of the person, although the work of understanding is carried out by knowledge from its contact with reality by different procedures.

Besides considering consciousness *prima facie*, Wojtyła also speaks of another modality that helps to explain the knowledge of subjectivity through experience. This has to do with "self-consciousness," which is obtained through self-knowledge. Let us look at this.

Consciousness allows one to realize what he knows, but it can go further; it can know the characteristics of subjectivity, of the comprehension of his own "self"; that is, it is conscious of self-knowledge. The act of cognition and the act of consciousness act in a conjoined way,[30] entering into contact with the "self" in the human being's subjectivity. In each human being the "self" is a point at which all the intentional acts of self-knowledge come together. Through an act of self-knowledge my action is objectivized in relation to my person—my action is the real action of my person, not something that simply "happens" in it; it is a voluntary act that also has ethical qualification. All these objective facts for my self-knowledge come to be "contents" of consciousness.[31]

30. "On this point the knowledge of oneself is identified with consciousness and, at the same time, is in a way different from it, given that the subjective union of consciousness with the 'I' itself does not cognitively direct it toward this as its object. One can even affirm that from the cognitive point of view consciousness is indifferent to the 'I' itself as an object. There are no intentional acts that objectivize the being of the acts of the 'I' itself. The acts of self-knowledge perform this function." PA, 77. See OC, 85; AP, 36.

31. "Concentrated in the 'I' itself as in its proper object, self-knowledge comprises together with this all the fields in which the 'I' itself unfolds." PA, 82. See OC, 88; AP, 39.

To see the pertinence of the human act as revelatory of the "self" in its own subjectivity, it is necessary to remember that in the realist philosophy:

the human being perceives himself, that he is and that he lives—first act—to experience his own operations—second acts—such as understanding and wanting. The soul knows itself through its own acts [per actos suos]. That is to say that we can know ourselves only in as much as we know, in as much as we are actualized by the species through which we know realities distinct from ourselves.[32]

Wojtyła indicates that self-knowledge is very special because it permits the development of self-consciousness. When we speak of self-knowledge, consciousness passes to a different dimension, because it does not simply reflect the contents of the things understood, but when one knows the "self," the self-knowledge is reflected and that implies what is known in consciousness. One is conscious of being conscious. This new dimension of consciousness, so closely joined to self-knowledge, is called "self-consciousness." Buttiglione's explanation is enlightening:

[S]elf-consciousness is strictly linked with the "I," as is the conscience. But this link should not lead us to forget that self-knowledge is always a cognitive act and therefore objectivizes man, in making his own consciousness an object of knowledge. Consciousness itself is the object of self-knowledge in the sense that in the cognitive act in which man knows himself, he knows himself as a conscious subject. However, there is a difference between knowing oneself as a conscious subject [in this case consciousness itself is, as it were, objectivized] and being aware of oneself. Self-knowledge gives the "I" the cognitive material which is reflected in one's consciousness of one's self.[33]

So, we have two modes of consciousness. The first mode is something objective, where something objective refers to the meanings of distinct objects that are contained in consciousness and come from different understandings of intentional knowledge. The second is also something objective—through self-knowledge—in relation

32. Alejandro Llano, Gnoseología [Gnoseology] (Pamplona: Eunsa, 2000), 143–44.
33. Buttiglione, Karol Wojtyła: The Thought, 130.

to the structure of meaning characteristic of the "self's" consciousness. What makes this special is the contact with the "self," which "constitutes something like a meeting-point of all the intentional acts of self-knowledge."[34] This mode of consciousness is called "self-consciousness."[35]

In summary, self-knowledge is a very specific type of knowledge.[36] Therefore the consciousness that is tied to this knowledge also acquires a specific character. This consciousness would be "the realm in which the 'I,' when it is manifest in all its specific objectivity [concretely, as object of self-knowledge] fully experiences its own subjectivity."[37] On this point Wojtyła makes a special qualification.

According to him, the functions of consciousness are not only the classical ones of reflecting and illuminating, as was noted above; rather, "the fundamental function of consciousness is to *form the experience* that allows the human being in a particular way to become aware of his own subjectivity."[38] It is here that the relationship between experience and consciousness is accentuated. "Through this role, consciousness allows us not only to look into the interior of our acts [introspection] and of their dynamic relationship with the 'I' itself, but also to *experience these acts as acts and as our own*."[39] Thus, the human being owes to consciousness the "subjectivization of the objective." This "subjectivization" can be identified in a certain way

---

34. PA, 81. See OC, 88; AP, 39.

35. Other authors name these two modalities, "consciousness" and "self-consciousness," as "spontaneous consciousness" and "reflective consciousness," respectively, but their functions are the same. Spontaneous consciousness: "When something is understood, there is perceived in a secondary way—concomitantly—that it is understood, for the subject knows that the thing is manifest to him, although he does not yet by this know the nature of the principle of understanding, that is of the subject. It is about a reflection that is exercised ... which accompanies the act of understanding something, but indirectly and conditioned by the determination of the object. [Reflective consciousness] Afterwards can come ... reflection *in actu signato*, by which the subject turns to his own act, and which requires a peculiar *intentio*, directed precisely at self-knowledge as such." Llano, *Gnoseología*, 145.

36. For a deeper look into self-knowledge see PA, 81–84; OC, 87–89; AP, 35–41.

37. PA, 85. See OC, 90–91; AP, 42.

38. PA, 86. See OC, 91; AP, 42 (emphasis in the original).

39. Ibid. (emphasis in the original).

with experience since it is in experience where the knowledge of it is had. Furthermore, everything that constitutes the intentional content of the person is subjectivized, since it is the material of experience and is incorporated into the individual subjectivity of each human "self."

Wojtyła takes us yet another step further. He speaks of a reflexive function that belongs to the same consciousness as that in which appears, not only the reflection and that which is reflected in a given moment, but also the lived experience in which, in a particular way, the subjectivity of the human being living that experience stands out. We should not confuse the reflection of consciousness with the human mind's reflection, which supposes intentionality and which is performed to know the object more deeply and even its character and structure. Wojtyła says that the reflection (of understanding) and the reflexivity (of consciousness) are insufficient of themselves to constitute an experience. For this it is necessary to turn especially to the subject, and in this turning, together with the experience, the subjectivity of the "self" who lives the experience stands out.[40]

Through the reflexivity of consciousness, the object—which is the subject—at the same time as it has the experience of its own "self" also has the experience of itself inasmuch as it is subject. This function of reflexivity appears especially in the moment of the act.

In this way we clearly distinguish that it is one thing to be subject and distinctly another to be known [objectivized] as subject [that which happens in the reflection of consciousness], and finally it is another thing vitally to experience oneself as subject of his acts and experiences [which we owe to the reflexive function of consciousness]. . . .

Self-knowledge confirms that "this being" that I objectively am is at the same time that which subjectively constitutes my "I," in that in it I have a living of my subjectivity. Therefore, I not only have consciousness of my own "I" [on the basis of self-knowledge], but also, thanks to [reflexive] consciousness, I have a lived experience of my "I," or rather, I experience myself as a concrete subject in that same subjectivity. Conscious-

40. PA, 87–88. See OC, 92–93; AP, 43–44.

ness is not just another aspect, but is rather an essential dimension or, which is to say the same thing, a real moment of this being that "I" am, given that it constitutes its subjectivity in an experiential sense.[41]

In consciousness the human being can encounter the experience of his own spirituality and the values that constitute it; on the other hand, we have to think that this captures not only intellectual experiences but emotional experiences as well. Here we can note Scheler's influence on the grasping of values and emotions. Wojtyła dedicates a special section of *Person and Act* to address the "emotionalization of consciousness."

Wojtyła shows through these reflections the place where Scheler's analysis of emotional consciousness should be incorporated into St. Thomas's objective personalism. Consciousness is founded on being but does not simply mirror it: it is a particular subjectivization and personalization which calls for an autonomous and accurate inquiry.[42]

In this way, thanks to consciousness, Wojtyła introduces experience as the fundamental point of support for knowing human subjectivity. Through self-knowledge and self-consciousness, I can know my "self." And through the reflexivity of consciousness I can attain to the experience of my "self" in its "existing" and its "acting," and in turn this will permit me to attain a better comprehension of subjectivity. With all this, Wojtyła finds a legitimate argument that permits him to include experience as an objective anthropological given and lays the foundation of its subjectivization, which is not a matter of a mere immanentist product but the natural result of acts of consciousness based on real lived experience.

However, at this point Wojtyła takes an approach that proves to be pertinent: "All analyses aimed at illuminating human subjectivity have their 'categorial' limits. We can neither go beyond those limits nor completely free ourselves from them."[43] My experience of my "self" is related to multiple objective experiences. Where do

41. PA, 88, 91. See OC, 93, 94–95; AP, 44; 45–46.
42. Buttiglione, *Karol Wojtyła: The Thought*, 133.
43. Wojtyła, "Person: Subject and Community," 221–22.

I sustain the unity of all my experiences that are given to my existence to comprehend my subjectivity in an integral manner?

In the history of philosophy many efforts have been made to achieve a comprehension of that subjectivity. For example: (1) From "pure consciousness" or the "pure subject": Here the problem is that objectivity is separated from experience based in reality, which is precisely what illuminates human subjectivity, and by this process the subjectivity is not attained. This is the immanentist proposal. (2) On the other hand, there is the intent to comprehend subjectivity through the particular sciences. There are consistent data which help this comprehension of the person and his subjectivity, , but comprehension of the person and his subjectivity is not an integral comprehension but only a partial, fragmentary one. (3) If we attempt a comprehension of subjectivity by way of phenomenology, we find a wealth of analysis which does put together a philosophical image of the person, but which is also resolved "in consciousness" but by performing an *epoché*. Here too there is a rupture with reality. To be valid, those contents should be transferred out of the level of consciousness and integrated into the reality of the person. There is an "almost" in phenomenology which turns out to be insufficient.

Finally, to solve the unity of subjective experiences, Wojtyła appeals to another classical concept. This concept focuses on that reality that enables us to link the concepts of experience and self-consciousness. The concept is *suppositum*.

Wojtyła appeals to the classical concept of *suppositum* as a realistic basis for the "self" of the human being with regard to his existing and acting. The *suppositum* is the human subjectivity in the metaphysical sense.[44] Wojtyła says that suppositum is the transphenomenal expression of metaphysical subjectivity and the ultimate guarantee of the person's existing and acting. If there were not a *suppositum*, we could not speak of a subjective experience in existing and acting. And if the *suppositum* is the fundamental expression of

44. Ibid.

the experience of man, it ought to contain every particular experience of his "self," facilitating the knowledge of the subjectivity of the person.

However, he adverts to a difference between the "self" and the *suppositum*. "Self" is a broader concept than that of *suppositum*, because it always designates a concrete person, combining the moment of experienced subjectivity with that of ontic subjectivity; by contrast, *suppositum* refers only to the latter characteristic. *Suppositum* prescinds from the experiential characteristics and speaks of the individual being inasmuch as he is the basis of existence and action. To highlight this characteristic the expression "ontic substrate" is used.[45]

We can say that the *suppositum* (metaphysical subjectivity or ontic substrate) is the ontological level where existing and acting interrelate. To show this, Wojtyła alludes to the well-known adage *operari sequitur esse* (acting follows upon being). This sentence expresses the causal dependence of the act with respect to being. Wojtyła especially emphasizes action as the most appropriate way toward knowledge of the being. This mutual ontological-epistemological relationship shows that the human being's *operari* allows us most adequately to comprehend human subjectivity. Here the acting, the "action" or human act, begins to take the leading role. Furthermore, the concept *suppositum* acquires another connotation; it is no longer the subject in the metaphysical sense but that which "makes the human being an individual personal subject."[46] Because the human being is manifest in his acting, everything that he does and that which happens to him give him a peculiar configuration, as much psychical as somatic, or, if we prefer, a somatic subjectivity and another, psychic subjectivity. At this point Wojtyła concludes:

45. I use the expression "ontic substrate"—instead of "ontic support," as it appears in the source in Spanish (1982) and also in *The Acting Person*—to avoid the physical connotation that the word "support" carries. The new edition in Spanish (2011) uses the word *suppositum*, which is Wojtyła's term in *Osoba i czyn*.
46. Wojtyła, "Person: Subject and Community," 223.

After all, metaphysical subjectivity in the sense of *suppositum* belongs to everything that in any way exists and acts; it belongs to different existing and acting beings according to an analogy of proportionality. We must, therefore, define more precisely the subjectivity proper to the human being, namely, personal subjectivity, taking as our basis the whole of human dynamism [*operari*], but especially the dynamism that may properly be called the activity of the human being as a person: that is, the act.[47]

The human act, about which we will speak below, allows the human being his dynamism in the most profound sense. In his act he is being constituted as subjectivity, and as he is being constituted he is revealed as a person. This self-constitution includes the entire psychosomatic dynamism, but there is no doubt that the metaphysical subjectivity should be manifest as a human "I," as personal subjectivity. For Wojtyła the strongest argument in favor of the metaphysical conception of human nature is this personal subjectivity: the human being is "by nature" a person.[48]

Once the *suppositum* is understood as metaphysical subjectivity, we can see better the distinction between the dimension of being a subject (*suppositum*) and that of experiencing oneself as a subject. The true reality of the human self can be reached only from the second—the experiential—dimension, even though the first is fundamental and constitutive. One could also say that the human *suppositum* becomes a human self and appears as one to itself because of consciousness."[49] The human being is a subject, and he is such fully *in actu* (in act) when he experiences himself as subject, and this is what makes consciousness.

To reach the full significance of the human being's personal sub-

47. Ibid., 224; translation revised according to Karol Wojtyła, "Osoba: Podmiot i wpólnota" [Person: Subject and Community], in *Osoba i czyn*, 380.

48. In passing, Wojtyła offers a comment that has important implications for bioethics: "The fact that the human *suppositum*, or metaphysical subjectivity, does not display the traits of personal subjectivity in certain cases [e.g., in cases of psychosomatic or purely psychological immaturity, in which either the normal human self has not developed or the self has developed in a distorted way] does not allow us to question the very foundation of this subjectivity, for they reside within the essentially human *suppositum*." Wojtyła, "Person: Subject and Community," 225.

49. Ibid., 227.

jectivity, it is necessary to study that which the *suppositum humanum* contains; it is necessary to enter through experience and consciousness into the person's interiority, into the deeper inner life.

Act and Operativity

Karol Wojtyła's personalist anthropology aims at comprehending the person through his deepest foundations. To fulfill these purposes, his chosen method was to study the person from the point of view of his act. But in what does the "act" consist?

We know that it is characteristic of the concept of person to emphasize the exceptionality that we find in every human being. Therefore this is not a phylogenetic study of the human being according to his nature, but rather it is precisely to descend to the ontogenetic characteristics of the being, into those which are found in "every" human being. This particularity, which even transcends the concept of mere "individual," is what the concept "person" intends to bring out.[50]

This particularity, which even transcends the concept of just the "individual," is what the concept "person" intends to highlight. How do we manage to study those aspects that are rooted in human subjectivity itself? For this Wojtyła relies on self-consciousness. But how will he prevent that self-consciousness from falling into immanentism? He does so by seeking for this subjectivity an ontological handle through the *suppositum* or ontological substrate. Self-consciousness reveals personal being through the person's experience. Wojtyła says that "every human experience simultaneously involves some understanding of that which is experienced."[51] Because experience shows the existence of a direct cognitive relationship with the object, and among those facts given in experience human acts (action) have especial relevance.

Wojtyła's point of view is that *"action serves as a particular moment of*

50. See LR, 22; AR, 28.
51. PA, 40. See OC, 58; AP, 10.

apprehending—that is, of experiencing—the person."[52] Action reveals the person, and we can see the person through his action.[53] He trusts experience as being something evident to everyone. Furthermore, that form of act that is called "action" refers necessarily to a person. It remains to show how.

"Only the *conscious actions* of the human being do we name act."[54] The term "act" comes from the Aristotelian metaphysical conjuncts, *energeia-dynamis* (*actus-potentia*) and the term "action" from the Greek concept *praxis*, which the Scholastics called *actus humanus*. Thomas Aquinas explains the distinction between "human acts" and "acts of the man" by saying that the former are voluntary acts, whereas the latter are involuntary acts that the human being realizes according to his nature without the action of the will—for example, digestion, blood circulation, etc. The power of human acts referring to the human subject lies in this, that in those acts is morality (the relationship of the human act with respect to good or evil).

However, the concept "act" in Wojtyła goes beyond simply the voluntary act. The task that he sets himself is to investigate the presuppositions of the dynamism of human acts as closely related to the human being inasmuch as he is a person. (The accent is placed on the term "person" and not on "human being.") He wants to examine those presuppositions from different perspectives. This is the point of *Person and Act*. He states further that the historical conception assumed that the human being is the source of the act. However, Wojtyła's objective is to show what that classical conception assumed, since this can serve as a "source of knowledge" of the person. In a footnote of the work he remarks: "We are dealing with the ontological interpretation of the person through the act as act. By 'ontological' interpretation we understand an interpretation that manifests what the reality of the person is."[55] For this reason, the concept

---

52. See PA, 40–41; OC, 58–59; AP, 10ff. (emphasis in the original).
53. PA, 41–42. See OC, 58–59; AP, 10ff.
54. PA, 61. See OC, 73; AP, 25 (emphasis in the original).
55. PA, 63n2. See OC, 75n11; AP, 303n12.

"action" will not be simply a "human act"—which is assumed—but the "dynamization of the human being as a person." The differentiating nuance lies in this, that the first speaks of the action as a specific form of becoming according to the potentiality of the personal subject, placing the emphasis on the dynamism in itself; however, with the second is indicated the ontic structure of the person.

If the "action" is voluntary, it is therefore conscious. From this it follows that the contents will have meanings both ontological (of the human act) and psychological (in consciousness) which will gradually be extracted in Wojtyła's work.

In order to integrate within experience the distinct actions what the human being accomplishes and to be able to arrive at an adequate unity of meaning, he will use the method of induction (in the Aristotelian sense), as well as that of reduction. The inductive method consists in "grasping the unity of meaning from this multiplicity and complexity of phenomena, its substantial qualitative identity."[56] Reduction does not mean diminishing the experiential content but a "converting into arguments and adequate demonstrative proofs, or in other words: explaining and interpreting."[57] Ultimately the investigation into the experience of the action of persons will be through analytic argument (based on induction) and reductive comprehension in the meanings explained.

The "act" has a special moment called "operativity." This concept is of the greatest importance in Wojtyła's anthropology, because through it the dynamization is converted into "act." Let us recall that we want to understand the person through his acts. However, the person has many types of acts, some of which are not "actions" in the sense of "human act" or "act accomplished voluntarily," as mentioned above. "Operativity" is a moment that manifests what is proper to "act," but to understand this better it is necessary to analyze the dynamic structure (of acts) in the human being.

56. PA, 47. See OC, 62; AP, 14.
57. PA, 50. See OC, 65; AP, 17.

Wojtyła finds two objective structures in the human being: "the human being acts"[58] and "something happens in the human being"; these are two fundamental aspects of the same dynamism; they indicate, in the first case, "activity" and in the second, "passivity." This double structure appears to be the most rudimentary datum of experience and is therefore evident to human knowledge.[59] Both find their source in the human being, and although "activity" and "passivity" show different aspects in the dynamism, they do not deprive the dynamic subject of unity. When the human being acts, he has the experience of being activated, of being the agent responsible for the dynamism that he performs: the human being is the conscious cause of his own causality. "By moment of operativity we should understand, in this case, the experience 'I am the one who acts.'"[60]

The difference between "the human being acts" and "something happens in the human being" is this, that in the first case the man is the subject of the performance by being its agent, but in the second case he is not—he is simply the passive subject. Something happens to him, but the "I" does not appear as the dynamic force for the action in which it is seen as responsible. Therefore, the human being who is the "I" has experience of himself as being the agent when he accomplishes an action and the moment of operativity appears.[61] By contrast, Wojtyła calls every dynamization in which the human being as "I" does not experience his operativity an "activation."

On the other hand, the moment of operativity makes manifest

58. Rendered as "man-acts" in *The Acting Person*.

59. Wojtyła appeals to Aristotle to support this affirmation: See Aristotle, *Metaphysics* 9.1. 1046a19–22. The metaphysical analysis of the human dynamism can be plumbed to its source—Aristotle's concepts of act and potency, which according to Wojtyła present the intellectual terrain in which are sunk the roots of all the domains of knowledge. "On the basis of this theory and with the help of its language, we can adequately conceive any dynamism that we meet in any kind of being whatever." PA, 117. See OC, 113; AP, 64.

60. PA, 120. See OC, 116; AP, 66. "*Jestem sprawcą*," literally "I am the agent (or performer)."

61. PA, 123. See OC, 118; AP, 67.

another characteristic aspect of the person, his "transcendence" with respect to his acting. "Together with operativity and transcendence there appears a peculiar dependence of activity with respect to the person. The human being is not only the agent of his activity; he is also its *creator*. At the essence of operativity belongs the birth and the existence of the effect."[62] The acting is a work created by the man which makes manifest his morality, although this is a theme that we do not treat here. Subsequently we will speak of the transcendence of the person in his action.

Precisely at this point can be seen a difference and a contrast between "subjectivity" and "operativity." The human being experiences himself as subject when something happens, but when he is acting he experiences himself as actor. Subjectivity points to what happens in the human being and operativity to his acting, both in his structural aspect. However, the one who acts continues being the same as the one to whom something happens. Both aspects are combined and linked in the same subject, since they have a common root. Wojtyła says that "this root is precisely that human being as dynamic subject."[63] Well then, the question that immediately arises is, "What is the ultimate foundation of this 'dynamic subject'?" Again, it is the *suppositum*.

Previously we saw how the *suppositum* appeared as the ontic substrate of subjectivity, and now we see that it turns out to be the ontic substrate supporting the structure of action. The two objective structures are supported in the *suppositum*, which is what gives unity to the person in his human nature. One of the constants throughout the length of this study will be the counterpoint between nature and person, different concepts but mutually necessary in the human being.

To continue on to explain the other concepts used in Wojtyła's personalist anthropology, we must point out the consequences of

---

62. PA, 124. See OC, 119; AP, 69–70.
63. PA, 127. See OC, 121; AP, 72.

action in the moment of operativity. This is a novelty of Wojtyła's, a new way of approaching the knowledge of the person through his actions. However, in order to discern with greater clarity those aspects of the person which are discovered in his action, it is necessary to distinguish them from other operations that happen in the human being under the concept of nature. For this reason it is appropriate to analyze, however briefly, this nature-person relationship.

Nature and Person

In his search for the roots of operativity, Karol Wojtyła found the ontic substrate of the man-person. However, "[w]e have understood person and *suppositum* not only as metaphysical subjects of existence and of the dynamism of the human being, but also as a certain kind of phenomenological synthesis of operativity and subjectivity."[64] If the person-ontic substrate relation helps us to understand operativity and subjectivity, how does the idea of nature work to explain the human being? Is it a further substructure? What is the person-nature relationship? Let us see how Wojtyła approaches this theme.

The concept "nature" has several different senses. In a broad sense, nature means the natural world, in another sense it is a limiting attribute of beings: human nature, animal nature, etc. Similarly, it suggests some specific property of a subject, that is, its essence. In this last sense, nature and essence do not mean the same thing but are used in different ways. Whereas "essence" points to the ontological constitution that distinguishes one being from another, "nature" indicates the principle of a being's operations, that is, its form of dynamism. We can focus on this by considering that "nature" relates to the given set of beings that possess common properties and ways of acting. When we say "human nature," the reference is to those beings that possess a specific common feature that makes them human beings.

64. PA, 132. See OC, 125; AP, 76.

In order to respect the methodology that originates from the human act or the human dynamism, the most adequate approach to nature would be derived from the etymological analysis of the term "nature" itself. "Nature" (from the verb *nascor*, "to be born") refers to that which is derived from birth. It makes manifest not only the fact of being born but furthermore the operative conditions of the being that is born. Birth is a dynamic act; this moment reveals the point of activation of the dynamism of the being that is being born. The initial dynamization caused by the *esse* will permit a certain kind of *operari* (according to its nature). In this birth is found the synthesis of "acting" and "happening." Wojtyła asks himself whether nature is at the basis of this synthesis or only refers to some determinate domain of the human dynamism. To analyze this point he turns to phenomenological reduction.[65]

If we understand the human being as a specific dynamic whole, we can rightly consider that when his "nature" is manifest most fully and essentially is not when the human being "acts," but when "something happens in the human being," not in the moment of acting, but in that of activation [as we called it earlier], not in the moment of operativity, but in that of subjectivity.[66]

This is because the concept "nature" includes the dynamism that is consequent upon birth itself. In this dynamism something is happening to the human being. The nature reveals the dynamism of the subjects, the activity that is completely contained in the dynamic disposition of the subject: "It is this activity as if already given beforehand to the subject, or rather, in a way prepared completely in its dynamic subjective structure."[67] Regarded in this sense, the nature refers to a moment of the dynamism proper to the human being and does not appear as the basis of that dynamism. At the same

65. "Understanding by phenomenological reduction an operation that leads to a fuller and at the same time essential manifestation of a given content." PA, 134–35. See OC, 127; AP, 78.

66. PA, 135. See OC, 127; AP, 78.

67. Ibid.

time, this dynamism does not depend on operativity, since there is no human act (that is, not voluntary).

Nature does not correspond to the structure "the human being acts," in which the predominance of the subject is displayed, but corresponds instead to the dynamic process that triggers it. It is worthwhile to pay attention to this point. The nature is manifest in the activation of the man-subject, while the actions show that he is a person. "In acts are contained operativity, and this manifests the concrete 'I' as the cause of activity conscious of itself. And this is precisely a person."[68] Then the person would be different from the nature and "even, in a way, opposed to it."[69] Experience shows us a difference between the structure of "something happens to me" and the structure of "a human being acts." If we separate these two experiences too much and fail to seek an integration between the nature—which manifests the moment of activation—and the person—which points to the moment of action—there will arise a relationship of opposition, as if there were one world of the person and another world of nature.

How can we achieve the integration of the two dynamisms? It must be by adequately respecting the complementarity of these two dynamisms as experience reveals them to us. Experience perceives a unity and identity in the man-subject. The synthesis of acting and happening is supported by the same ontic substrate. The mutual complementing of actions and activation, operativity and subjectivity, requires the integration of person and nature.[70] It is always the human being who acts; there cannot be a rupture between nature and person, because the nature of the human being is personal.[71] Contrary to functionalist theories, the fact that at some moment in the stages of his development the human being cannot act does not mean that he has ceased to be a person. The entire potentiality of the nature is oriented toward its personal unfolding. It is not a mere

68. PA, 135. See OC, 127; AP, 79.   69. Ibid.
70. PA, 138. See OC, 129; AP, 81.
71. See Buttiglione, *Karol Wojtyła: The Thought*, 138.

individual of the species, not a "something." The human being is a "someone." Let us recall that "[t]he person may be identified as *suppositum* through an appropriate analogy; that is, the *suppositum* 'someone' indicates not only likeness, but also difference and distance from every 'something' *suppositum*."[72]

The "I" is the agent of the actions and the "I" is also what experiences that which happens in it, although not in the form of operativity. He has the experience of himself along with what is happening, and this is manifest in his consciousness.

What happens under the form of various kinds of "activation" is a property of my "I"; what's more, it comes from it. . . . The experience of the unity and identity of my own "I" is objectively prior to and more basic than the experienced distinction between acting and happening-in, between the operativity and non-operativity of the "I."[73]

In the *suppositum* the nature shows the form of dynamism that derives from it (activation), differentiating it from the person who is manifest in the action, but integration avoids considering the nature and the person as two independent or separate objects.

However, Wojtyła notes the priority of some nuances in his consideration of action. Without a doubt, the first is existence and afterwards the action, because logically, in order to act, it is necessary to exist. Here we should note another distinction: "the man who exists" is not equivalent to "the man who acts," although "the man who exists and acts" is one. When the man acts, it seems that he has his own form of existing. His activation certainly depends on his existence; but this "acting," for being a mode of existing, makes the man develop existentially throughout his life in a particular way, as such and such a person. In some way the person is a living synthesis in continuous expansion through the very dynamism of the human being. Likewise, there is a radical precedence of the human nature that becomes the metaphysical basis where the cohesion of nature with person is achieved.

72. PA, 130. See OC, 123; AP, 74.
73. PA, 137–38. See OC, 129; AP, 81.

[Integration] cannot consist only in the individuation of nature through the person, as someone could imagine strictly attending to the words of the Boethian definition.... The person is not simply "individualized humanity." He is also [among the beings of the visible world] a specific mode of individual being of humanity. This mode of individual being proceeds from the fact that humanity's mode of individual being is personal existence. The first and fundamental dynamization of any being proceeds from its existence, from *esse*.... The dynamization from personal *esse* must be rooted in the integration of humanity by the person.[74]

With this he affirms that human nature is endowed with properties that allow the human being to be a person, and which are distinguished from that which prevents his being able to act in a way that he would not be (a person). Acting and happening take place within the person, but they proceed from the nature, from the humanity of the human being. "The specific operativity of the human 'I' in act, which reveals to us the transcendence of the person, does not separate the person from the nature."[75]

Finally, it is necessary to allow a difference between nature and person, where the nature works as the causality of the ontic substrate, and the person manifests himself in a process of dynamization of this substrate. For this reason, Wojtyła devotes the third part of *Person and Act* especially to the integration of both. What we have as yet not commented on is the underlying potentiality in the nature which allows the "happening" and "acting" of the man-person, since the entire dynamism of which we have been speaking supposes something that sustains it. This is not the ontic substrate or *suppositum*, but rather the levels of potentiality that are generated from the ontic substrate on the level of nature.

74. PA, 141. See OC, 131; AP, 83–84. It should be noted that Wojtyła by "*esse*" understands "existence." He does not enter into the Thomistic debate concerning the real distinction between *esse* as the act of being and existence. On this aspect of the history of philosophy, see Etienne Gilson, *Being and Some Philosophers* (Toronto: Pontifical Institute of Mediaeval Studies, 1952); as a general feature of Thomism, see Fernando Ocáriz, "Rasgos fundamentales del pensamiento de Santo Tomás" [Fundamental Features of the Thought of St. Thomas], in *Tomás de Aquino, también hoy* [Thomas Aquinas, also today], ed. Cornelio Fabro et al. (Pamplona: Eunsa, 1990), 49–94.

75. PA, 143. See OC, 133; AP, 84.

Levels of Potentiality and Dynamisms

Wojtyła uses the Aristotelian term *dynamis* to signify force or power. In his work, this term is related to the concept of "dynamism." On the other hand, the Scholastic term *potentia* signifies power or faculty, and in his work this is referred to as "potentiality."[76]

In Wojtyła's anthropology, action indicates an underlying potentiality. With this we cannot say that he leaves to the side the consideration of the faculties; even less does he ignore them. Quite to the contrary, as we have already seen, nature represents the anthropological terrain of these faculties, but his anthropology is centered in the personal aspect, and therefore he follows another method.[77]

One cannot speak of the dynamism of the person without considering the underlying potentiality. An adequate integration of nature and person suggests at the same time an adequate relationship between potentiality and dynamism, to which I will refer briefly at this point. Wojtyła is faithful to his methodology; that is, the interpretation of the source of the dynamism departs from the global consideration of experience. When the human being "acts" and when "something happens in him" we have a direct experience, but the sources of such dynamisms arise in consciousness indirectly. We know that these manifestations proceed from our interior but in a form that is at times confused. We perceive that the "acting" is different from "happening," and so we infer that, since the two are not homogeneous, they must arise from heterogeneous sources. The roots of action and of activation are different.

Wojtyła finds two structural levels of the dynamic human being,

76. "'Dynamism,' as we can see, indicates above all the present dynamization of the subject 'human being,' which proceeds from his interior and assumes the form of acting or that of happening-in. On the other hand, 'potentiality' refers to the same source of the present dynamization of the subject. The source that is found in the interior of the subject, something that pulses stably in it and is manifest in one or another form of dynamization." PA, 145. See OC, 134; AP, 86.

77. Wojtyła explains that the study of the faculties has been abundant, explored in its totality, but in his work he desires to focus on the person, his transcendence and manifestation in act. See PA, 147 and 147n8; OC, 135–36 and 135n32; AP, 87 and 308n33.

which are the "somato-vegetative" and the "psycho-emotive" levels. The "I" has the experience of these two levels of being a subject, but the "I" is not their author. If he were the author, he would have a conscious activation and we would speak of a kind of action, but this is not the case. To study these he will intend to discern how consciousness reflects the experience that comes from each level (and not which faculties or powers act in these levels).

The events of the psycho-emotive level are clearly reflected in consciousness, and the subject perceives them as different experiences. Not only do we have knowledge of these facts, but consciousness reflects them as necessarily arising from the interior of human subjectivity. By contrast, the events of the somato-vegetative level are more obscure to knowledge and even appear inaccessible to consciousness. "The somato-vegetative dynamism is the human being's specific form of dynamism, which decides concerning the life of the human body as a concrete organism and also inasmuch as the organism conditions different psychic functions."[78]

The human being is conscious of his body, but he does not have detailed consciousness of his organism; he is not conscious of the concrete dynamic events at work in it. These act spontaneously and even without coming to the level of consciousness. One cannot "see" his internal organs or what goes on in their physiology. Only by means of certain sensations (on the psycho-emotive level), through pain or physical well-being, can we have any idea of what is occurring in the organism. In general we have consciousness that something has happened on the vegetative level when there is a sickness and it comes to our attention through pain, thanks to the intervention of the psycho-emotive functions. Wojtyła therefore says that the total experience of the body and the consciousness of the body appear to be based largely on what corresponds to the bodily sensations. Regarding the psycho-emotive level, the activity of consciousness is more direct, making the dynamism more effec-

78. PA, 149. See OC, 137; AP, 89.

tive. The human being can experience the elements of this level with more intensity, whether they are sensations or emotions.

The formation of the psycho-emotive sphere performs a peculiar kind of human becoming, since its conscious activation will be of the "what" and "who" he really is.[79] At this point, Wojtyła recognizes one of the moments of morality. His conscious acts are what bring the human being his own goodness or evil. "The quality of the acts, which depends on the moral norms and ultimately on the conscience, passes to the man—the author of the acts."[80]

Wojtyła also alludes to another human dynamism to which consciousness does not reach but which is present in the form of sub-experiences in the subconscious.[81] The subconscious is a kind of space where are contained certain objects, some of which are retained so as not to reach the threshold of consciousness. There are certain mechanisms that prevent them from crossing this threshold. Still, one can see that the contents of this subconscious continue to hope to be able to cross the threshold of consciousness and appear to it; for example, "when consciousness is weakened or inhibited by weariness and especially during sleep."[82] The subconscious manifests the subject's potentiality in its internal aspect, since in its ongoing relationship with consciousness the human being manifests itself as interiorly subject to time, and furthermore:

[B]ecause it helps to perceive ... the interior cohesion and the continuity of this subject; thanks to the subconscious, there is made manifest the passage of that which happens in the human being only as an effect of natural vegetative activations—possibly emotive—and that of which the human being has a lived consciousness and considers as his act.[83]

79. PA, 161–62. See OC, 146–47; AP, 98.
80. PA, 162. See OC, 147; AP, 99.
81. Here we clearly see the contribution of Freudian psychology (and before this of the understanding of human nature especially in the study of the subconscious). Buttiglione also indicates the philosophical tradition, from Leibniz to Schopenhauer, that refers to this part of the psyche. See Buttiglione, *Karol Wojtyła: The Thought*, 139.
82. PA, 155. See OC, 142; AP, 94.
83. PA, 156. See OC, 142; AP, 95.

The constant tendency of the subconscious to come to consciousness shows that where the human being attains his most adequate realization is in consciousness. The subconscious is like a depository in which are stored what the man-subject retains in the hope that it will appear in consciousness, at which point is will acquire a fuller significance. In the passage of these contents into the ambit of consciousness there also intervene the factors of morality and education. Buttiglione writes that "[p]sychological energy needs to be disciplined and sublimated but not repressed if one does not want to block off one of the primary sources of the general human dynamism."[84]

Up to this point of the First Part of *Person and Act* we have examined those concepts that we consider to be "keys" for understanding his anthropology. We have been introduced to his methodology and have seen the efforts to develop a unitary thought in conceiving the man-person. In the next part we will see more clearly the scope of the personal dynamism by displaying what Wojtyła called "self-determination."

84. Buttiglione, *Karol Wojtyła: The Thought*, 140.

9 ∾

TRANSCENDENCE

Self-Determination: Horizontal and Vertical Transcendence

The human being is not a being finished in itself, and neither does he attain his fulfillment in a natural, instinctive way through simply biological development. Rather he is formed and transformed by the work of his own dynamisms. The man-person realizes himself throughout his life. That is, every form of dynamism that there is in the human being has a relationship to his "becoming." By "becoming" (*fieri*) is understood the characteristic centered in the human being himself—who is subject—insofar as he is affected by a process of change. This subject is not someone "indifferent" to what happens, but rather one who participates in his dynamization and can direct himself in the formation of himself.[1]

The first dynamization is his coming into existence, which is given, but in each subsequent dynamization there begins to exist something new that modifies this subject over time. This becoming is achieved on two levels of potentiality—with their corresponding dynamisms—which we have already seen: the somato-vegetative (and its organic dynamism) when the human being develops or regenerates biologically (at the cellular level), and the psycho-emotive

---

1. PA, 158. See OC, 144; AP, 96.

potentiality (and its emotive dynamism), which has especial relevance in the area of morality, as we also noted earlier.

Let us take another step. When this becoming is found in the realm of conduct and morality, it makes manifest another decisive and primordial component: freedom. Freedom is a basic factor of human action and of morality. Wojtyła refers to fundamental freedom with the expression "I can—I do not have to";[2] it is a matter of a dynamism in the line of the act to which the man-subject's potentiality called "will" corresponds. In this moment we touch the position of that freedom and speak of the will from the perspective of the person in act.

Wojtyła analyzes in depth the human will from the perspective of the person, and he does so by making manifest a new personal structure.

The will is not only a "capacity of nature" but also a "property of the person." This means that the activation of the will has as its source the person who possesses this natural property. Not only is the will "deduced" from the accomplished action, but when the will is realized "in" the act, there is revealed the person acting voluntarily. "Every act confirms and simultaneously concretizes this relationship in that the will is revealed as a property of the person; and, for his part, the person is manifest as a reality with relation to its dynamism, which is itself constituted by the will."[3] This relationship in which the will is manifest as a property of the person in act is "self-determination."[4]

2. In Polish "mogę—nie muszę." The Italian version translates this as "posso ma non sono costretto" (see PEA, 966), which differs significantly from the English version, "I may but I need not" (see AP, 105), because, to my mind, it gives greater force to the sense of interior freedom: "I can, but I am not bound."

3. PA, 167. See OC, 151; AP, 105.

4. "Self-determination is an act of the person, even if, materially speaking, it belongs to the will. In this sense, Wojtyła says that choice and decision intrinsically define the essence of the will, without replacing the orientation of tending toward the act, but instead personalizing it, that is, giving it freedom. By this, the better or worse decision is correct or incorrect. Thus, as recta ratio requires active intellectual virtues [synderesis and prudence], the right decision requires the acquisition of active practical virtues [justice]." Franquet, Persona, acción y libertad, 208.

Let us now study a more complex aspect of the will. The moment of "I want," which refers to the will, points to a personal structure that sustains all its content and fullness—wherein is included the "I can—I do not have to," which is the fundamental freedom. It is not a matter of a simple "I want"; beneath this expression lie several personal structural elements that are detected phenomenologically in the voluntary act.

Let us recall that Wojtyła does not make his study of the will from the point of view of a faculty.[5] His method takes another approach, that of the will from the point of view of the act tied to the concept of the person. Within this perspective are discovered two elements: "self-possession" and "self-dominion." Together these two constitute the will as "self-determination."

Indeed, through self-determination, the human being develops, in the future becoming what he himself chooses by his freedom. The person is such when he possesses himself and is his only and exclusive possession. The expression "I want" makes manifest the self-possession in which a person determines himself. Only that which is possessed can be determined; if one is capable of saying "I want" he is determining his person toward something. Furthermore, the voluntary "I want" reveals the self-dominion of one's own person through self-possession. Self-dominion goes beyond self-control, because while the latter refers fundamentally to the control of the dynamizations of nature, the former directs the future becoming in the personal sense, which affects the realm in which fundamental freedom operates.[6]

Another difference between the will as faculty and the will as self-determination relates to intentionality. The will as faculty possesses intentionality, which means that through its acts the will is

5. According to Thomistic philosophy the human will is considered a faculty of the rational nature and is composed by diverse acts that are situated in the *voluntas ut natura* (*simplex voluntas, intention, fruitio*) and the *voluntas ut ratio* (*consensus, electio, usus*). The acts accomplish specific functions which complement each other and the understanding during the volitional process. On acts of the will, see Aquinas, ST I-II, qq. 8–17.

6. See PA, 169; OC, 152–53; AP, 106–7.

directed to an object outside itself. One cannot desire in a vacuum; he desires "something," an object that the intelligence presents to the will as a good. Now if we consider the will as the "person who possesses and governs himself," it is possible to think that this self-determination is also intentional. However, this is not so. More than being directed toward "something" outside, self-determination is directed to itself, revealing another reality in the dynamic order: the objectivity of the person. Let us analyze this "objectivity" and that in which it consists.

"Every actual self-determination realizes the subjectivity of self-possession and self-dominion."[7] This means that in each of these intrapersonal structures, to the person as subject (that which possesses and governs) there corresponds the person as object (that which is possessed and governed).[8] Objectivity is correlative to the subjectivity of the person, and, of the two, subjectivity seems to be especially emphasized. In each moment in which is produced an "I want," the "I" is constituted as object and subject at the same time, and this is what "self-determination" means. This does not happen in other acts of the will (as a natural faculty), because they are turned "toward without"; in them we speak of volitional intentionality. On the other hand, self-determination is not "directed toward" an "I," but in it and through it "reality is conferred upon objectivity" in there being conferred in the "I" the relationship of self-dominion and self-possession, not seeking it without but affirming it within.

By means of self-determination—will as property of the person in act—each one governs himself.[9] This self-determination, which is found at the personal level, is what integrates the different manifestations of the human dynamism and is at the same time "that

7. PA, 171. See OC, 154; AP, 108.
8. Ibid.
9. "... 'persona est alteri incommunicabilis.' This expression encloses a yet richer content than what we are treating here, even if the latter is included within it. The human being owes his structural 'incommunicability' [incommunicabilitas] to the will to the extent to which through it self-realization is realized; at the same time this is expressed and manifested in action as self-determination." PA, 170. See OC, 153; AP, 107.

which constitutes, defines and manifests this level."[10] Also, self-determination, in the dynamic order, shows the objectivity of the person, which is the concrete entire "I" that acts consciously; therefore, when this objectivity is concretized in each moment in which the human being says "I want," there is produced an "objectification," and in his realizing an act at the same time the person is realized.[11]

I repeat that the objectification does not indicate the presence of an intentionality as such understood as the natural volition *ad extra*; there is no orientation "toward" the "I" as an object, but rather reality is conferred on the objectivity of the "I" already present, contained in the intrapersonal relationship of self-dominion and self-possession. It is an effect *ad intra*.[12] Objectification points to the interior objectivity; it is found in the volition in itself and therefore cannot "be directed outside." The emphasis on interiority shows that the voluntary act affects the becoming of the person who is realizing himself through the act.

Wojtyła stresses that this manner in which self-determination affects the future has important consequences, especially in morality, because when I want something I am seen as determined by myself.[13] As an objective being, the "I" is contained in the voluntary act. Self-determination not only comes from the "I" but also turns back upon it as its basic object (as contrasted with the intentional objects, which are transitory and external to the "I"). "At this point we touch the deepest personal reality of the act, because making his own "I" in one way or another, the human being simultaneously becomes someone."[14] To the extent that he possesses consciousness, the person lives in a special way. We must remember that by his consciousness the person has the experience of himself as a sub-

---

10. PA, 170. See OC, 152–53; AP, 107.   11. See PA, 175; OC, 157; AP, 111.
12. See PA, 172–74; OC, 155–56; AP, 109–10.
13. "This actualization has a fundamental significance for morality as a specifically human dimension of personal existence, a dimension that is a once subjective and objective. The entire reality of morality, of moral values, sinks its roots here." PA, 172. See OC, 155; AP, 109.
14. PA, 173. See AP, 110; OC, 155.

jective "I." The human being also has the experience of each of his volitions; each is the interior objectivity of the act made manifest by consciousness (consciousness reflects the subjective "I" but also objectivizes subjectivity). This act is interior operativity.

In this way, in considering the integral dynamism of the will—the moment of "I want"—self-determination is contained as well as intentionality. "Turning oneself toward any external object as a value and an end presupposes that one is directed toward one's own 'I' as the object."[15] In this self-determination is presented a new dimension of operativity and subjectivity.

Consciousness plays a concrete role in the operativity of objectification. Thanks to consciousness, the person "lives in a peculiar manner." He does this not only in his own reflection as image of himself but also in the specific experience of self that results from the reflexive function of consciousness.[16] Thanks to this, the man-person experiences himself as subject. He also has the experience of his volitions, which are converted into a subjective fact, and which sees itself in the objective construction of its own "I." When consciousness manifests this entire objectification of self-determination in the orbit of experience, we clearly note the person's full subjectivity which is being experienced in the act. "Then, too, the person, the agent 'I' has the experience of deciding about himself and in the function of his self-determination becomes somebody, who at the same time possesses certain qualities (good or bad)."[17]

Although the experience of self-determination is conditioned by consciousness, it seems that it is led, not by it, but rather by self-knowledge, since the "light" of the cognitive function does not come from the reflection of consciousness but from the acts of intelligence that show to the will the character of the good of an object to which it is directed as an end.

15. PA, 174. See OC, 156; AP, 110.
16. See the section "Consciousness and the *suppositum*" in the previous chapter, "Consciousness and Operativity."
17. PA, 177; OC, 159. See AP, 113.

Then if there is anything that directs self-determination and the entire dynamism of the will ... this is directly and above all self-knowledge. However it is indirectly the entire knowledge of reality, in particular the knowledge of values as possible ends and as foundations of the different norms by which the human being is guided when he acts.[18]

Knowledge directs the will. Only through its capacity to objectivize and present objects to the will can it act (*nihil volitum nisi praecognitum*).[19] For its part, consciousness accompanies the act by its subjectifying function, although it neither directs nor controls the will. In the conscious act the person appears as a specific unity of self-determination and consciousness, or, from another perspective, as a particular synthesis of objectivity and subjectivity.[20]

Having arrived at this point, we can summarize, saying that the will ("I want") manifests itself under two aspects: on one side as a power or faculty whose function is the intentionality of the object to which it tends as an end; on the other it is a property of the person in his self-determination, whose function is the person's self-possession and self-dominion. The two aspects of the will are mutually complementary. We cannot speak of "two wills."

Once the meaning of self-determination is known as form of the will, its relationship with freedom acquires greater relevance. Freedom is linked with the will and is manifest in the experience of "I can—I do not have to." The person's freedom, which proceeds from the will, turns out to be identical with self-determination; freedom

18. PA, 178. See OC, 159; AP, 113–14.
19. The Latin adage reminds us that nothing can be desired if it is unknown beforehand. This derives from the Aristotelian theory of knowledge.
20. If we consider human experience, especially moral experience, in its two aspects (interior and exterior), we can see that there is a certain complementarity between subjectification and objectification. Wojtyła says that consciousness and self-determination balance each other; the first provides a certain degree of interiority and the second a certain exteriority. "And not only is the person objectivized in each one of his acts, but he is also exteriorized, even in the case when, by the criterion of observability, the act was absolutely interior. On the other hand, any act, even one that would be external in the light of that criterion, undergoes a certain interiorization through consciousness." PA, 179. See OC, 160; AP, 115. "Interior acts" have no external perceptibility, but this is no proof of exteriority in relation to the person who is found in action.

is not a matter of mere choice, for, if it were, then it would be circumscribed in the functions of the will as power or faculty.[21] The freedom of "I can—I do not have to" is based in the person, which is subjective in itself, where the person's most autonomous center is revealed. It is a type of real property of the human being, more complete and fundamental, and it is also a real attribute of the will. This double situation of freedom avoids the consideration of it as a species of idealism, where freedom has no "link," since one cannot speak of a "pure" free will, but one speaks rather of a "reality that is the human being" who works in freedom.[22]

Wojtyła integrates the will and freedom, showing them as powers, but at the same time finding their roots in the person, placing them at the basis of the man-person's becoming. These are manifest not only under the aspect of intentional tendency (*appetitus*) [23] and the "I want" as the capacity for choice (*electio*), but also as structures of "self-determination" and of the "I can, but I do not have to" (fundamental freedom). Self-determination keeps the human dyna-

21. Wojtyła emphasizes that he is dealing with freedom as a reality, as a real property of the human being, not with pure freedom in itself, as some idealist philosophers are accustomed to consider it. Moreover, to understand freedom as only the capacity to choose would be to reduce it to the voluntary act called *electio*. This type of reduction would be the proposal of John Stuart Mill, when he speaks of freedom as "*choice*." Further on Wojtyła will show that not just any election whatever is an act of freedom, although it may be a sign of it, since the action of a bad man instead perverts freedom. Self-determination—and finally freedom—is oriented toward truth and self-realization.

22. See PA, 180–81; OC, 161; AP, 115–16. On this point, Wojtyła refers to Kant as the exponent of the "apriorism of freedom," where "pure freedom" (autonomy) is the end which leads to the categorical imperative. Only by arriving at this kind of freedom can "pure morality" be realized. He recognizes that Kant contributes to highlighting the personal significance of self-determination, especially thanks to the "second imperative" rather than to his theory of *a priori* freedom. See also PA, 180n3; AP, 309n40.

23. *Osoba i czyn* makes clear that Wojtyła does not repudiate the Latin *appetitus rationalis*, even if the cognate expression "rational appetite" may be misleading. The classical conception of the will is as "rational appetite," a tendency toward an end known at a level superior to the sensible. Wojtyła does not very much agree with the literal meaning of this concept in Polish (but we also can say the same of the English and Spanish renditions), because this expression "rational appetite" (as well as its equivalent in Polish) tends to imply the dimension of "horizontal transcendence" and so does not allow for perception of the profound roots in the subjectivity of the person ("vertical transcendence"). See PA, 193; OC, 170–71; AP, 125.

mism integrated at the level of the person and thus makes manifest the ontological density of the will and also of freedom.

On the other hand, and by way of *excursus*, he makes a provocative comparison between instinct and freedom. Let us recall the distinction between the dynamism of nature and that of the person. Whereas in the first there is "activation," in the second there is "act" (operativity), that is, voluntary acts. In the dynamism of nature there are activations that have a determinate direction. The potentiality of nature is in turn the integrator of the activations that are sustained in it. Everything that happens in the individual is directed toward a determined objective. "The subjective basis of both integration and finality exclusively at the level of nature [particularly in animals] we call instinct."[24] Everything that happens in the animal is circumscribed by the directionality that its instincts provide. We cannot say that the animal has self-determination. The animal's actuation has the appearance of "action," but it is not act as such, because what differentiates the dynamism of the nature (where instinct is found) from the dynamism of the person (where the act takes place) is self-determination. If the animal does not have self-determination, then its freedom is very different from that of the human being.

The most interesting analysis arises when our author demonstrates that the basis of freedom is the "dependence" of acting that the human being has with respect to the "I." Paradoxically, this dependence is what allows him self-determination. By contrast, when there is not a dependence on the "I," one falls into necessity, because there is the possibility neither of self-possession nor of self-mastery. Animals are situated in the plan of actuation by necessity—where freedom is beyond their scope—in virtue of having no relationship with the "I"; then their activations are found to be directed by instinct, which depends on the dynamism of their nature.[25] This "de-

24. PA, 182. See OC, 162; AP, 116.
25. "To constitute the 'I,' that is, the person is his strictly experiential profile and content, consciousness is indispensable ... and so too is self-determination." PA, 184. See OC, 163–64; AP, 118.

pendence" with respect to the "I" is contrasted with the conception of freedom as an "abstract and independent" notion of distinct factors; in reality what freedom does is to establish a link with the "I" to achieve a deeper dimension of operation and to be "more free."

Now we have the elements to understand the two modes of transcendence in Wojtyła's anthropology. The classical concept of transcendence means "to go beyond." Realist philosophy has used this concept to explain, for example, the subject's capacity to go beyond his limits and direct himself toward objects.[26] Wojtyła accepts this kind of transcendence and calls it "horizontal transcendence," in which is found intentionality, both cognitive and volitional; however, he adds a second kind, which is "vertical transcendence," a fruit of self-determination. Here it is not a matter of a transcendence "toward something"; vertical transcendence is not directed toward an end or object but is "a transcendence within whose framework the subject confirms himself [and in a way surpasses himself]."[27] This new aspect of transcendence, verticality, indicates that there is a movement toward the deepest interior of the person, where the person is known as the object of his own subjectivity.[28]

Wojtyła affirms, "Man is free, which means that in his dynamism the subject himself depends on himself,"[29] and adds:

To be free, it is necessary that we constitute a concrete "I" that would be simultaneously subject and the first object about which we decide by an act of the will.... [W]hen something only happens in it, the *suppositum* manifests only subjectivity; on the other hand, when it acts its operativity is manifest along with subjectivity. Given that operativity is based on self-determination, since in acting we decide concerning ourselves, it follows that the subject himself is also the object for himself. And this

26. In Scheler's phenomenological philosophy we also find the same sense of transcending: the individual passes beyond himself intentionally toward the object that is exterior to him. See Buttiglione, *Karol Wojtyła: The Thought*, 145–46.

27. PA, 185n4. See OC, 164n40; AP, 309n41.

28. It is called vertical transcendence in contraposition to the horizontal, to show that it is based in self-determination and holds ascendency over the human dynamism, which it allows to remain free. See PA, 191–92; OC, 169–70; AP, 124.

29. PA, 186. See OC, 165; AP, 120.

is how "objectification" is introduced into the fundamental meaning of freedom.[30]

Self-determination brings into being a dominion of the "I," counterpoised to the dominion of the instinctive. Therefore we can use expressions that differentiate persons ("*persona in actu*" or "human act") from non-personal individuals ("*individuum in actu*" or "individual action"). The former depend on the dynamization of the person and the latter on the dynamization by nature.

The consideration of the will does not end with emphasizing the aspect of "property of the person"; will also is presented under the aspect of "strength," as when we often say "strength of will." For the human being, the will is a strength that carries him to attain his objectives; in this sense the will is subordinated to the person. The person is capable of controlling his will, and the will "is *the person's faculty of freedom*."[31] This facet of the will as strength is especially relevant in relation to the dynamism of self-determination and the dynamism of the human act. For this reason, the classical authors in a special way circumscribed *praxis* and *poiesis* within the ambit of the will.[32]

The root of the act is found in the will. As the knowledge of the interior structure of the person deepens, the transcendence of the person in act becomes more manifest, perhaps not so much in spontaneous liberty but rather in the assistance of reflection in the act of self-determination (fundamental freedom) and in the presence of cognitive acts.

At this moment of his work *Person and Act*, Wojtyła plunges deeply into the analysis of the volitional act and carefully studies the acts of choice, decision, motivation, and deliberation, among others. I will refer to these only tangentially and then focus on other concepts of his anthropology that are, in my view, more innovative.[33]

30. Ibid.

31. PA, 189 (emphasis in the original). See PA (1982), 142; OC, 167; AP, 122.

32. *Praxis* concerns the way that a person does something, while *poiesis* is the final result of that action.

33. To consider more deeply the volitional act, see PA, 186–206; OC, 165–79; AP, 120–35; PEA, 984–1003; PA (1982), 141–57.

Truth, Responsibility, and Self-Realization

"To want means to tend toward a good that thereby becomes an end."[34] In a simple act of the will (*simplex voluntas*), the step between detecting the good and the desire for its possession produces in the human being an almost immediate decision. However, if there are several values, it is necessary to *choose* among them, and in order to do this the person must *deliberate* beforehand and come to make his final decision. Every decision implies the renunciation, the setting aside or postponing, of other values. In this dynamic deciding, choosing, or suspending of desire, are found in the ambit of the will, but these cannot be considered acts exclusively of this faculty; nor can they be circumscribed by the limits of this potency. In fact, deliberation, which intervenes in the decisions, is an act that pertains to the understanding just as does also the cognitive grasp of the value.[35]

Although we referred earlier to the relationship intelligence-will when we spoke of the *nihil volitum nisi praecognitum*,[36] we should linger more thoroughly in the analysis of one aspect of the will that is found intrinsically in decision and is manifest in a special way in choice: the "implicit reference of the will to truth."

The will does not have a cognitive function, but it establishes a strict relationship with the intelligence at the moment of the recognition of truth, and it depends interiorly on it.[37] Wojtyła's analysis

---

34. PA, 198. See OC, 174; AP, 129. However the English translation is misleading, rendering "*chcieć*" ("to want") as "to will" and "*dobru*" ("good") as "value."

35. "Regarding the impulse related to the decision, of which Wojtyła speaks, it suffices to say that it cannot be identified with the instinctive activation of the human being, for to pertain to self-determination has the sense of a personal moment. The instinct of the will refers rather to the traditional thesis that the will as nature [*voluntas ut natura*] is inclined toward the good. In *Person and Act*, we do not find a study of the will as natural; however, this thesis is developed more fully in *Love and Responsibility*." Franquet, *Persona, acción y libertad*, 217–18.

36. "Nothing is desired except that which is known beforehand," explained in note 19 in this chapter.

37. See PA, 210; OC, 182; AP, 138.

helps us to understand, in the unity of the person, the difference between "knowing the truth" and "the disposition in the face of the truth." They are not the same; one can give an account of the conformity between the intellect and the thing, but at the same time there is an inclination of the person which indicates to us the degree of truth of this conformity. In this moment the will intervenes and the affections concur, but by this we are saying that the person intervenes. In the moment of the conformity of intellect and thing, the person establishes a gradation of the truth that ranges from the complete denial of this conformity, that is, its falsity, to the maximum degree of acceptance, which is called certitude, passing through intermediate states such as doubt or opinion.[38] The fact that the will is dependent upon the truth renders it independent of objects, and thanks to this we can explain the transcendence of the person in the act and its influence over his own dynamism.

The person is transcendent in his own acting because he is free, inasmuch as he is free. Freedom in the fundamental sense is equivalent to self-reliance. Freedom in the developed sense is independence in the intentional realm. To be directed to different possible objects of volition is something that neither these objects nor their presentation determines.[39]

The dependence of the will upon the truth is what helps decision and choice and in the end directs moral conduct, which is related to good and evil. However, although in the human activation the will is realized according to the truth about the good, this truth is the object of the intelligence and can contain errors or mistakes if its conformity is not based on the evidence,[40] which would lead one to make decisions that were not completely correct and to make inadequate choices. In this sense, often cognition is specifically influenced by the requirements of the will, which at times come from

38. On the dispositions of the person in the face of truth. See Llano, *Gnoseología*, 51–70.

39. PA, 210. See OC, 183; AP, 138, but again the English translation is misleading.

40. Evidence is the "patency" of the mind before the object of cognition. It is the form of conformity in which the intelligence does not doubt but rather submits completely to that which is presented so clearly.

lived experiences or from the potentialities of nature (somato-vegetative or psycho-emotive), both of which can cloud or clarify the judgment.

All knowledge is contained within the limits of experience, and to speak of knowledge is to admit to being in the presence of truth; without truth there is no knowledge.[41] When the human being is found before the truth, not only is he in possession of knowledge, but also the subject's experience in relation to that truth reveals his spiritual nature and thus his transcendence. Thus truth constitutes the basis of the transcendence of the person in act, because the moment of the truth about the moral good makes the act what it really is. This moment is that which gives the act the authentic form of "actus personae."[42]

In the experience of values is contained knowledge of the truth about the objects to which the will is directed in virtue of its specific intentionality. It is the intentionality of wanting, which is a wanting precisely as a consequence of the experienced values, and takes the form of decision or choice, through the moment of the truth about the good which is constituted by the respective objects. We have already noted that the characteristic of the will is not the intentionality of wanting in itself or rather in the being directed to objects that have a value of certain sort, but the orientation through a decision or a choice. It is always the person's "directing himself."[43]

Wojtyła recalls that truth in the axiological sense is not the same as ontological or logical truth. In axiological truth the value of an object is affirmed, not what the object is in reality or the object as known. Neither is it the same as practical truth or knowledge of "making,"

41. Falsity is a kind of knowledge by the via negativa: it is known that something is false because there is some true knowledge in contradistinction to it. Otherwise the falsity would not be noticed. The lie is not the same as falsity, since the lie is ethically qualified: a person says something untrue with the intent to deceive.

42. See PA, 220. See OC, 189; AP, 146 (but the English edition also translates the Latin phrase "actus personae" as "the act of the person.")

43. PA, 216. See OC, 187; AP, 142. Although the Spanish uses "volición" and the English "volition," the Polish is "chcenia" from the verb "chcieć," which means "to want." The more accurate rendering would therefore be a "wanting," which is a weaker term than "volition."

but it is a theoretical knowledge and essential element for the act in which "knowing" is converted into "wanting." In a way, it is a mixture of acts of both powers, but without a confusion of the two.[44]

When we say that the act of thinking is principally receptive, this does not mean that the understanding has only a passive function by which it simply waits to be affected. Although Wojtyła's phenomenological analysis states in a first moment that thought seems to be something that "happens" in the human being, denoting a certain character of passivity, he subsequently clarifies that we must also admit another moment in which the human being has the experience of being agent of his thought and knowledge.

That moment is in the elaboration of judgments, during the act of judging, to which he gives the highest importance.

The act of judging is also the cognitive act most specific to the human being; it presupposes—as the analysts of knowledge highlight to its full extent—another activity of the intellect that is even more elementary, namely simple apprehension. But the experience of this act lies in the act of judging, and by this is it known in consciousness in which the "I" is distinguished not only as subject but also as the agent.[45]

In Wojtyła's example, "the wall is white," the judgment is made when a real property (whiteness) is attributed to a thing (the wall). It is a logical structure contained both in language and in thought. However, in the judgment there is something more than simply the exterior logical structure; the judgment captures the truth about the object. A computer can detect that logical structure (logical truth), but it cannot capture the sense of "truth," because while the computer makes a connection according to pre-established (a pri-

---

44. These acts are different when they are analyzed in terms of the faculties. From this point of view we can appreciate the distinction, for example, in the form of being directed to an object. While desiring implies "going out and being moved" toward an object (intentionality) as a centrifugal effect, thinking and knowing "introduce" the object into the subject as a centripetal effect. For this reason we say that the will "moves" the act, and intelligence "receives" external data through the senses to produce sensation and perception (then, on another level, comprehension and understanding are developed). See PA, 217–18; OC, 188; AP, 143–44.

45. PA, 219. See OC, 189; AP, 145.

ori) rules to realize the relationships of attribution, truth requires an interior penetration that attributes the properties to a thing as something adequate to its reality (ontological truth);[46] the rules are inferred *a posteriori*.

Let us remember this point, then, that to attain the truth is the same as to introduce an object into the person-subject according to an essential property of the person-subject. This relationship of the person-subject with truth— not only transcendental (from inside the subject to reality) but also experienced (conscious of the act of knowing)—reveals the person's spiritual nature. Also, from another point of view, the will is possessed by the truth, which orients it in relation to the good; facing decision and choice of self-determination, the will is an inclination that recognizes the value. Let us look at this more slowly.

Cognitive transcendence (*praecognitum*: known beforehand) conditions the specific transcendence of the will in action (*volitum*: to want). A judgment about value is presupposed as much in the act of decision as in the act of choice. Not only is this judgment pre-constituted in and by itself through the truth about the objects, but also it makes possible and conditions the proper relationship of the will toward the objects on the basis of truth. Whenever a person chooses or decides, he has had to make a judgment of value beforehand. "'To want' means not only to move toward an end, but to move by deciding. Precisely for this reason the will is integrated so profoundly in the structure of the person, and every authentic 'I want' that is full of value actualizes the person's self-dominion and self-possession."[47]

Thus, once we have understood the strict relationship between truth and self-determination, we can move on to refer to the objec-

46. In the realist theory of knowledge, logical truth indicates the adequate construction of the syllogism, which avoids fallacies or formal errors; by contrast, ontological truth refers to the transcendental property *verum* (truth) that each being possesses according to its act of being and its essence. Intelligence is capable of capturing both characters of truth, because in correct argumentation they are complementary.

47. PA, 221. See OC, 190; AP, 147.

tive to which the reality of the person and his action points: his "realization."

Every act that is a consequence of the operativity of the agent (the person) has a beginning and an end that are made manifest in an external or interior way. In this study of the person and his act, the interior dimension of the person is more interesting than the result that these activities produce in the external world. In its interior dimension, the human act is transitory, but it also leaves an imprint that can be enduring to the extent that its effects remain longer than the act itself. The effects of the act should be considered in relation to operativity and self-determination, that is, with the person who acts in freedom. The implication of freedom is objectified in the person, concretely in its character of morality, because—depending on whether the act is morally good or bad—the human being himself, as a person, becomes morally good or bad. For this reason we say that in every act that is executed there is achieved a certain "realization," because the person's self-determination establishes a specific form of being. "To fulfill oneself, meaning to realize oneself, in some way means to bring to its own fullness the structure that corresponds to being a person, because he is someone and not something. It is the structure of self-dominion and self-possession."[48]

Human acts that have been already performed leave their traces; in its wake the act leaves an imprint that has a moral value. This moral value is an objective reality related to the person, and it is at the same time profoundly subjective. "As a person the human being is someone, and as someone he is good or bad."[49]

The relationship of the human being with his morality is so close that the execution of his acts and his realization as a consequence of those acts are accomplished in the same existence. The realization is put into practice in his self-possession and self-dominion, as con-

48. PA, 226–27. See OC, 195–96; AP, 151.
49. PA, 227. See OC, 196; AP 151.

sequence of his self-determination. This conclusion opens a field of concrete study called ethics, which denotes a reality adequate uniquely to the person. Through the ontological structure of self-dominion and self-determination, the person is the only being that can support moral value as existential reality. Now we understand better why morality is intrinsic to the act, the human act (willed and free). We can also understand the natural end of the human being to be his self-realization, which in its axiological sense can be obtained only through the good, since moral evil is equivalent to non-realization, to a truncated end. "Self-realization includes the perfectible dimension of the human being in his fullness."[50]

When we say that the entire dynamic of the person and his action point to self-realization, which for its part is linked to morality, we discover the relationship of dependence between self-realization and conscience. This is because the conscience has the function of distinguishing the character of good in the act and of forming a sense of obligation in relation to the good discerned. "*Duty is the experienced form of dependence on the truth,* on which the freedom of the person depends."[51] Freedom, in the fundamental sense of the self-determination that is found in dependence on conscience, also shows that the transcendence of the person in the act does not consist in an ontological "autonomy" centered in the "I" but includes the moment of essential dependence on the truth that we have seen before. Dependence on the truth routes the person's autonomy in a direction appropriate for freedom. "The freedom that corresponds to the human person is not pure independence, but self-dependence, which includes dependence on truth."[52] This moral freedom is what constitutes the spiritual dynamism of the person and shows us his realization or non-realization.

Therefore the subordination of freedom to the truth passes through the conscience. Wojtyła says that the conscience has not

50. Franquet, *Persona, acción y libertad*, 223.
51. PA, 232. See OC, 199; AP, 156.
52. PA, 230. See OC, 198; AP, 154–55.

only a cognitive function, by which X is distinguished as a genuine good because it is good or Y as a genuine evil because it is not good; it also impresses a sense of duty, which urges the will to subordinate itself to the genuine good, or to the truth about the good. This surrender to the truth in good forms a new reality inside the person. It is the "normative reality" that we can see in the formulation of norms and its application in human actions. The object of study of the "normative reality" falls within the ambit of moral philosophy and is manifest in conscience.[53]

At this point it suffices to remember that, besides configuring thought, the intelligence has as an essential function the evaluation and distinguishing of what is true from what is not. In this sense, the intelligence gives the human being the basis for a certain dominion of reality, of the objects of his knowledge. Consciousness is also a mental function, but its objective is not only to participate in the distinction truth-falsity—by this its principal office is judgment—but furthermore by means of its reflexive function,[54] it receives its significant contents of the active intellectual and practical processes directed toward truth. Therefore, not only does it have a relationship with truth but, further, through its reflexive function it conditions the experience of truth. "The activity of the intellect, of the entire power directed toward the truth—and not exclusively consciousness—seems to be the foundation for the transcendence of the person."[55]

When consciousness experiences the truth it also experiences duty. It is inclined to the perception of truth primarily in the sphere of values, principally moral values. This is not about a "clear and dis-

---

53. Wojtyła also extends the normative factor into other realms, such as the norms of logic, aesthetics, and others—some related to the realm of theoretical knowledge and others to the realm of beauty and art. He establishes a kind of association of the normative order with the ambit of the transcendentals and human activities. See PA, 233–34; OC, 200; AP, 156.

54. On the functions of consciousness see the section "Consciousness and the *suppositum*" in the previous chapter, "Consciousness and Operativity."

55. PA, 236. See OC, 202; AP, 159.

tinct" perception, but rather about a search in which there is margin for error and doubt. Therefore it is necessary that the consciousness not act alone, autonomously, but in congruence with the truth. It seems clear that intellectual consciousness assures to judgments of moral conscience the subjective experience of truth (veracity); thus as it assures the experience of certainty, and if it does not meet the truth in pure form, it allows for the experiences of uncertainty, vacillation, bad faith, and even error.[56]

Moral conscience introduces into [self-fulfillment] the normative power of truth, which not only conditions the fulfillment of the act on the part of the person, but also the fulfillment of self through the action.... Truthfulness, the normative force of truth contained in moral conscience, constitutes the keystone of this structure. Without truth ... it is impossible correctly to perceive or interpret the conscience or, more generally, the entire system specific to its function and the moral order.[57]

When conscience notes the character of veracity, it leads to a kind of obligation or command to accomplish the act that leads to the realization of what is good, and in doing so it is linked directly with the dynamism of the realization of the personal "I" in and through the act. This is the sense of truth, obligation, and self-realization of the person in act. However, conscience is not a legislator. It does not create the norms; rather, it discovers them in the objective order of the morality of the law. In this, Wojtyła opposes Kant, who maintained that conscience is an autonomous legislator that grants unlimited freedom to the person, which comes to break the "ontic and ethical equilibrium of the person."[58]

In line with this theme there arises a reflection on the responsibility that we have to see with the consciousness of duty and self-realization. We have seen the intimate relationship between values and duties, which is not something merely cognitive: through one's

56. See PA, 238; OC, 204; AP, 160. In ethics we speak of certain, doubtful, deformed, and erroneous conscience.

57. PA, 239–40. See OC, 205; AP, 161–62.

58. PA, 244. See OC, 208; AP, 165.

actions, duty introduces the person into the drama of reality (*dramatis persona*).[59] The act of the person who fulfills his duty toward the attainment of values that his conscience claims for him—that act is accomplished in the terrain of reality, which is the terrain of his self-realization. At the same time, in this process, the person's maturity is developed. This means that the person realizes himself most adequately when he fulfills his obligations in the drama of life, and that realization refers more to the person who acts than to the act that he accomplishes. "Neither through the pure intentionality of wanting nor even thorough self-determination, but through *duty as a special modification of self-determination and intentionality*."[60]

This also means that freedom is not so much the capacity to "do what I want," as to "do what I want in order for my self-realization to be committed to the truth, value, and the good." This "commitment" of freedom is to protect the person from the natural activations that can orient him toward his own non-realization. If the person chooses evil for himself, he does not realize himself but is non-realizing and even destroying himself, which runs contrary to the tendency toward his own perfection as a person. Either way one can choose what harms him; this choosing is a "sign" of his personal freedom, but it is not its correct use in the moral sense.

Obligation is found to be linked with the idea of responsibility. Addressing this point, Wojtyła pays close attention to the phenomenological reflections conducted by Roman Ingarden.[61] The

59. See PA, 248. See OC, 211; AP, 168.
60. PA, 249. See OC, 211; AP, 169 (emphasis in the original).
61. In a footnote to Wojtyła's text is an extensive commentary indicating several of Ingarden's points relating to responsibility. In the context of a discussion of *Osoba i czyn* in *Analecta Cracoviensia*, several authors agreed on having found certain methodological analogies between this work and that of Ingarden. Basically, Ingarden says that a free act is one which results from the initiative of the person. This act is independent of the state of affairs of the situation of the exterior environment, which could exercise an influence on its realization. This supposes two aspects, on the one hand "a determinate formal structure of the person and, on the other hand, a certain structure of the real world in which he lives and works." Roman Ingarden, *Über die Verantwortung. Ihre ontischen Fundamente* (Leipzig: Philipp Reclam, 1970), 66. Karol Wojtyła cites the Polish edition, *O odpowiedzialności i jej podstawach ontycznych* (Kraków:

responsible human being is the one obliged by truth and called to act accordingly; the response to his responsibilities will have consequences with respect to happiness and the transcendence of the person. Let us see how our author develops this.

Every human act has its consequences. The one who performs the act is implicated and obliged by his act. He has to answer for it; he is responsible for it. Further, there is a responsibility implicit in the value that also generates an obligation, even if the obligation has not yet been acted upon. Responsibility is a consequence of the obligation and the operativity of the person. "The human being is responsible for x when he ought to realize x or in the opposite case, when he ought not to realize x. The one can be included in the other because the passage of the value to duty takes place not only by the positive way, but also by the negative."[62] Wojtyła gives the example of the man who tells lies. He is responsible for deceiving others; he ought not to have done this because of his obligation to be faithful to the truth. In the responsible act, obligation is presupposed.

Responsibility is a response to the "should" that is contained in obligation. The will attends to the call of the values that engender the obligation, and it is converted into a form of responsibility before those values. It is true that the will has an intentional relationship with good or value, but above all it influences the aspect of veracity, which warns the conscience before the truth of the object. The conscience having been faced with this warning, obligation arises, and at the same time responsibility is constituted. Responsibility is conditioned by the obligation and at the same time participates in the constitution of an obligation. Here we must distinguish two aspects. There is, on the one hand, responsibility toward the value in conformity with the object of the behavior, and, on the

Książeczka o człowieku, 1973), 132; Spanish edition: Sobre la responsabilidad, trans. Juan Miguel Palacios (Madrid: Caparrós Editores, 2001), 63. Here in this way our author situates responsibility within the structure of the person, in addition to the relationship between obligation and responsibility based on value that also appears in Ingarden's study. See PA, 262n9; OC, 222n58; AP, 312n59.

62. PA, 250. See OC, 212; AP, 170.

other hand, the responsibility that is at work in the subject himself. This latter is inferred from the first property of the will, which is the objectification of the "I" or reference to the "I" in the act and not only the intentional reference toward external objects. This means that the root of the person's responsibility in act is that which arises from his self-determination owing to the moral value of the agent. Responsibility is not to be separated or idealized but rather to be rooted in the person. This is called moral responsibility.

Based on these premises, the ambit of responsibility increases; it is not only a matter of "responsibility for" but also of a "responsibility to," since we are always responsible to someone. On this point Wojtyła brings to light the interpersonal structure of the world of persons. We are not isolated beings enclosed within ourselves; our life unfolds in a social environment, and necessarily we have a series of obligations to others. The recognition of responsibility to others begins with the recognition of each person's responsibility to his own "I." The experience of the "I" as person comes from conscience and from the veracity of the value of oneself. "This 'someone,' before which I am and feel myself to be responsible, is also my own self."[63]

Finally, to close the analysis of the will in relation to truth, responsibility, and self-realization, it is appropriate to note that we all experience the judicial function of our conscience. Indeed, the voice of conscience stands as judge of oneself, appealing to one's responsibility. According to Wojtyła, this self-responsibility seems to come from the person's self-dependence and self-determination.[64] If the person governs and possesses himself, then also he is responsible not only for himself but also "to" himself. From this we infer that if we diminish responsibility, we diminish personality.[65] The human being is responsible as much for his behavior as for that which hap-

63. PA, 254. See OC, 215; AP, 173.
64. Ibid.
65. Not as we ordinarily understand "personality" as a kind of "tone" or "color" to one's appearance in the world. The Polish word here is "*osobowości*," which might better be rendered as "person-ness," or as Wojtyła puts in the text, "in the sense of being a person." PA, 255. See OC, 216; AP, 173.

pens in him as a consequence of his behavior. This responsibility, which is rooted in the interior of each one, founds the intersubjective nexus of moral and social participation and collaboration in the human world.[66] Self-realization necessarily has the character of the person's openness to others.

Felicity and Spirituality

There is a close relationship between the transcendence of the person in act and felicity. One can say that self-realization approximates well to the meaning of felicity, which is the sense of greatest fullness to which we are called as human beings (similar to the Aristotelian *eudaimonia*).[67] In *Person and Act* Wojtyła compares two terms that connote subtle differences: happiness and felicity.[68] Felicity in not precisely "happiness." While the former expresses the

66. Here too there is the consideration of the relationship of the responsibility of the man-person before God, but this requires an analysis of a theological rather than philosophical nature.

67. It is not the same as the Aristotelian *eudaimonia*, because for Wojtyła the concept of happiness is not confined to the natural realm but also admits a theological approach, which is open to the supernatural dimension where grace is at work.

68. On this point there is a new inconvenience with the terms used in different editions translated from *Osoba i czyn*. In the Spanish versions (1982 and 2011) we find *"felicidad"* and *"dicha"* (see PA (2011), 255ff.; PA (1982), 202ff.). In *The Acting Person* they are translated "happiness" and "felicity" (see AP, 174ff.) and in the Italian as *"beatitudine"* and *"felicità"* (see PEA, 105iff.) Confusion arises about the meaning that both terms have with respect to what Wojtyła wants to emphasize. He himself changes one word for the other in the subsections, for example when he refers to the happiness that derives from the relationship with others. When Wojtyła uses the Polish terms *"szczęśliwość"* and *"szczęście,"* each means felicity, but the first appears to refer to the maximum human fullness (beatitude), while the second word, *"szczęście,"* has a weaker sense, referring rather to a concrete state of well-being in a given moment. The clearest indication (for the translator, at least) of Wojtyła's intention can be found in his own choices to translate this term. In his Polish manuscript, Wojtyła/John Paul II, *Mężczyzną i niewiastą*, 47, 52, he uses the term *"szczęśliwość"* to describe the original state of Adam and Eve's relationship. Subsequently as John Paul II, when he used this material in his series of audiences on the Theology of the Body, he chose the Italian term *"felicità."* See John Paul II, *Uomo e donna lo creò* (Rome: Città Nuova, 2011), 74, 83. In any case, the term most used is *"szczęśliwość,"* which the Spanish editions render as *"felicidad."* Although the English term "felicity" could be ambivalent in its connotations, we prefer to use it, as the cognate of the Italian term that John Paul II himself chose.

maximum human fullness in the general and, if you will, final sense, "happiness" places the accent rather on an affective character, which can be concrete or temporary. In felicity the person is happy. Felicity includes happiness, and happiness is a certain manifestation of felicity.

When a person realizes himself, he increases his felicity. Self-realization pertains to doing the good, and in doing the good the man-person is made good. However, that the act contributes to felicity does not mean that the act would be felicity's source, nor that it would lead automatically to it. It is appropriate to remember that the act has a double effect of operativity and self-determination, one external and the other internal, one transitive and the other intransitive. Felicity refers rather to the internal and intransitive in the act, in which it is identified with the realization of the person's "I."[69] The realization of the "I" is complex and is constituted by numerous characters, but we can identify two of those clearly: truth and freedom.

By itself freedom is insufficient to make a human being happy, but it is a condition for felicity. It is true that if a person is deprived of freedom, his felicity can also be seen as in danger. However, more fundamental is that one's freedom be realized through the truth. If there is no truth in the free act, then the interior realization of the person is attacked, and even the sense of freedom fades away.

Besides freedom, relationship with others also contributes to felicity. Aristotle said this already, especially concerning friendship, a virtue necessary for felicity.[70] Human relationships are complex and of different levels, from interpersonal and social relationships to relationships with beings of nature—the person's openness does not remain only toward living beings, but there is also a certain participation with the nonliving beings that nature comprises.[71] In this

---

69. See PA, 256; OC, 216; AP, 174–75.

70. See Aristotle, *Nicomachean Ethics* 1170b15–19.

71. On this point we can discern Karol Wojtyła's ecological consciousness, which can be seen reflected later on in various documents during his pontificate as John Paul II.

last case, Wojtyła says that "personal" felicity is not equivalent to that of "non-personal" beings, for instance, that of animals. There can be no doubt that animals can experience natural satisfactions and pains (comfort and discomfort), but they do so on a sensitive level distinct from our experience. Personal felicity requires a structure in which one can base the realization of the "I," which transcends the sensitive. This personal structure is not observed in the animals, plants, or inanimate beings. The felicity that arises from the relationship with non-personal beings would rather be a kind of "joy,"[72] which would contribute to but not complete our deepest personal felicity.

We can also mention the level of the encounter that can be established between the man-person and another personal being superior to the human being, that is, with God. In this case the interactions and the communion are those occurring not between equals but between inferior and superior, in which God is the cause and source itself of all felicity. The man-person participates within his limitations in the sublimity of this relationship, which represents a greater felicity than that generated between fellow humans. In this case we speak of beatitude or felicity in the religious sense.[73]

Another recurrent theme to address concerning felicity is pleasure. Its treatment is ancient in the history of thought and is very pertinent to anthropology.[74] Wojtyła also paused in his analysis with an explanation in line with his methodology. But first, to emphasize

72. Wojtyła refers explicitly to the explanation of "joy" in his *Love and Reponsibility*, 60–61. See AR, 32. Here he also explains the relationship with things and beings that are not persons.

73. See PA, 257; OC, 218; AP, 175–76. If we consider the etymology of the term "religion" as "*re-ligare*" (to tie or link again), we can better appreciate the meaning of "relationship" that is established between the man-person and God. Wojtyła indicates that the deep comprehension of the person influences the revealed Christian truth that speaks of eternal felicity or union with God.

74. Wojtyła specifically mentions the evolution of the term *eudaimonia* through history and refers to the work of Władysława Tatarkiewicz, *O szczęściu* (Warsaw, 1962); in English, *Analysis of Happiness*, trans. E. Rothert (The Hague: Martinus Nijhoff, 1976). See PA, 260n8; OC, 220n57; AP, 312n58.

the contrast and to accentuate the line of premises, let us recall the pronouncements of three philosophical theses with respect to the pleasure-felicity relationship.

The first thesis says that felicity is an elevated kind of pleasure. Wojtyła analyzes Kant's critique of Jeremy Bentham and the theory of the emotions proposed by Max Scheler. He judges that there is a confusion in treating felicity as if it were only a kind of pleasure or that pleasure is a component of felicity.[75] Fundamentally this view derives from the principle of maximization of pleasure and minimization of pain based on the hedonistic calculus worked out by Jeremy Bentham and later advanced by John Stuart Mill in utilitarianism.[76]

The second thesis proclaims the now-widespread conception that compares the levels of intensity between the two. Pleasure is more superficial and less profound than felicity. This comparison comes out of the analysis of the emotive characteristics of the human being; it is found, for example, in the analysis of Max Scheler. Just as in utilitarianism, so also in Scheler's comparison of emotions, felicity and pleasure are considered to be elements of the same kind. They are comparable because they differ only "by degree" (intensity, composition, etc.).

The third thesis holds that felicity is a spiritual fact and pleasure is something merely sensual or material. Here, it is a matter of qualitative differences, and the separation is not one merely of degree. They are of different "kinds."

Wojtyła proposes a different approach in his analysis of the pleasure-felicity problem. First of all, he affirms that felicity and pleasure are not the same. But where is the difference rooted? Felicity is structurally linked to the act and the transcendence of the person in the act. The accent is placed on "the human being who acts" and not on "something happens in the human being." In felicity, the

75. Ibid.
76. Wojtyła's critique of utilitarianism can be found in his work *Love and Reponsibility*, 34–39; 292–93n13.

principle of self-determination governs where freedom prevails. This freedom may or may not be in accord with conscience (be true in the normative sense) and the human being may or may not fulfill himself, but the basis for his act is free. (Therefore, if the human being does evil and places obstacles to his fulfillment, he can fall into the extreme opposite of felicity, that is, into despair.)

On the other hand, pleasure (or its contrary, discomfort) is not found in the foregoing structure, but in that which indicates what "happens" in the human being, on the level of nature. The line of demarcation between "felicity" and "pleasure" has to do with the structures in which these experiences are contained. But we must be careful. It would be a mistake to say that pleasure has to do only with what "happens" in the human being and not with the person, because it is indubitable that it also accompanies the human act. In acting, the human being also seeks "pleasure" and he avoids "discomfort." We cannot establish a relationship of exclusion, because that would be like trying to separate "person" from "nature," creating a dichotomy within the human being. This is not the idea. The meaning of the distinction that Wojtyła intends is "to show that the fulfillment of the act and one's own personal fulfillment of self through the act are related to felicity [or its opposite] as with something absolutely specific, something that cannot be resolved into the elements pleasure-discomfort and be reduced to them."[77]

In other words, Wojtyła shows that the end of fulfillment through action consists in felicity. Felicity is found to be framed by the personal structure where the act is performed. For its part, pleasure indicates something that "happens" in the human being and, as with all human experience, it forms part of the part of the person, showing or signifying an aspect that can accompany felicity or not. However, it is present and affects him. The person integrates the experience of pleasure and it can form part of the act. However felicity does not only attend this experience but can assimilate it without

77. PA, 261. See *OC*, 220–21; AP, 178.

being reduced to it. Felicity cannot be reduced to pleasure because there is no structural correspondence with the person in act. Hence, Wojtyła affirms, "Precisely this specificity and irreducibility of felicity seems to be found in close relationship with the transcendence of the person."[78]

This allows him to explain some cases of persons who feel discomfort and pain at the somato-vegetative level, and yet are happy because they have been fulfilling themselves throughout their lives, working to be good persons. Pleasure and pain form part of the potentialities that indicate the functioning of our organism, and they also manifest themselves on the psychosomatic level, but they are to be subordinated to the affectivity of the personal level, where are situated self-fulfillment and felicity.

Felicity makes manifest the transcendence of the person in act. However, our analysis of the key concepts of Karol Wojtyła's anthropology would be incomplete if we were not to mention that this transcendence of the person in act also makes manifest another essential aspect of the human being, his spirituality. The term "spiritual" in Wojtyła refers not only to an immaterial factor, something intrinsically irreducible to matter. He connects the spirit with rationality and especially with our orientation toward truth and goodness.[79] That which constitutes and in which consists transcendence of the person in act is something spiritual, not material. Wojtyła arrives at this conclusion by way of phenomenological intuition and not by means of abstraction.[80]

78. Ibid.
79. In *Love and Responsibility* and *Person and Act* Wojtyła gives to the word "spirit" the real meaning in his philosophical personalism.
80. Ordinarily many people connect "spiritual" with "religious," which creates confusion when they come to philosophical analysis. In philosophy, "spiritual" commonly means that which transcends the material. They differ from each other, although the two—matter and spirit—are not absolutely opposite, since in the human being, they interact in that form of existence that is called "substantial unity." The ontological degree to which the spiritual surpasses the material escapes quantitative analysis and the methodologies of the positive sciences. Therefore the sciences cannot analyze it, and sometimes cannot even localize it, since the study of it belongs to

Human existence itself is manifest in the form of transcendence. "The human being as a person lives and fulfills himself in this form."[81] The human being could not show the spiritual aspect of his nature if he himself were not in some way spirit. Phenomenology allows the relationship "manifestation-explanation"; the manifestation allows the explanation.[82] Applying this method, Wojtyła states that the manifestation of immaterial aspects of the human act, such as self-dominion and self-possession in the man-person's vertical transcendence, explain spirituality. Thanks to the human act, and through the effects that it entails, we can infer his spirituality. And spirituality refers to the idea of person.

If there is a condition of spirituality in the human being, then the existential modality adequate to this spirituality cannot be other than that of the person. This affirmation is confirmed in the definition of person (Boethius) since the "spiritual nature" (natura rationalis) indicates an essential ontological character. The person is that which acts and therefore is a "someone."

The person has the peculiar capacity and power of self-determination in which he himself has the experience of himself as a free being. Freedom is expressed in operativity, and operativity brings with itself responsibility, which for its part reveals the dependence of freedom on truth. However, this relationship of freedom with truth constitutes the proper meaning of conscience as the decisive factor of the transcendence of the person in his acts.[83]

---

metaphysics. In virtue of having this spiritual character, the human being is capable of interacting with other spiritual beings, such as God, and this relationship is called "religion." When the study of God is undertaken in philosophy it is called theodicy or philosophy of religion, but when supernatural faith intervenes in this study it is called theology and does not form part of philosophy (although theology utilizes philosophical elements in developing its logical argumentation).

81. PA, 265. See OC, 223; AP, 181.

82. Wojtyła especially emphasizes the viability of the phenomenological method intuitively to approach the idea of spirituality and, ultimately, the person. He refers to how Roman Ingarden, starting from responsibility, deduces the idea of the person. See PA, 262n9; OC, 222n58; AP, 312n59.

83. PA, 264. See OC, 222; AP, 180.

That the person is "someone" is independent of the fact of his having a distinctive structure in act or in potency. His own essentiality identifies him from the beginning of his existence. Therefore, although the actualization in fulfilling what is proper to him may be interrupted or impeded, he continues to be a man-person. The fact of acting or of doing does not found his nature, but it uncovers its operative principles, which refer to a kind of personal being. There is an ontological basis of the person which permits his existential development. This is the core of the argument that makes manifest the dignity of human life in virtue of the sole fact of having been conceived as a member of the human species.

The act of being permits the existence and potentially contains multiple possibilities for this man-person that he will develop throughout his life. There is something "sacred," "untouchable," of "intrinsic value" in that first vital operation which is the act of being. All this is contained in the material-spiritual conception of the man-person. From this arise the other operations of the human being; this initial act of being is a foundational ontological act, in which is rooted the dignity of the human person. As we can see, these considerations can be understood only on the basis of a metaphysical explanation.

At this point in the analysis, there again arises the relationship between nature and person. Earlier we saw the difference between the two,[84] and now the point of reflection consists in seeing how they are integrated. We can admit that some structures appertain to the character of nature, as for instance the free will; however, others would be located better in the ambit of the person, such as self-determination (fundamental freedom). Freedom, as we have studied it in relation to transcendence, goes beyond the natural scope of free will. However, we cannot think that the two would be distinct in such a way that there would be generated a dichotomous vision of

84. See the section "Nature and Person" in the previous chapter, "Conciousness and Operativity."

the human being. This would bring about anthropological dualism. Wojtyła always affirmed the unity of the man-person, even though there is a dual composition in virtue of the material and spiritual dual condition of the human being. If it is true that unity is made manifest especially in the human act, in the analysis of this action we discover a certain complexity inherent in his potentialities and dynamisms.

In order to avoid confusion, it is necessary again to emphasize that the act makes transcendence manifest and uncovers human spirituality, but far from being a consequence of the act or even of any human dynamism, this spirituality is its source. As there is a proportional relationship between potentialities and their dynamisms, we can infer that a spiritual dynamism originates from a potentiality of the spiritual nature.

In the cognitive function, to these [spiritual] faculties there corresponds the dynamic reference to truth, and in the function of self-determination, freedom and the dynamic dependence of freedom on truth. The first we equate with the concept of intellect, and the second with the will. Therefore, the powers of intellect and will evidently form part of a spiritual element and manifest themselves as such.[85]

The fact that the intelligence and will are spiritual supports the idea that these powers are not based only in nature. The condition of spirituality that is manifest phenomenologically points to an ontological explanation of the matter-spirit relationship in the man-person. No one has had direct contact with the "soul" or the "spirit";[86] one has, rather, the experience of spirituality. Indeed, the

---

85. PA, 269. See OC, 226; AP, 184.

86. The concept "soul" (psyche—ψυχή) comes from ancient Greek philosophy and is a concept that refers to the vital principle of some beings. It is a metaphysical concept which can neither be treated by the positive sciences nor equated with the elements of particle physics, because it is a unifying and organizing metaphysical principle that allows beings to live from themselves (self-transformation) and in themselves (material and immaterial immanence). For a basic anthropological approach on life see Jacinto Choza, Manual de Antropología Filosófica (Madrid: Rialp, 1988), 21–40; 49–70; José Ángel García Cuadrado, Antropología Filosófica. Una introducción a la Filosofía del Hombre, 6th ed. (Pamplona: Eunsa, 2014), 44ff. Aristotle defines the soul in general as "the

concepts that we have seen—consciousness, self-determination, veracity, obligation or responsibility—show us an experience of interiority and refer us to an idea of spirituality.[87] But in order to go more deeply into this character, which transcends the material, we must resort, not to the senses, but to metaphysical reflection, as we have already shown.

---

primary act of a physical bodily organism," *De Anima* 412a27–b5. As we see, it is a type of philosophical, not scientific, explanation, about an immaterial reality; for this reason Wojtyła says that no one has had direct contact with the soul. We come to understand it indirectly, from the effects that refer us to it.

87. See PA, 270–71; OC, 227–28; PA, 185–86.

IO ∾

INTEGRATION

Integration

In the Sixth Chapter of *Person and Act*, Wojtyła analyzes a complementary aspect of transcendence that he calls "the integration of the acting person." We will look first at the basis for such integration and afterwards, at some concepts of each of the moments into which integration is divided, the soma and the psyche.

In general, the term *integration* (from the Latin *integer*) means entire, complete. To integrate is to assemble the parts in a whole, denoting a process and a result. From the psychological and philosophical point of view, the word *integration* is used to speak about the attainment and manifestation of a whole and a unit that is constituted by certain complexity.[1]

Having said that, to speak about the unity of the human being, the natural aspect must be integrated in the person and vice versa. That is, the somato-vegetative and the psycho-emotive aspects that form the levels of natural potential have to be integrated together with transcendence. It is not only about how they relate to each other, but about how they complement each other and interact mutually in order to attain the unity of the person. A person is not only something "spiritual," but a "soma-psycho-spiritual" synthesis. Un-

Translated from Spanish by Paul Gordon and Ángela Gimeno Nogués.

1. See PA, 278; OC, 231; AP, 191.

der this perspective, Wojtyła tries to avoid the recurrent dualisms (e.g., Plato, Descartes, some current proposals in the philosophy of mind . . .) or monisms (e.g., Spinoza, De la Mettrie, Russell, Monod . . .) that have arisen throughout the history of thought in relation to anthropology. Our author admits the Aristotelian-Thomistic idea of the human substantial unity, but wants to show how it may be presented from the viewpoint of the person in act. This is what the present chapter is about.[2]

Karol Wojtyła says that act is accomplished through self-determination, which, at the same time, permits us to discover, as a base, a personal structure of self-dominion and self-possession. These structural characteristics overstep what is merely natural, since freedom, consciousness, and self-determination are alien to nature. We should keep in mind the difference of experience that there is between "a human being acts" and "something happens in a human being." Whereas the first is placed in the sphere of the person's operativity, the second is placed within the scope of nature. This means that there is a part of the man-person that is not included in transcendence, and that is what has to be integrated.

Which part is not included in transcendence? "[F]or we call transcendence only the character of the active possession of self and the active dominion of self, which are related to self-determinations, that is, with the will."[3] Therefore, the "I" dominates and possesses the "I" itself in an act of reflexiveness in which transcendence is accomplished. But the "I" is not transcendent until this "I" is self-determined by governing and possessing itself. If it does not obtain this self-determination, the integration of the person in act cannot be accomplished.

Another way to consider integration is through the act of reflexiveness of the operativity and subjectivity of the acting human "I."

---

2. See PA, 275; OC, 227; AP, 189. In the last section of the chapter "Consciousness and Operativity" we mentioned only "the levels of potentiality and dynamism"; in this chapter, the idea is to show how they can be integrated in the person in act.

3. PA, 276. See OC, 230; AP, 190.

In this reflexiveness one experiences himself as an agent of his action; for this reason he is his own subject. And, in addition, the human being experiences what is happening in himself, where he is not the protagonist of the action, but someone who simply realizes that something is happening on the margins of his will. "Just as operativity is disclosed as the domain of transcendence, so subjectivity is with integration."[4]

When someone acts, the person's transcendence is revealed and, logically, the "I" is involved in such action. Integration occurs when there is unity of my "I" and my action. I commit myself in my action, and my own operativity contributes to the dynamism of my "I."[5] All the effort that leads to self-realization must pass through integration as well as transcendence. I perform acts on the one hand of horizontal transcendence (level of nature) and at the same time of vertical transcendence (level of person); these acts must be integrated in the man-person. That means that the person cannot be some kind of a dweller inside a body, but there is a unity between the person and his psycho-somatic character; only thus do we attribute the action to the human being and to the person as well.

In order to understand this human unity, Wojtyła turns to the opposing term: "disintegration." Disintegration shows an incapacity of the person for self-dominion or self-possession. It is a lack that limits his action. This disintegration can have a wide range of forms and levels of intensity that affect the development of "personality."[6] A man who is integrated is a "normal" person; if, on the other hand, he is disintegrated, he cannot reach normality.[7] Some human scienc-

4. PA, 278. See OC, 231; AP, 191.   5. PA, 279. See OC, 232; AP, 191–92.
6. Wojtyła deepens the characterization of disintegration and offers more nuances, which we will not treat in this study. See PA, 283ff.; OC, 235ff.; AP, 194–96.
7. It seems that the criteria of normality should come from the disciplines that study the human personality; thus Wojtyła says that, besides this, in most cases the criteria are established by intuition. "[S]imply put, it is common sense that indicates who is a normal human being and who is not, whether partly or entirely." PA, 280. See OC, 233; AP, 192. In the same place he adds that the criterion of normality, "as [this term] is used in the particular human sciences, including medicine [psychiatry]—frequently emerges from facts of ethical nature." Ibid.

es such as psychology and psychiatry help to establish the parameters that determine those grades, and these parameters are what we use to discover pathologies. A possible example of disintegration can be observed in the mental illnesses that have several causes, among them disorders on a natural-organic level. But leaving aside these more extraordinary situations, it is possible to speak about disintegration when the person cannot achieve the self-governance and the self-possession of his natural dynamisms. Many times, one can have natural impulses that can induce desires against one's personal intentions. For example, when one feels the desire to go on eating (natural tendency) but knows that he should not do so because he is full and does not need to eat (personal intention), but even so goes on eating (disintegration).

This "independence" of the natural movements can be understood because of the specific scope of their operations, which are referred to specific objects and addressed to them—or react to them—in an automatic way. Without an adequate integration of such movements from a higher power—as would be the person's self-determination in relation to his action—disintegration would go directly against the psycho-somatic unity of man. Integration does not mean a direct control of the natural potentialities; the "I" does not have access to vegetative potential levels and can hardly have an impact on some of the psychic processes. For this reason, the ancients already talked about a "political control"—not "direct"—over the passions; and we can talk of no control at all over certain physiological operations such as the blood circulation or operations at cellular level.

The person's integration is referred to a higher order where the "I" intervenes in relation to human action in such a way that the transcendence of that action is accomplished within a psychosomatic unit. "Activations" that overcome the division between what "happens" in man and his "acting" are produced through the integration of the person in action.[8] "If the integration of the per-

8. See PA, 288–89; OC, 239; AP, 199.

son in the act is not accomplished, and by this the very dynamisms of the psycho-somatic composition of the human being, then in his ontic *suppositum* only subjectivity can be realized and not operativity. We know from experience that operativity is dominant in it."[9]

Prior to his study of the characteristics of integration related to the soma and the psyche, Wojtyła makes a very pertinent methodological and epistemological commentary, from my point of view, with respect to the situation of philosophical anthropology and its relationship with the rest of the particular or positive sciences. It is understood that they are not exclusive but complementary disciplines. "[T]he particular sciences investigate each of the singular elements of the person's psychosomatic unity and each of these psychic or somatic dynamisms by itself. They do not specifically consider the totality of the person, that which is most essential for us."[10]

The results of the investigations carried out by the particular sciences with regard to somatic and psychic aspects are very useful for understanding the integration of the person in action. Because of the different methodologies and objects of study, the sciences have a more specialized approach and focus for practical applications. By contrast, the approach of philosophical anthropology achieves a vision of the whole. It does not need to enter into technical details because that is the scope of the particular sciences; rather, it expects to see the complete relationship between the person and his action. Those sciences are charged with the individual study of the different somatic and psychic dynamisms, but it is philosophical anthropology whose charge is the essential aspects of the dynamisms and their integration in the person. Philosophical anthropology cannot distance itself from the results that are offered by the particular sciences, and it must agree in some way with them, but, at the same time, neither must it neglect its rigor in its critical reflection related to them.[11]

9. Ibid.
10. See *PA*, 290; *OC*, 240; *AP*, 200.
11. "This characteristic cannot be separate from the examination of the particular sciences nor can it be in contradiction to them; but neither can it share the minute

Reactivity of the Body

When Wojtyła starts to analyze the integration of the soma, he makes two aspects clear that will support all the line of argument of his exposition. The first is that "we cannot investigate the human body separately from that totality which is the human being, that is, without at the same time understanding that he is a person."[12] Second, he assumes the general principles of reality proposed by Aristotle and Thomas Aquinas, in which are recognized in all the beings of the visible world a material element (*hyle*) and another immaterial (*morphé*). However, he will not repeat the hylomorphic theory but will analyze the dynamic of the human being from the reality of the person in action, that is, according to the methodology that he uses in *Person and Act*.[13]

Man is realized and manifested in his body. In the classic Aristotelian definition of "rational animal,"[14] the concept "animal" is attributed to the body and corporeality.[15] Right from the start, the human being appears in this world and before himself in an individual physical form with a double aspect. There is the external aspect, wherein he shows a unity of different members coordinated amongst themselves, visible to the external senses and discernible like other sensible realities. We can see arms, legs, a head, etc. Additionally, he presents an internal aspect, which also reveals diversity and complexity such as were seen with the body organs. These body organs determine the vitality and dynamism of the body along

---

accuracy of their methods." Ibid. With this we better understand the need to establish principles of unity of knowledge and new discoveries of the positive sciences in a more integrated epistemological level provided by philosophy—and in this specific case, philosophical anthropology.

12. PA, 294. See OC, 243; AP, 203.

13. See ibid.

14. Let us recall that this Aristotelian definition is logical (proximate genus-specific difference), not anthropological, as some contemporary philosophers propose (e.g., "the being that laughs," "the being that talks," "*Sein-zum-Tode*," etc.)

15. Wojtyła also admits the metaphysical doctrine of individuation by means of matter (*materia signata*).

with its potentialities. Both aspects constitute the human body, and the term "somatic" covers the entire whole.

Corporeality also fulfills an important role regarding personal identification, since as much through the internal somatic structure as through the external mobility are differences amongst people established. This had already been considered in the physiognomic studies in ancient times and in Aristotle's and Hypocrite's famous theories of temperaments.

The relationship between the visible exteriority (somatic realm) and the invisible interiority (subjectivity) of the man-person has to be integrated in the action.[16] In other words, how can a relationship be established between the body and the person in order to say that there is a unity of action? Wojtyła's answer is that the personal structure of self-possession and self-governance "passes through" the body and expresses itself through it.[17] The dynamic transcendence of the person is spiritual, and its unity with the body is perceived when this (the body) responds to the person's self-governance. "[The body is the terrain and in some way the means for accomplishing the act and, with this, for the fulfillment of the person in the act and through the act."[18] The person makes his choice and exercises his decision—both of them subordinated to the truth—making them manifest through the body. The body belongs to and is subordinated to the person.

Wojtyła does not make a metaphysical analysis of the soul-body relation, although, as we already said, he adheres to the doctrine of their substantial unity. With his method he makes clear the necessity of this unity (integration) in the man-person; otherwise the person would not be able to reveal or to express himself, and finally he would not be able to achieve his realization. "And thus [the body] is also converted into the means and the terrain by which the soul is

16. This is the central problem of philosophical anthropology that distinct approaches, including dualisms and materialisms, have tried to solve.

17. See PA, 297; OC, 245; AP, 204.

18. PA, 297. See OC, 245; AP, 205.

exteriorized into the proper dynamism of spirituality and freedom in its dynamic relationship with truth."[19]

It is not a question of "objectification" of the body, but of seeing how it is objectivized in a special way in the action.

The person becomes for himself the object of his act. The body participates in this objectification in a particular way. Every time the person exteriorizes himself through his body, the body simultaneously becomes an object of the act. The objectification of the body constitutes a particular aspect and even an integral element of the objectification of the entire personal subject, to whom the body belongs and in which subjectivity penetrates structurally. The body's belonging to the subjective "I" does not consist in being identical with it. The human being is not his body; he only *possesses* his body.[20]

The fact that the person expresses himself through his body should not be interpreted as if the body were a "mere instrument of," as if it were devalued in relation with the spiritual. Nor does it mean that I can do whatever I want with my body since it is subordinated to my desires and it is obedient to the expression of my self-governance. The way to interpret the "having" of the body is not only treated by Wojtyła, but it has been a topic of discussion within the scope of personalism.

In a footnote of *Person and Act*, Wojtyła presents two positions in this regard—those of W. Luijpen and of H. Bergson[21]—that I believe to be appropriate to bring up, since his discussion there facilitates the understanding our author's attitude. Luijpen clarifies that it is not possible to have the body at one's disposal as if it were something external like a car, a pencil, or a book. This kind of having is said in a literal sense and does not express the anthropological meaning of what we are speaking about. I do not have "a" body but I have "my" body; somehow my body "incarnates" me. Nor can it be said that I "am" my body, because that would mean that the self-

19. Ibid.
20. PA, 298. See OC, 246; AP, 206 (emphasis in the original).
21. PA, 298n4. See OC, 246n62; AP, 314n65.

consciousness would materialize somehow and disappear as such. Luijpen prefers to say that to understand the situation of the body it must be thought as a trade-off between those two opposite sides. For his part, Bergson thinks that the spirit rules the body. In his work *L'énergie spirituelle* he says that the life of the spirit cannot be considered a fact of the life of the spirit, but rather that the body is used by the spirit. Bergson affirms that there is no reason for the two of them to be indissolubly linked. With regard to both positions, Wojtyła finds it necessary to insist: "When it is said 'the human being is *not* his body; he only possesses it,' this affirmation is a consequence of the conviction that the human being 'is' his own self (that is, a person) only insofar as he possesses himself, and in the same sense, he *does* possess his body."[22]

M. J. Franquet, in his study of Wojtyła's anthropology, says that man is conscious of using his body with regard to self-governance, which is related to the responsibility—and this is due to being ruled by the truth. "For Wojtyła, the possession and use of the body does not have the meaning of ethical utilitarianism, but the personal disposal. The corporeal having has, in Wojtyła's thought, the meaning of the personal self-possession and the self-governance necessary for one's own realization as a person."[23]

In any case, it is necessary to remember that the body can perform certain operations outside the person's voluntariness; we call this "natural action." These operations have been and still are stud-

22. Ibid. See PA, 299n4. On this point Julián Marías says: "I do not *have* a body, nor *am* I my body, with which I find myself as the rest of reality. I *am* corporeal; if you prefer, *someone corporeal*" Julián Marías, *Persona* [Person] (Madrid: Alianza Editorial, 1996), 135. Gabriel Marcel is another contemporary philosopher who has emphasized the idea "I am my body," but he differentiates between the body-subject and the body-object, where the first has an intimate and personal character, whereas the second is that which enters into spatial contact. Both of them are inseparable and complementary. For a synthetic approach, see Julia Urabayen, "Gabriel Marcel: Una imagen digna del hombre" [Gabriel Marcel: An image worthy of man], in *Propuestas antropológicas del siglo XX* [Anthropological Proposals of the Twentieth Century], ed. Juan Fernando Sellés, 1:327–43 (Pamplona: Eunsa, 2006).

23. Franquet, *Persona, acción y libertad*, 241.

ied in great detail by the particular sciences, including the ones that affect the human psyche, as we will see further on. The integration of the person in action cannot ignore these natural dynamisms, because it is precisely the linking of them that explains the whole that the man-person is. The body, from the point of view of nature, is our point of juncture with the rest of living beings, and this fact situates us in the historical natural order, as biology and the evolutionary theories teach us.

The common aspects of the natural dynamics of the body, in both animals and human beings, are oriented to the development and conservation of life, and to this end they respond to external stimuli. "Reactivity" is the term used by Wojtyła to describe this dynamism of the human body as such.[24]

The life of the body is essentially vegetative and reacts to external conditions as other bodies do, which means that it is determined by the environmental conditions of food and drink. The organism adapts to those conditions so that, besides self-preservation, it can reproduce as well. In the case of man, such reproduction is possible thanks to the sexual differentiation of his body through the specific organs, a gestation period, and the birth of an autonomous life. The urges that inspire and initiate this entire process, as well as the subsequent development of the new life, follow the course of the organic reactions imposed by nature. That is, "they happen in the person" without a special influence of the will. The person's self-dominion is not observed; they are acts of the person, but not operativity (act).

Very much linked to the vegetative and reproductive dynamism is the reaction to environmental stimuli. Dynamism and reaction to stimuli are not the same. In the first case, there is a submission of the body to the physio-chemical processes and to the external conditions of the organism. In the second case, there is a perception of the stimulus and an "instinctive" response. In human beings, the

24. "It seems that this dynamism can be grasped and expressed with the concept of 'reactivity' and with this attribute it is 'reactive.'" PA, 302. See OC, 249; AP, 208.

capacity to react to these stimuli is related to the nervous system and does not appear in a passive way, as in the vegetative sphere. Therefore, it involves another kind of dynamism.

The faculty of will is not the cause of the organism's operative dynamism. We notice this in experience, because there are acts that occur in us without our intention; sometimes we do not even realize them. When contrasting this kind of experience with the person's operativity, we come to realize the ontic complexity of man. In this complexity (acts that "happen" and acts that are "operativity"), it can be seen that the body is at the base of what determines the person's structure. Together, acts that "happen" and acts that are "operativity" form a unity.

The fact that the human body's own reactive dynamism and its own vegetative vitality "happen" in the person independently of his self-determination, without the will's active intervention, does not at all annul the person's unity. Neither does the fact that all the vegetative vitality and reactivity of the body occur in the human being outside the radius of action of consciousness annul that unity. This fact ... does not in any way annul the personal unity of the human being, even though to some extent it characterizes it.[25]

This vision of human unity is opposed to dualism. Indeed, this vision does not depict a kind of "harmony" of two elements that are joined momentarily but can separate again, each one keeping its own proprieties. In the ontological unit, each element depends on and conditions the other. Without the one there is not the other. In order to see how it can be this way, we merely need to think of something that is one although it has a complexity of parts. "Its unity with the ontic subjectivity of the human being, with the human *suppositum*, allows no doubt."[26] Even when the experience of subjectivity—through consciousness—tends to include only the external aspects of the body and its mobility, this is enough to contrast with the interior and to know its subjectivity.[27]

25. PA, 306. See OC, 251–52; AP, 211.   26. Ibid. See OC, 252; AP, 211.
27. On this point, Wojtyła offers a parenthetic commentary about some practices

Thus, Wojtyła speaks of two distinct "subjectivities," one that would correspond to the person's integral subjectivity, but another that would correspond to the body's subjectivity as such, as it is subject to reactions. This latter somatic subjectivity is reactive, vegetative, and external to the consciousness. In the acting person's integrity, the somatic subjectivity has to be in tune with the operational subjectivity; otherwise there would be a shortcoming and the person would run the risk of disintegration. Here, an important reflection arises: when the body's subjectivity escapes the person's control in a harmful way, it would go against the very nature of the man-person, because "in itself, the harmony of the body's reactive and vegetative subjectivity with the person as a subject active and conscious of himself appears as something natural, in the sense of corresponding to the nature of the human being, who is a person."[28] On the other hand, we would be breaking the man-person unit as a consequence of disintegration. One example of this is anorexia, when a person has an eating disorder related to anxiety or an emotional illness, the reaction of the body goes contrary to the sense of its nature and rejects eating any food. This will damage not only the body but the entire person. It is a kind of disintegration.

The unity to which our author refers is made clear in the synthesis of action and movement. When one voluntarily wants to perform an activity or accomplish some movement or shift, the body goes along with him, is involved in, and is predisposed to carry out, the person's intention. For example, if one wants to jump over a puddle in order not to get wet, then the somatic dynamism is placed at the will's disposal to execute the action, even at the vegetative level, where greater glandular secretions are produced or the heart rate increases—and the psychic aspect has to be included as well. The

---

that come from oriental culture: "It is well known that the ascetic exercises of yoga are focused also on controlling the internal reactions of the organism, but that control does not at all mean that they generate these reactions, which always belong to the operativity of the body." PA, 307. See OC, 252; AP, 211. In any case, these practices reinforce the idea of dominion of the person in the body and its unity.

28. PA, 307–08. See OC, 252–53; AP, 212.

execution of the action will be favored when the body is better disposed and ordered. Most of the time we do not pay any attention to those intermediate acts that make up all the action. But in reality, the body goes along with, and makes it possible to achieve, the aim.

With this, we assert that the integration of the person in act presupposes the integrity of the body. In Wojtyła's anthropology, the body acquires a great importance, and its care contributes to the realization of the person. The body cannot be treated in just any way, because the whole person is affected by this treatment. This idea represents again a rejection of the dualistic and dichotomist positions where the physical is "independent" from the metaphysical. Additionally, the somatic reactions must be in accord with personal integrity; here I am referring to the instinctive orientations that can undergo modifications by voluntary acts and lead human conduct to disintegrated forms. We will encounter this below when we deal with ability (habit or skill) and impulse-instinct.

In the analysis of the action-movement dynamic there appears the classic concept of habit (habitus). Habits allow man to have more skill in his acts and movements, hence the term "ability," which is also related to the concept of "virtue." "Ability" refers to the body, "virtue" to the spiritual and moral life.

"Motor abilities are created very quickly, as the result of instinctive reactions and drives. Also very quickly in this entire process of forming movements, the will, which is the source of motor impulses that arise from the 'interior' of the person, is integrated. These impulses bear within themselves the mark of self-determination."[29] The corresponding abilities are formed in the synthesis of act and movement. Abilities allow the motor dynamism to be fluid and spontaneous. As we have just indicated, sometimes habits are almost imperceptible, but sometimes they claim the attention of the consciousness because the situation is one of importance, such as

29. PA, 310. See OC, 254; AP, 215–19. Here for "impulse," the Polish word is "impulsów."

performing delicate surgery or practicing a high-risk sport. In these moments, conscious operativity is more or less clearly experienced. A certain degree of "habituation" is important to perform with effectiveness some acts without having to pay close attention. By the repetition of acts a certain automatism is eventually developed, a kind of reflex act where will does not seem to take part. Because of this appearance of quasi-unconsciousness, the classics called habits "second nature."

Forms of activity are affected not only by the habits or the abilities but also by the bodily dispositions and the specific characteristics of the organism. Not everybody reacts or acts in a similar way to the same stimuli or events; there are psychical factors that intervene here, such as those related to temperament. There can also be as well merely somatic deficiencies or forms of disintegration that affect and condition the action. For example, the absence of an organ or a body part prevents certain kind of activities from being performed and strengthens others. An example would be those blind persons who develop a special ability to hear. In any case, these kinds of impediments have only a physical significance, never a moral one; therefore they do not deform the conscience or impede its self-dominion. There can even be cases with a high level of somatic disintegration but with a personality of great value.[30]

Drives and Instincts

Wojtyła differentiates between drive and instinct.[31] The term "instinct" refers to human being's responses to stimuli. Instinct auto-

---

30. See PA, 311–12; OC, 255; AP, 215.

31. In *The Acting Person*, the concept "impulse" is misleading—in fact, wrong. The Polish original is "popęd," which the *New Kosciusko Foundation Dictionary* translates as "drive" or "urge." Besides this, the distinction between instinct and urge is very clearly discussed in *Love and Responsibility*, chap. 1, part 2. The 1980 translation uses "urge" and the new (2013) translation uses "drive." Although "impulso" may render "popęd" well in Spanish (the Italian also uses "impulso"), "impulse" is not quite right in English. "Drive" is much to be preferred. See PA, 312–18; OC, 255–59; AP, 215–19.

matically produces reactions that come from the soma. When one feels a burn he immediately takes his hand away, in an instinctive manner. On the other hand, the term "drive" aims to go further, covers more, and involves even the psyche. Drive indicates a dynamic orientation of nature, a determined direction. "A drive is a form of dynamism of the human being precisely in virtue of his nature, and it maintains a close union with it. However, at the same time the drive is not an exclusively somatic dynamism."[32] Let's explain this more thoroughly.

Drives have their own conditioning factors in the human body, but Wojtyła wants to distinguish them from the instincts in order to show that, while there is an automatic reactivity that affects the somatic part especially, there is as well another, more profound, form of reactivity that affects in a more direct way the person's operativity. It is true that, on a certain level, the human organism has mechanisms of self-protection and self-defense that care for its survival, as if they were the operativity of the human body. But other types of dynamisms can be found, too, in which the psychic part of the human being intervenes as much as the personal part. This demands a different structure from the merely instinctive, and for that reason the term "drive" is used. *Person and Act* there is a reference to two of them: the drive for self-preservation and the sexual drive.

In the self-preservation drive there is a fundamental value, a principle, which makes the obligation to exist manifest; this "subjective necessity" to live pervades the entire human structure. It is felt at the somatic level, but there is further an emotive desire and even an intellectual assertion of existence, "the consciousness that to exist and to live is good, and it is bad to lose existence and life."[33] Self-preservation is not only a "drive" but also a "drive" that takes the form of a need, of fundamental value in the human being. That does not mean that the person has absolute control of that value, because experience shows that its assertion can be changed for its denial.

32. PA, 313. See OC, 256; AP, 216.
33. PA, 315. See OC, 257; AP, 217.

About the latter, Wojtyła considers whether the intention of people who commit suicide is to cease completely to exist or, perhaps, only to cease to exist in a form that they consider unbearable.[34]

In human sexuality it is possible as well to see the amplitude of the dimension of drives. "Just as the drive for self-preservation is founded on the natural inclination to preserve one's own being, so too the sexual drive is founded on the inclination to be with another human being, based on the profound likeness and at the same time the diversity that results from the difference of the sexes."[35] However, "[t]he sexual urge in this conception is a *natural drive born in all human beings, a vector of aspiration* along which their whole existence develops and perfects itself from within."[36] With this definition from his work *Love and Responsibility*, the author stresses that human sexuality does not strictly remain on the biological level but also affects the existential level where "that which happens" is referred to a broader end, in this case, personal love. Wojtyła maintains that this desire constitutes the natural basis of marriage and that in married life it is also the foundation of the family.

The reproductive characteristic is clearly revealed in the dynamism of the drive where "something happens" in the human being automatically. This automatism permits the person a certain measure of control in adapting the body's dynamism to its own aim. Wojtyła never ceases to mention that sexual control can often pose complicated problems, above all with individuals whose sexual desire is especially strong. Here we are speaking not only about somatic reactions, since there is a great psychic component that has an emotional character. The ethical aspect in relation to the need to control the sexual drive is addressed not in *Person and Act* but in *Love and Responsibility*.

So far we have considered the concepts related to the integration of the soma in the person in action; now we must take another step

34. PA, 315. See OC, 258; AP, 218.   35. PA, 316. See OC, 258; AP, 218.
36. LR, 46. See AR, 59 (emphasis in original).

to complete the unitary aspect that integration demands. This is the integration of the psyche.

Psyche and Emotivity

The complementary aspect of the person in act's integration concerns the psyche. In order to understand how this integration is accomplished, we first have to explain the concept of psyche and its principal characteristic, which is emotivity;[37] secondly, we have to analyze the relations between the soma and the psyche; finally, we will conclude with the subject's emotions and the person's operativity.

Initially it should be pointed out that in Wojtyła's anthropology, "psyche" is not synonymous with "soul." Even if etymologically they are the same, this concept "psyche" cannot be compared to the "vital principle"; it will be considered under its metaphysical, not its phenomenological, aspect. Here, the concept "psyche" refers to what allows the integrity of man in the order of nature and is not corporeal or somatic. "In the concept of 'psyche' and in the adjective 'psychic' are mixed the elements of human nature and of the concrete human being that we discover in our experience of the human being as if they were in some way connected and integrated with the body, but which, at the same time, are not of themselves in the body."[38] As, in this context, the psyche is related with the body, it should not be confused with the relations soul-body or material-spirit.

Whereas the externalization of the soma is evident and constitutes an organic system having clearly differentiated parts, this does not occur with the psyche. We cannot speak of a "psychic constitution" of a man that can be compared with his corporeal con-

37. The Polish word is *"emotywność,"* which corresponds precisely to the Spanish *"emotividad."* The Acting Person renders this as "emotivity," a neologism that works better than "emotion," especially considering that the Polish suffix "-ność" has exactly the same effect as "-ity" in English.

38. PA, 321. See OC, 263; AP, 221.

stitution. The concept is elusive, the psyche having no physical or material outline to be compared with the body. The psychical functions are internal and immaterial, and therefore irreducible to the somatic. Nevertheless, they have a close relation with the soma; for that reason it is pertinent to study them in the integration of the human being in act, so much so that we cannot speak about a complete integration if the psychical part is excluded. In addition, it is appropriate to consider that the psyche's functions operate rather in the corporeal scope, as they are revealed and externalized through the body. "[T]here is a just tendency to express all the psychical functions of the human being in union with the somatic constitution, which has found ancient expression in the different conceptions of the problem of so-called temperaments."[39]

We saw that, in the integration of the soma, Wojtyła identifies "reactivity" as a principal characteristic; now, in the integration of the psyche, "emotivity" will be principal. In this context, emotivity includes the sensations, emotions, sentiments, behavior, and attitudes related to affective phenomenon. The affective range is so varied and there have been so many divisions and classifications throughout history that this very fact reveals the difficulty that its treatment supposes from an intellectual point of view. Emotivity is, by definition, different from understanding; its study, moreover, is necessary if we are to situate it adequately in anthropology.

39. PA, 323. See OC, 264; AP, 223. In relation to the temperaments, it is common to mention the Hippocratic theory of humors, better known as the study of temperaments, which even nowadays—with some changes—is useful in psychology. In this theory, Hippocrates establishes a relation among soma, psyche, Empedocles's four elements, and even the seasons of the year, with the object of determining the sort of temperaments that correspond to human beings. For a synthetic approach see Giovanni Reale and Dario Antiseri, *Historia del Pensamiento Filosófico y Científico.* [History of Philosophical and Scientific Thought.] (Barcelona: Herder, 2001), 1:114–15. The relationships between body and psyche had already been studied by the ancient Greeks. At the beginning, they thought that passions were something corporeal, with a subtle consistency but corporeal. It is Plato who moves away from this conception when he considers passions as movements of the soul. He situates them in specific organs of animals and men and says that they are the cause of illnesses (*Timaeus* 86e ff.). For a synthetic approach see Miguel Acosta, *Los afectos inferiores* (Madrid: Publicep, 2006), 18ff.

Reactivity is not the same as emotivity, although the two act together and at the natural level. Emotion is not a reaction, because psychic dynamism does not belong to and is different from the body, though it (emotion) is rooted in and conditioned by the somatic. They are two different spheres, and Wojtyła never tires of repeating that the person in act's integrity implies the complementing of the somatic dynamism and the psycho-emotional. At the same time, this integrity is complemented by the person's transcendence. We can say that there is a principle of complementarity between them.

If we consider this well-known anthropological distinction: corporeality, sensibility, spirituality—then emotivity will be situated between corporeality and spirituality, mixing with both but without being identified with sensibility.

As for corporeality, it has already been seen that reactivity acts though stimuli that allow the motor activity in the corporeal level. In the same way, emotivity reacts to those stimuli providing the "sense" effect in man,[40] which does not refer to the direct somatic effects but accompanies those corporeal movements. "This is a psychical effect, expressed in a sentiment. And although this psychical effect may be conditioned at the somatic level by some reaction, nonetheless it surpasses it completely."[41]

With regard to spirituality, when the man-person acts, he expresses his transcendence by self-governance and there is produced in him a personal emotional resonance that gives rise to a specific expressivity different from the somatic. This expressivity leaves an experiential imprint that cannot be found in the body but is situated

40. In Aristotelian-Thomistic anthropology, the external and internal senses are part of the cognitive potencies. The traditional five external senses (sight, hearing, smell, taste, and touch) have been amplified by psychology and the discoveries of neuroscience (algesia, synesthesia, hyperesthesia, kinesthetic senses, etc.) Although Wojtyła's point of departure is based on the Aristotelian-Thomistic conception, in the analysis of emotions he more closely follows Max Scheler's phenomenology; this is because the sentient is situated in the sphere of emotions and in some way includes the sensory data (sensory perceptions and cognitive sensory faculties). See PA, 336–37 and 337n3; OC, 274; AP, 232.

41. PA, 330. See OC, 269; AP, 227–28.

in the person. This is evident in the person's emotional attitude toward intangible values such as truth, goodness, and beauty. There is no doubt that emotivity also has a close relation with the spiritual realm.

With this global vision of the situation of the psyche in relation to the body and the spiritual, we are going to analyze first the relations between the soma and the psyche and then the peculiarities of the integration of the latter in the realm of corporeality.

In this sense, a first step that consists in the affective answer that accompanies motor action has already been mentioned. Such an answer is called "sensation" and it is a first level of feeling.[42] Referring to the somatic reaction, I mentioned the "subjectivity of the body," which in a certain way is independent of the "subjectivity of the person" and which is kept away from consciousness. How is it possible to integrate these two subjectivities?

When a somatic reaction is produced which is accompanied by a sensation, the sensation, which forms part of the emotivity, is what is empowered to overcome the subjectivity of the body for this experience to be included in consciousness. Wojtyła's simile is the

42. Owing to the variety of terminology with regard to the human affective side and to avoid confusion, it should be clarified that in the Spanish translation of *Person and Act* the terms "sensation" and "feeling" in a few passages are synonymous. By contrast, in the Italian version the concept of "sensation" is more clearly distinguished from "feeling." This is pertinent because some of the anthropologies related to the Aristotelian-Thomistic tradition, within the wide range of the affective classifications, tend to establish a difference amongst sensations, emotions (passions), and feelings. Sensations are acts that have a direct relation with the sensible impressions that come from the exterior or interior environment of the body through the senses and form part of the cognitive sphere (e.g., hearing sound waves or feeling a stomach ache); the emotions are affections that are closely related to the soma and that have as characteristics their intensity and brief duration and are accompanied by somatic changes (e.g., sweat and trembling in "fear"); finally, feelings are located in a higher level than emotions, and in them intelligence and will intervene directly—these are what give them a certain stability, for they are longer lasting than the emotions and they cannot be accompanied by emotional affections in a specific moment (e.g., vengeance, friendship). Wojtyła makes reference to these affective differences according to his methodology (this will be seen when we come to deal with excitement and emotion). See PA, 348, "The richness and differentiation of the world of sentiments," and PA, 349, "Some criteria for differentiating sentiments."

subject-object relationship in knowledge; the somatic aspect would be the "object" which receives the "subject" (emotivity) by means of which the consciousness is made present and is integrated as an experience of the individual. We are dealing with a psychological response that accompanies a motor response, although they occur at the same time.

The different corporeal dispositions are the origin of the sensations by which one has experience of his own body. Consciousness becomes aware of the feelings of one's own body, but in a different way from mental knowledge. That is to say, the presence of the corporeal aspects that are related to reactivity is determined by the feelings as they are manifested in consciousness. If such reactions do not enter into the field of feeling, neither will they enter into the field of consciousness. For this reason a person can become aware of his organic interior and of his interior dynamism through the sensations or feelings that are produced by organic movements. Pain, pleasure, and the state of the body's wellbeing provide the information about what happens in the subjectivity of the body. Without this mediation of the psyche, the person would not be able to realize what happens in his body, for good or for bad. How many times, only because of a sharp pain, does an illness come to light which has been developing over time, but without the person's having been aware of it? And suddenly, thanks to this information one stops to think about the cause of the pain and discovers, for example, a cancer. If the sensation were not present, one would not be able to treat the illness.[43]

Wojtyła emphasizes that the "autosensation" of man expresses a qualitative value and characteristic by means of which his general state can be evaluated, "I feel well"—"I feel bad," including his state

43. An extreme and uncommon example is that of persons who suffer congenital insensibility to pain with anhidrosis (CIPA), a pathology of the nervous system that produces a lack of sensibility to pain. It is a rare disease; those who suffer it can neither feel pain nor distinguish heat, cold, pressure, etc. In this case, the problem is located in the somatic level, where there is not the proper reactivity for the feelings to be manifested in consciousness.

of tiredness, happiness or weakness, amongst others. "The human being also feels able or unable, which shows—through psychical reflection—the meaning of ability in the reactive-motor dynamism of the body."[44] Furthermore, the way we feel psychologically because of our soma can influence other higher psychic functions. The fact that we feel tired can lead us to a reduced intellectual performance, or, on the other hand, the sensation of wellbeing helps us to have more mental agility. These are experiences that help us better to appreciate the soma-psyche interaction in the act of the person.

In the sensation of one's own body, the body and consciousness are united through the psyche. We can admit a certain predominance of consciousness (the realm of intelligence) with respect to the sensations, since owing to consciousness we have knowledge of them, whereas we have no sensation of our consciousness. This primacy of consciousness supposes a certain order and subordination of the sensations with respect to self-determination. But in certain moments, sensation can predominate in the sphere of the intelligence, up to the point of influencing choice and decision. Although such influence can be of great intensity, the structures of self-possession and self-dominion can dominate them.[45]

The last aspect mentioned is connected with the relations between feelings and intelligence. Before dealing with this let us stress that, by means of auto-sensation, Wojtyła finds another way of showing that "integration in this case is equivalent to the normal experience of one's own body, which is conditioned by sensation and by consciousness."[46] That which impedes an adequate sensation can also be considered a disintegrating factor.

Not only the emotional experience of one's own body, but also the integral experience of one's self and of one's "I" as a being-in-the-world, is present in consciousness. That is to say, the emotional sphere is not closed to the information that arrives from the cogni-

44. PA, 332–33. See OC, 271; AP, 229.
45. Here we are not considering pathological cases.
46. PA, 334. See OC, 272; AP, 231.

tive sphere—quite the opposite; they are related in such a way that the information received from the senses in the cognitive aspect also has an affective effect. We are not talking about closed spheres, and this is evident from their reflection in consciousness. Here we enter into an important aspect in the study of the integration of the psyche which has to do with the feelings and the intelligence or, as Wojtyła suggests, with "sensibility" and "truthfulness."

Sensibility, in addition to its emotional aspect, can be understood also as "the different intentional directions of human feeling, deeply rooted in man's spiritual life."[47] Let us remember that Wojtyła's study of the integration of the psyche in some points appears to be nearly identical to Scheler's phenomenological approach. In both there is a close relation between emotional experience and values.[48] Wojtyła, though, does not agree that the emotions are the only source for detecting values, as some emotionalists, including Max Scheler, maintain.[49] Scheler considers that "[e]very one of our sensations is directed to an act in the subject himself or outside him, but always with that 'inclination toward a value,'"[50] to the point that a feeling can be the way to sum up an experience of values.[51]

The problem that arises here is that if man discovers the experience of value in emotivity, there would be a primacy of the feelings in the moment of the person's act. The realm of "something happens

47. PA, 336. See OC, 274; AP, 232.
48. In an essay on Max Scheler, Wojtyła offers a definition of value that stresses that it is not the same as "good." "Rather, a value is the content given in our lived experience when we come in contact with a good—with a thing we experience as a good." Karol Wojtyła, "On the Metaphysical and Phenomenological Basis of the Moral Norm," in Person and Community, 92. In any case, Person and Act sometimes uses the word "value" as a "good."
49. In Person and Act Wojtyła does not explain the problems of emotionalization in relation to feelings (for example, by admitting that the only cognitive source of values is the emotions), because to do so would be to venture into epistemological as well as ethical issues. Our author treats the rupture of the ethical norm in Scheler's philosophy not only in his doctoral dissertation but in several of his essays. Certain approaches about this topic it can be found in Wojtyła, Person and Community, 23–44, 45–46, 73–94; and Wojtyła, Metafisica della persona, 1421–35.
50. PA, 337. See OC, 274; AP, 232.
51. PA, 337. See OC, 275; AP, 232–33. We will comment again on this point later.

in man" would condition the structures of transcendence and, consequently, self-dominion. Wojtyła rejects this position and affirms that this integration is insufficient in itself. In order not to fall into this situation, it is necessary that there be produced, at the same time, another integration through "truthfulness." Remember that the person's integration in the action refers above all to the "truth," which makes possible the authentic freedom of self-governance. The supremacy of sensibility cannot be permitted, but the very opposite. It has to be subordinated. "The penetration of sensibility in truth is a condition for the person to have experience of values."[52]

This is how we might resolve the error of anthropological emotivity. There can be authentic freedom only when self-governance is directed to truth and therefore refers to an authentic value. The grasp of a value only from the point of view of sensibility, which already ceases to be the ultimate criterion of values, is displaced to give way to a superior integration that operates on the basis of truthfulness, where a decisive signification of value is given to the person in act. For that reason, man should not exclusively rely on the way his feelings develop, but he must go through the integration of truthfulness. Wojtyła's posture in this sense is so clear that he affirms: "Self-determination and the self-governance related to it require, on occasion, that one act in the name of 'naked' truth about the good, in the name of values that are not felt. At times this even requires that one act against the perceptions of the moment."[53]

With this in mind, there is no question of denying the value or place that sensitivity and feelings have in the integration of the person in act, nor is an "intellectualist" attitude being proposed. Intelligence can discern about values but it cannot obtain greater expressive capacity than that which the emotions offer, or the proximity, intensity and concentration that these give them in experience.

Wojtyła sums up an adequate integration of the person and the

52. PA, 338 (emphasis in the original). See OC, 275; AP, 233.
53. PA, 339. See OC, 275; AP, 233.

psyche: "To the extent that one governs himself more fully and possesses himself with more maturity, to that extent he will feel all values more truly, and in his experience of those values will be reflected more deeply the order that exists among them in reality."[54]

Excitement and Emotion

In the study of the emotional nature of the human psyche, Wojtyła analyzes two emotional phenomena which are related to sensibility and about which he goes into detail using his method in order to shed new light to show the complexity of this human dimension. In his explanation we can perceive the ambiguous and subtle character of affective movements. We are talking about excitement and emotion.[55]

Thomistic tradition establishes a typology of the passions that depends upon whether the objects to which they are directed are easy and pleasurable (concupiscible desire) or arduous and difficult (irascible desire).[56] This traditional definition in Scholasticism highlights the inherent intentional sense in all sensitive appetite. An appetite can be a desire or impulse toward a concrete object perceived cognitively. However, Wojtyła recognizes a type of phenomena that lacks this intentionality and seems to respond to a certain cause in which the cognitive aspect cannot clearly be determined. It is called excitement;[57] it includes elation[58] and excitability, and it requires special treatment.

Excitement is "something which happens" in man and is different from sensation (or feeling), in that sensation has certain cogni-

54. PA, 339. See OC, 276; AP, 234.
55. Translates the Polish "wzruszenie"—rendered as "conmoción" in the original Spanish text. We ordinarily render this as "emotion," but see note 64 in this chapter.
56. Wojtyła acknowledges that this traditional classification of the Medieval Scholastics continues to be confirmed in experience. The concupiscible and irascible sentient appetites are related to the soma and act also in the realm of the will (that is, the rational appetite). On this see Aquinas, ST I-II, qq. 22–28.
57. In Polish, "podniecenie."
58. In Polish, "uniesienie."

tive intentionality of the psyche that excitement has not. Excitement cannot be identified with desire, given that desire is directed toward a concrete object whereas excitement manifests itself as being "self-sufficient," follows its own course, and is at times ambiguous. In excitement there appears to be an appetitive inclination, although, in reality it is not an appetite, but is rather an emotional-reactive characteristic. It is an emotional "activation" of the human psyche.

The characteristics of excitement seem to align with somatic reactivity, since it is exhibited with determinate conscious bodily reactions. They are somatic signs that accompany excitation as an extension to the body of something that is really psychical (heart rates, breathing, etc.).[59]

Wojtyła distinguishes between a "corporeal excitement," which is a phenomenon that produces only an emotional resonance and "psychic excitement," which is more complex. This latter includes a peculiar transmission of its effects to the body, rich in sensations that increase the experienced intensity of this excitement.

In addition, this excitement appear to have levels whose origin in some cases is not found in the stimulus of the senses, but which can originate from a value experienced beyond the senses. When we are talking about this type of experience, rather than speaking about excitement we refer to "elation," because it exhibits a spiritual nature.

Elation may or may not be accompanied by sensory, even corporeal, excitement, which could favor elation. Only if elation becomes very intense, though, would it constitute more of a hindrance by impeding its spiritual aspect.[60]

The integration we are studying should also account for this excitement and elation, which together take the name of "excitability." Excitability is the capacity for excitement that is especially rooted in human potentialities and is connected with sensitivity.[61] As I have

59. See PA, 342; OC, 278; AP, 236.
60. See PA, 343; OC, 278–79; AP, 237.
61. See PA, 343–44; OC, 279; AP, 237.

said before, it is necessary to note how "excitability" and "sensitivity" differ, since "excitability" refers to different emotional events than those to which "sensitivity" refers. Wojtyła states that excitability (and excitement, which is its nucleus and dynamic catalyst) tends to refer to a certain emotional awakening, in a sudden way; for this reason it has an "explosive" character. In this way, emotion arises in an irrational way in the manner of the passions.[62]

According to Wojtyła, excitement has its roots in human impulses, although it does not appear to meet the necessary conditions to be considered an impulse in the sense studied previously. As excitability is related to the somato-reactive stratum, where the self-preservation and reproductive impulses are located, everything points to its being due to basic forces of nature oriented to the most fundamental value, which consists in maintaining one's continued survival.[63]

In conclusion, excitability—which includes excitement (very connected with sensitivity) and elation (an aspect more distant from sensitivity and with spiritual manifestations)—is not a passion in its own right, as it does not possess cognitive intentionality; neither can it be reduced to corporeality, because it is a psychic phenomenon. More than anything, it is a diffuse and intense (explosive) reaction, which appears to be caused by the impulses of self-preservation and reproduction.

"Stirring emotion"[64] is another psycho-emotional phenomenon that makes manifest a type of peculiar affective experience. It is an experience of profound emotional impact characterized not only by its intensity but also by its radical effect on the human being. "Stirring emotion" erupts on the "surface," disposing the person af-

62. See PA, 344; OC, 279; AP, 237–38.
63. See PA, 345; OC, 280; AP, 238.
64. This phrase is used in The Acting Person, 238, to translate the Polish "wzruszenie," which the New Kosciusko Foundation Dictionary (as well as others) renders in English as "emotion," but the connotation is of deep or powerful emotion. In Spanish it is rendered by "conmoción" and in Italian by "commozione." Unfortunately, the English cognate, "commotion," of these terms has a completely different meaning.

fectively in a temporally more enduring way and overcoming other affective states, which, in comparison, seem to be lesser and momentary. Wojtyła states that stirring emotion is the point of origin and development of the emotions, which later can be eliminated although, occasionally, can be established as an "affective state."

"Stirring emotion" is different from excitement. The psyche is the clear sphere of action of "stirring emotion"; excitement also intervenes in the psyche (especially in its aspect of elation), since it is an affective phenomenon, but it has a greater relation with sensitivity and is presented as an "explosive" affection. "Stirring emotion" is more specifically psychical; because of this, Wojtyła identifies it as a source of affective movements. "Stirring emotion" can act far from sensitive movements; for this reason, profound and higher emotions can be experienced as emotions related to the spiritual life of man. "And thus there is an experience of aesthetic 'stirring emotion' tied to the contemplation of the beautiful, of cognitive 'stirring emotion' tied to the discovery of some truth, and different kinds of 'stirring emotion' tied to the sphere of moral good and evil."[65]

To order the emotions, some have proposed "levels" of depth, of inferiority or superiority, and even ways of tracing them in an immaterial space where the emotions are located in a more central or peripheral way. This kind of cognitive recourse illustrates in a certain way the differences among different emotions. "Stirring emotion" would be located in an upper zone, more central and deeper; it would be a more stable and durable form of psychic movement than a sensitive emotion,[66] which would be the emotion of passions and excitement. Wojtyła agrees with Scheler on the depth of these emotions (stirring emotions) and on their special relation with the processes of moral conscience: "The moral remorse produced by a fault is not only a judgment on oneself, but also the experience of demonstrated truth, which is, as we know from experience, an

---

65. PA, 346. See OC, 281; AP, 239.
66. In some authors there would be the difference between emotions and feelings. See García Cuadrado, *Antropología Filosófica*, 119–21.

exceptional component of 'stirring emotion.'"[67] The same experiences are verified in a personal conversion process: mental peace, joy, and profound love. None of them can be considered in the sphere of excitement, but rather they must be considered in that of "stirring emotion."

This does not mean that there is an impassable barrier between excitement and "stirring emotion"—quite the opposite, as both are emotional dynamisms that "happen in man" and are largely accomplished outside the person's operativity; one emotion can be transformed into another one. There is talk of inferior and superior emotions, and the human being is capable of achieving, for example, "sublimations" and passing from excitement to emotion.[68]

Every sentiment has its emotive marrow in the form of "stirring emotion," from which it radiates. And on the basis of the "stirring emotion," each sentiment defines itself as a totally original psychical fact. If a determined content belongs to it—and it is clear that a content corresponds to the emotions ("wzruszenia") and to the sentiments—it also belongs in an emotive manner: neither cognitive nor appetitive, but precisely emotive.[69]

Thus, we have seen some special psycho-emotional movements where the human being manifests his subjectivity in a special way. The sphere of emotions is where the tension between the human being's operativity and subjectivity are best confirmed. There is no need to be reminded of the importance that integration has in this realm of the human being so that he may accomplish his realization.

Spontaneity and Experience of Value

The passions, excitement and emotions that "occur in man" as a subject, therefore, do not form part of his personal operativity. That is to say, they act in a spontaneous manner; the human being sees himself affected and realizes that without his voluntary desire he participates despite such emotions. "In the face of this, we must ac-

67. PA, 346. See OC, 281; AP, 239. 68. See PA, 350; OC, 284; AP, 241.
69. PA, 350; OC, 284; AP, 242.

knowledge a certain operativity of the psyche at the root of the emotive dynamism, without which it would be impossible to understand everything that happens emotively in the man-subject."[70]

Emotionality, for Wojtyła, is the spontaneous efficacy of the human psyche, and with this is emphasized the idea of an activation independent of the psychic sphere in relation to self-governance. Just as in corporeality there is a sphere in which human efficacy cannot intervene, so also in the psychic sphere; there is a sphere in which the person "loses control" or should have control in an indirect manner, and then integration becomes more difficult.

In any case, this entire affective sphere does not of itself represent disintegration. As we already know, the Stoics maintained a negative vision of the emotions and desired to suppress them in order to achieve *ataraxia* or imperturbability of spirit. In modern times Kant also affirmed that for a human being to be able to act with complete liberty he should do it with the force of reason alone. According to these philosophies, emotivity represents in itself a source of disintegration that goes against the person in action. But, because they deny an important aspect of human nature, Wojtyła is opposed to approaches that try to eliminate affections as a part of self-realization, and he agrees with Aristotle's criticism of Stoic pessimism and with Scheler regarding Kant's pessimism.[71]

It is clear that the tension which exists between the spontaneity of the affective sphere and the operativity of the person makes self-realization more difficult. This is not a new topic; in traditional anthropology the opposition between the sensitive appetite and the rational appetite (will) is treated. Only seen from Wojtyła's perspective does such tension occur between subjectivity (regarding the experiential, and not as a supposed ontic, aspect) and the operativity of the person. Achievement of the person's dominion over his subjectivity is what is understood as integration, and it is not exempt from effort.

It is also necessary to consider that although the psychic effects

70. PA, 351; OC, 284; AP, 243.   71. PA, 352; OC, 285; AP, 243–44.

are manifested spontaneously, according to the type of passion, excitement, or emotion involved, these effects tend to become fixed in the experience of the "self" where the habit becomes present. A particular type of emotion can be fleeting; or, according to the habit's dynamic, by means of its intensity and repetition, it becomes more permanent and develops an interior attitude in man. "Thus, for example, the immediate and fleeting sense of anger is different from being permanently angry; the anger becomes an interior posture of the human being. We must also distinguish between a passing feeling of love or hatred and love or hate as the permanent interior stance of the human being."[72] In this type of emotional fixation the will can eventually give way and incline toward the position of such emotions presenting an "emotional attitude" of the person. This would constitute a clearly "subjectivist" attitude, as there would be a dominance of subjectivity over the operativity of the person. This subjectivity would be preponderant over the transcendence of the person and its result would lead to disintegration.

Yet, this does not lead us to conclude that the emotions constitute the cause of disintegration. As we have seen, the emotions can be in some cases an impediment and in others an incentive to action of the person. It is certain that an "emotionalization of the consciousness" can be produced,[73] but also there can be integration if the person knows how to orient these psychic movements that occur in his interior. The positive aspect is that the emotion gives a special intensity to operativity and, with this, to all of the personal structure of self-dominion and possession, but it is necessary that the person know how to direct it.

72. PA, 354. See OC, 286; AP, 245.

73. "The emotionalization of consciousness begins when the meaning of every one of the emotive acts and their objects disappears, when in a given moment, sentiments are somehow placed above comprehension on the part of the human being. This implies that self-knowledge is disrupted. As a result, consciousness no longer reflects those emotional facts as they 'happen' in the man, but it loses its relation of dominion, its objective relation with them; for it is well known that objectification in these cases is a specific function of self-knowledge." PA, 101. See OC, 102; AP, 53. For full explanation also see PA, 97–105; OC, 99–105; AP, 53–56.

Although Wojyla's intention in the analysis of emotivity does not consist in deepening or exhausting the richness of psycho-emotive life, the anthropological approach that he carries out from the person in action reveals a series of new elements for the dynamic operativity of the human being and helps us to understand the complexity and repercussions that the affections cause in the person. We have just seen this with his presentation of excitement and of emotion; now we are in a position to add another extra element that intervenes in this dynamism: the experience of value.

Emotivity is a source of spontaneous subjectivities that can act independently of the person. Moreover, it could happen that man performs acts that in reality are not the result of his operativity, as he does not perform them voluntarily, but conditioned by the subjectivity of the emotions and even by the emotionalization of consciousness. Something occurs in him, but he is not fully responsible for it. We can even arrive at pathological extremes that are not attributable to the will of the person. We are speaking about extreme cases where emotivity can oppose and destroy the operativity of the person. But what we cannot believe is that there is a clear and direct opposition between emotivity and operativity.

We already know that a large part of somatic reactivity is not directly connected to consciousness and that the perception of value is indirect; the same cannot be said of emotivity. The psychic-emotional aspect is directly related to consciousness and, I repeat, has a special force due to its value experience. This is the force that influences consciousness; it both permits a cognitive approach to the emotions and also gives experience a special subjective intensity. The experience of values can direct the emotions.

The emotions always refer to a value and proceed from this relation.[74] Value's character is not cognitive or appetitive, as we saw in the case of emotion. "We can only say that the emotions 'show' in a particular, experiential way the existence of values beyond them-

74. See PA, 357; OC, 289; AP, 248.

selves, outside of the subject who has the emotional experience."[75]
For this reason we can have an experience of a value and indirectly, in consciousness, have the experiential knowledge of the value. Even so, if an emotionalization of the consciousness is produced, the experience of value is made more difficult and its realization can even be impeded. This emotionalization confuses or distorts the value—which coincides with the good—especially when the subjectivity of a rooted emotion is imposed.[76]

Therefore, in normal situations, when an emotion arises, it is spread and spontaneously provokes a value reference. Such spontaneity tends to adapt itself to the necessities of the human psyche and is oriented to emotional realization. "Emotional fulfilment is at the same time a specific fulfilment of the very subjectivity of the human 'I'; it creates the feeling of being entirely within oneself, along with greatest closeness to the object—precisely to that value with which it is then put spontaneously into contact."[77]

In the integration of the emotions and its reference to value, the transcendent relation with the truth is also at work, along with its corresponding obligation and responsibilities. The intelligence has the role of "putting them into order," not of "opposing them"; through the ordering of the elements by intelligence, choice and decision are made. The complementarity between transcendence and integration is also clearly seen here.

The education of affectivity and its adequate orientation toward values facilitates integration. If from childhood a person is oriented toward a positive value and feels repulsion toward another, negative one, the corresponding attitude and inclination of the person's subjectivity is formed. In considering these inclinations Wojtyła ap-

75. PA, 358. See OC, 289; AP, 248.
76. "The essence of the problem is rooted in this, that the emotions ... not only have their reflection in consciousness, but also that they influence in a specific manner of their own the conscious reflection of distinct objects, beginning with the 'I' itself and its actions. The different sentiments emotionalize consciousness, which means that they insert themselves into its two functions, of reflection and reflexivity, and in some way modify its characteristics." PA, 100–101. See OC, 101–2; AP, 52–53.
77. PA, 359. See OC, 290; AP, 249.

peals to the most profound roots of nature, which go beyond the deepest emotions or the emotions in general and, at the same time, give preponderance to the knowledge of the truth.

In this sphere emotions go according to the orientation of nature, which—as we have already shown—is expressed in drives. . . . We are referring above all to the drive proper to human nature "toward" good and "against" evil. Furthermore, the attraction of repulsion of which we have treated here very generally is not defined immediately in relation to its object. To define it is the specific task and function of the person and thus pertains to the intellect, which forms the human being's cognitive reference to the truth, in this case the truth about good and evil.[78]

The education to which I referred has to do with the development of skills and abilities that facilitate the development of self-dominion and self-possession. Although this integration may take a whole life, there are moments in which it is verified more clearly, as happens in some phases in the formation of the personality (appearance of the moral conscience, puberty, old age . . .).

In every moment of the man-person's integration, the ethical aspect is present, with reference to which this study has not gone into greater detail. Although the ethical theme is not treated directly in the anthropology of the person in action, Wojtyła maintains that it is present in an underlying way throughout his work. In order to do so he refers to a mathematical resource, supposing an expression x $(a + b)$; although the variable x is outside the parenthesis, it equally affects both the variable a and the variable b; it does not become meaningless or belong to the expression because it is outside, but it is present in a common manner.[79] Ethics deserves a separate and detailed study, to which our author has dedicated many pages and years of study. Nevertheless, in his anthropology he prefers to focus on the philosophical aspects that explain the anthropological phenomenology of the person, leaving aside the x (ethics), not because

78. PA, 361–62. See OC, 292; AP, 251.

79. Wojtyła refers to the anthropology-ethics relation at PA, 42–46; OC, 59–62; and AP, 11–14. "Those elements of a mathematical function are placed before the parentheses which are in some way are found in all elements of the polynomial and are a

it is not important, but because he prefers to focus on the aspect in brackets (the anthropology). Anthropology and ethics go together and interpenetrate each other.

Thus, in the sphere of action of virtues and skills that are reinforced by human strengths and affect the transcendence and integration of the person, ethics is directly present. "The integration of the person in act on the basis of the emotivity [emotionality] proper to the human psyche is realized through abilities which, from the ethical point of view, are called virtues."[80]

At this point, the key concepts of Karol Wojtyła's philosophical anthropology have been almost totally analyzed. With the integration of the person in action, we have tried to show the great unifying task of the "diverse complexity of the human being"[81] and how it constitutes a complementary aspect of transcendence. We can say that in the study of the man-person conducted from the experience of his operativity, we have realized the importance of the unity of the natural dynamisms and the personal structures in order to achieve our own self-realization and, ultimately, our happiness. There is lacking, however, a central point, which Wojtyła addresses in the last part of Person and Act, titled "Participation," since it manifests the character of man's openness toward others. The central idea is that we are not isolated beings but each of us is a being-with-another.

To finish with integration, before revising the related concepts with the participation of the person in action, and to respect the explanation of our author, we shall summarize some ideas that were introduced in the final paragraphs of the study of transcendence. This summary concerns integration and the soul-body relation.

---

common factor for those elements that remain within the parenthesis. Excluding the common factor has for its object the facilitation of the operations; it does not at all seek to eliminate the element found outside the parenthesis nor to break the relationship that exists between that element and [the] part found within the parenthesis. Quite to the contrary, when the common factor is excluded its presence and importance for the entire operation remains particularly evident." AP, 45–46. See OC, 61–62; AP, 13. "It is a matter of separating the essentially ethical problematic from the essentially anthropological." PA, 46n4. See OC, 62n4; AP, 301n4.

80. PA, 363. See OC, 293; AP, 252.   81. PA, 367. See OC, 296; AP, 255.

Wojtyła recalls that all the complexity of the psycho-somatic structures which we have seen is not equivalent to discovering the adequate relation between soul and body or vice versa, which can only be discovered in the total experience of man.[82]

In the integration of the soma and the psyche we have attempted to deepen the understanding of the dynamisms that come to us through human experience. These dynamisms, which have their roots in the natural potential of man, are intimately related with the person and his transcendence. For this reason they find a place in the structure of self-possession and self-dominion, just as we have been analyzing. But understanding this panorama does not mean perceiving the body-soul relation in the human being. We have already said that man does not have a direct experience of his soul, and neither is the experience of transcendence of the person in action an equivalent of it. No direct experience of the soul can be found in the integration of the person in action.

Nevertheless, one can say that in both there is an intuitive content that includes the reality of the soul and its relation with the body. For example, while the body is the source of reactive dynamism and of emotional dynamism, the integration of these two claims a common origin in the transcendence of the person. Wojtyła asks if the soul is the transcendent beginning and the origin of the integration of the person. "Under this aspect, the subordination of integration to the transcendence of the person in act is very significant. Its complementarity is significant. This fact tells us much, that the human being as a person may be at once that which possesses and governs himself and is also that which is possessed and subordinated to itself."[83]

All of this "prepares the way" and brings us closer to an understanding of the soul-body relation, although we cannot comprehend this relation. To proceed further into the reality of the soul-body relation it would be necessary to undertake metaphysical reflection.

82. See PA, 367–68; OC, 296–97; AP, 256–57.
83. PA, 370. See OC, 299; AP, 257.

II ∾

PARTICIPATION

Intersubjectivity and Participation

The last chapter of *Person and Act* studies a characteristic of the person that can appear to be a side issue, but that in reality is unavoidable in Karol Wojtyła's anthropology. This characteristic deals with the intersubjectivity of the person through participation or, what is the same, the person who acts together with other people. Man is not an isolated being and, although his acts can be individualized and even personalized, as has been seen throughout these pages, it is evident that the human being "acts together with" other human beings. His action is "affected by" and, at the same time, "has an effect on" other people's actions. Here there is stressed the idea that the intersubjectivity of the person in action is achieved through participation, which is not an accidental but a fundamental and determining attribute in the realization of the man-person.

In his chapter, Wojtyła does not intend to focus either on the sociological analysis or on founding the bases to explain society or the community; his objective is rather to broaden the field of "the person's action" or "the persons' action in community." While it is true that the dynamic interrelationship of person and action is a fundamental relation in itself, it is possible to add one more ele-

This chapter has been translated from Spanish by Ángela Gimeno Nogués and Paul Gordon.

ment that is not foreign to the already stated interpersonal relationship, but rather is, in some way, included in it—included, because it starts from the basic idea that man is a social being by nature.[1] From this point of view, Wojtyła could not omit the analysis of the interpersonal relationship and, although he himself admits that it is an introductory approximation, he offers some concepts that provide a suitable framework for understanding the anthropological basis of the action of the person who lives in society.

We must, here at the beginning of this study, emphasize again the fundamental value that the action undertaken by the person has in itself. This value is intrinsic to the realization of the act; therefore it differs from the moral values that arise once the action has been carried out according to a norm. The value of the acting person is prior to and manifests self-determination; Wojtyła calls it "personalistic value."[2] This "personalistic value," inherent in the realization of the person's action, contains a number of values related to the transcendence or the integration of the person, and although, for example, we talk about spheres of integration in the soma and the psyche, all the values implicit in these realms condition the self-determination as an action of the whole person. The personalistic value synthesizes the rest of the acting person's values.

Although "*operari sequitur esse*," and according to this the person and his value is anterior and more fundamental with respect to the value of the act, nevertheless the person manifests himself simultaneously by his act.... [T]he personalist value of the act, strictly linked to its *realization* by the person, is of itself the origin and concrete basis of both the knowledge of the person's value and of the very values that are found in the person according to their specific hierarchy.[3]

In the previous chapter it was said that value has a relationship of dependency with the action of the person, but the "personalis-

---

1. See Aristotle's classic definition *zoon politikón*—ζῷον πολιτικόν in *Politics* 1253 a2–3.
2. See PA, 379; OC, 304; AP, 264.
3. PA, 380. See OC, 305; AP, 265.

tic value" is prior to the moral or axiological values. The aforementioned value is analyzed at an ontological level that affects moral values. Undoubtedly there is a relation between the two, because there must be an action in order for there to be an ethical value, but here Wojtyła is referring to the fact that one must first determine if there has really been operativity, self-determination, and responsibility on the part of the person; that is, if the man-person has really carried out an action. Therefore, "the personalistic value" cannot be identified with "moral value"; the terms indicate different aspects. They cannot be radically separate, though, since every personalistic value points to the self-realization of the person, which in essence means acting morally and avoiding the evil that prevents one's non-realization.

This reflection about the personalistic value and its distinction from moral value aims to highlight the richness contained in human action. In fact, traditional anthropology attributes self-determination to the will; however, in Wojtyła's anthropology the volitional content is understood in part as the effect of the will as a natural power and faculty, but beyond that, it displays the entire structure of self-control and self-possession that horizontal and vertical transcendence allow. This anthropology complements the traditional anthropology by more clearly revealing the nature-person complementarity. Wojtyła highlights a practical application of this reality: "The analysis of human acting conducted at the level of the will as a faculty seems to limit the significance of the act both insofar as pertains to its ontology as to its axiology, as well as to its 'ethical axiology'. Furthermore, at times it could seem as though the act had only an instrumental significance, with respect to the ethical order."[4] By contrast, the personalistic idea of action shows the authenticity of the personalistic value, which is not in itself ethical, "but it flows from the dynamic interiority of the person; it reveals and confirms it. And consequently it allows us better to understand ethical values in

4. PA, 383. See OC, 307; AP, 266.

their strict relationship with the person and with the totality of the 'world of persons.'"[5]

Nevertheless, what happens with the personalistic value of a man when he enters into relationships and interacts with other men? Here arises the phenomenon of participation that deserves an approach according to Wojtyła's methodology. First of all, we will look at what is meant by participation and then consider its relation with personalistic value.

The classical definition of person refers to his rational and social nature. Wojtyła's anthropology does not deny those essential notes but assumes them, but it must explain them from the perspective of the act. Specifically, to reflect about social nature from the act, he resorts to the concept of "participation" (etymologically: "to take part"). The action of the person in social life requires the cooperation or the participation with others. Before going on, we need to clarify what is meant by "participation," as this concept has a long philosophical and theological history that has different nuances and applications. In this anthropology, the concept "participation" indicates that man, when acting with others, keeps the personalistic value of his own action and at the same time affects the realization and results of the common action.[6]

Participation, as Wojtyła sees it, is an attribute of the person, "that innermost and homogeneous feature which determines that the person existing and acting together with others does so as a person."[7] The expression has substance, since it implies that the person constitutes himself thanks to the participation within his own being. Therefore participation is a specific and fundamental attribute of the person. This assertion is completely opposed to the idea of the person as some kind of a monad, closed in on himself and self-sufficient; the man-person is an open and inter-subjective being that cannot self-realize itself without the action of other men. Moreover,

5. Ibid. See *OC*, 307; *AP*, 266–67.
6. See *PA*, 385–86; *OC*, 309–10; *AP*, 268–69.
7. *PA*, 387. See *OC*, 310; *AP*, 269.

an adequate self-knowledge allows a greater understanding of human intersubjectivity.[8] In this manner, we can perceive that participation has a sense of directedness toward others, but at the same time of a fundamental attribute of the person.[9]

Participation has an intrinsic correspondence with transcendence and integration. On the other hand, when a kind of cooperation is established with others in which there is not any participation, the person's actions are deprived of their personalistic value.

In the act itself, acting "together with others" corresponds to the person's transcendence and integration in the act when the human being chooses what others choose or even when *he chooses because others choose*, always because he sees in the chosen object a value in some way his own and homogeneous. To this is linked self-determination which, in the case of action "together with others," contains and expresses participation.[10]

If participation is so decisive for the person, we infer that in some way the normative principle is true, not as a simple theoretical concept but as a practical one, too. That is to say, every man should try to exercise his action "along with others" to achieve his realization; and also, the entire human community must ensure that its members are self-realized through participation. Strictly speaking, this is not an ethical norm but a norm that establishes the necessary conditions for the person to participate with the full exercise of his self-determination. It would be like the norm that safeguards his self-determination.[11]

With these foundations, Wojtyła deduces that, since the personalistic value conditions the ethical order in action, the person not only must act according to such an ethical order, but also has "the fundamental and 'natural' right of the person [that is, the right

8. In *Person and Act*, Wojtyła comments on the discussions that arose concerning this concept, although there was positive acceptance of it. See PA, 387n2; OC, 310n74; AP, 316n77.

9. Likewise, other persons also help us to know ourselves better, because they see us "from outside," which is a perspective that we will never be able to have from our individuality.

10. PA, 388–89. See OC, 311; AP, 270.

11. PA, 390. See OC, 312; AP, 272.

that results from the fact of being a person] to realize actions and to realize himself in those actions."[12] In this way, the importance of persons' action in society can be seen more clearly. Their self-realization depends on their action, and their action is "together with others." In this regard, two obstacles can arise that prevent the fulfillment of this objective. On the one hand, there is the difficulty that comes from the particular person who is not capable of joining a society with his actions, who isolates himself. And on the other hand, there is the difficulty that comes from the community that cannot allow for the possibilities of the action of its members, the people. These are two possible sources of frustration for personal action. Let's see how they may occur.

Individualism and Totalitarianism

Considering the two difficulties that prevent the self-realization of the acting person, Wojtyła identifies two systems that have continually emerged throughout history: individualism and totalitarianism (or anti-individualism). In individualism, the individual is the supreme good to which all interests in society must be subordinated. In totalitarianism, it is the individual or individuals who must be unconditionally subordinate to the good of society. These are two extremes, which nevertheless have in common that they go against the person by limiting participation, since they hinder the person's action "together with others" and their way of living in community.

In individualism, the person is isolated because he focuses on himself and on his own good. This isolation limits (or prevents) participation in the personalistic sense. In individualism, living "together with others" represents a difficulty, a brake, a limitation. Other people are an obstacle to reaching one's own aims and therefore they represent a danger for what one considers his "realiza-

---

12. PA, 390–91. See OC, 312; AP, 270.

tion." In this manner, individualism encounters people and considers them an impediment to its objectives.[13]

In totalitarianism, there is also a denial of the participation that we are studying. Wojtyła calls it "inverted individualism," inasmuch as its principal characteristic consists in "being protected" from the individual. Here, the individual is the enemy too, not for another individual but for the whole of society. Totalitarianism presupposes that each individual seeks only his own wellbeing, that his action is opposed to any participation and cooperation, and that the lives of others are indifferent and alien to him. For that reason, the only way to achieve the common good in society is to limit the individual. Therefore, wellbeing, for totalitarianism, is opposed to the individual's desires and to the good that he can freely choose. Hence, totalitarianism also does not fit in with the concept of personalistic participation. It restricts the conditions of actions in such a way that it limits that "freedom of action" and, in general, does so in a coercive manner.

Individualism is a matter of safeguarding the good of the individual in the face of the community; in totalitarianism—as various historical experiences will confirm—it is a matter of being protected from the individual in the name of a peculiarly conceived common good. But at the root of these two orientations, of both systems of thought and behavior, we find the same manner of thinking about the human being.[14]

13. When Buttiglione comments on this part of Wojtyła's work, he brings up Sartre's maxim: "hell is other people," which could very well synthesize the point of view of individualism. See Buttiglione, *Karol Wojtyła: The Thought*, 171. At the antipodes of Sartrian thought is Lévinas and his philosophical proposal about the "Other." Although Wojtyła and Lévinas concur in their valuation of the "Other," their approaches are different, Julia Urabayen says: "Lévinas criticizes Western humanism and proposes the humanism of the other, in which he stresses the absolute responsibility for the other. Wojtyła, on the contrary, begins in the acting person and tries to complete the classic perspective. Thereby he delivers an image of man that emphasizes his conscience, his capacity for action, his self-determination and self-possession and, finally, his transcendence and his participation in the community." Julia Urabayen, "Emmanuel Lévinas y Karol Wojtyła: Dos comprensiones de la persona y una misma defensa del ser humano" [Emmanuel Levinas and Karol Wojtyła: Two understandings of the person and a single defense of human beings], *Persona y Derecho* 56 (2007): 409–42.

14. PA, 393. See OC, 314–15; AP, 275.

We can call this way of understanding man "impersonalistic" or "antipersonalistic" due to the fact that it is opposed to the adequate form of participation that corresponds to it. Needless to say, it also confronts the personalistic value that implies freedom of action. For this reason, the anthropological position of Wojtyła directly opposes these two kinds of social systems. For him, society must take care of the ethical order that allows freedom of action, since only moral good enables the realization of the person, whereas moral evil is always a non-realization. From this we can also deduce that man has the freedom and the right of action, but is not entitled to do evil. Only then is the personalistic value protected.[15]

Communities of Existence and Communities of Action

United with the concept of "participation" is that of "community," the opposite of what happens in the anti-personalisms (individualism and totalitarianism). Participation is a constitutive factor of human community, where the expression "together with others" applies more properly.

Wojtyła explains that, in a community, each person is a member and, according to the relation that they maintain amongst themselves, members can express their condition, e.g., what kind of member that person is: if they are members of a family there is a "kinship" that identifies fathers, mothers, daughters and sons, etc. As members of a national group they are "compatriot," as, belonging to a state, one is a "citizen." Depending on the type of association and based on the principles on which societies are established, relations with their own characteristics arise. This is studied in a specialized way in sociology.

Once this point is understood, it is easier to grasp the difference that exists between a "community of existence" and a "community

15. See PA, 394. See OC, 315; AP, 275–76.

of action." The "community of existence" highlights a more stable and intense common link, depending on the type of factor that binds people together and to which group they belong (family, city, country, among others). On the other hand, the "community of action" refers to the way of acting in a community whose links are given by an aim that brings its members together into that community. The terms "apprentice," "assistant," and foreman refer to a kind of relation established in a group according to the type of operation that each performs. The emphasis is on the action, although logically, the existence in common that is the community of existence is implied: the community of existence always conditions the community of action.

If we focus our analysis on the community of action, we can distinguish two aspects that are important to highlight participation. Wojtyła gives the examples of a team of workers digging a trench and a group of students attending a conference. They are two communities of action. In each, an objective meaning can be observed— that is, what is proposed as a common aim: digging a trench (that may be part of a bigger aim: building a foundation) and learning something about the subject of the conference. These aims define the community in which persons act together. But in addition to this "objective" aspect detected in the community of action, there also arises, from the point of view of a person and his action, a "subjective" aspect that is the "participation." The important thing here is to know whether that person, "in acting, completes an authentic act and realizes himself in the act. Because participation consists in this."[16]

This "subjective" aspect is key in every community of action. Let us remember that participation presupposes choice because this is inherent to it, even when the person chooses what others choose (and sometimes because others choose it); even in this case, one adheres to the choice others have made because he sees his own good

16. PA, 399. See OC, 319; AP, 279.

and sees that, through those actions chosen by others, he will reach his self-realization as a person. It is then that there is participation when it is said that there is "cooperation" in a community. It is not only acting "together with others"; this aspect indicates only the objective aim of the community. Rather the aim of the community must include participation to reach the subjective aim. There are many communities, both of existence and of action, that remain in the objective level and never pass to the subjective.[17]

Authentic Attitudes and Non-authentic Attitudes

The way to consider society and participation goes beyond acting and existing "together with others"; it is also necessary to pay attention to the "common good" or, to be more precise, to the "good of the community." In this sense, Wojtyła holds a reinterpretation of the "common good" concept that will especially illuminate the analysis of authentic or non-authentic attitudes that we will see in this section.[18]

It is insufficient to identify the common good with the common objective of action performed by a group of people who constitute a community. Let us recall the example of the workers and their objective of digging a trench and the students and their goal of learning about the subject of the conference. It is necessary to add the other moment, called the "subjective aspect." "We need to understand the common good in a twofold sense, at once objective and subjective. The subjective meaning of common good is intimately related to participation as a property of the person and his act. In this approach we can also maintain that the common good is something that responds to the social nature of the human being."[19]

In line with the methodology of *Person and Act*, Wojtyła has intended not to stop in the ethical and axiological field, although at

17. See PA, 399–400; OC, 319; AP, 279–80.
18. See PA, 400n3; OC, 320n75; AP, 316n78.
19. PA, 401–2. See OC, 321; AP, 281–82.

this point he recognizes that this task is especially difficult when it comes to "the common good," since it is a concept directly associated with the ethical. In order to concentrate his analysis, he highlights once more that his objective is to know the personalistic structure of human existence inside every community to which man belongs.

The common good creates the conditions for social existence in an axiological sense. It belongs primarily to the sphere of the being "together with others"; but, from the point of view of the action of the person "together with others" only, this aspect is insufficient to discover the whole reality that comprises the so-called common good. The members of the community not only aspire to reach the common aim but also manifest forms of participation adequate to the members of a community of action, and this is because they want to develop as persons.[20] It matters not only that the aim is achieved but how it is achieved.

Moreover, it is important to distinguish the type of community we are speaking about, as not all of them are the same. This is noticeable, for example in the number of members comprising a community or how long the community lasts. Thus, the type of participation is different whether the community of action is sporadic or more stable over time. For example, a family or the citizens of a state require a much deeper common good, because their aims have a long life span. In this way, it can be said that the most stable communities are the communities of existence that, responding to the social nature of man, are also called natural societies. In these cases participation is stronger and more necessary. Consequently, if a member will not come to participate in them adequately, their realization may be affected in a more serious way than in the temporary communities of action. And the contrary: when members thoroughly participate in them they are capable of making sacrifices, willingly giving up the individual good for the good of the community.

20. See PA, 402; OC, 321; AP, 283.

On the other hand, the priority of the common good over individual goods derives not only from the quantitative aspect of the members of a community; what matters is the intrinsic character that determines the very nature of the common good that is given in participation as a quality of the person and act. That is what constitutes the foundations of every authentic human community.[21] We must also keep in mind the personalistic value of the community members.

After making this basic approach to the requirements of the common good, we can talk about the two attitudes that are manifested in favor of and against action in community. Wojtyła calls them "authentic attitudes" and "non-authentic attitudes." The study of these will be, as in the case of the common good, pre-ethical in relation to the personalistic meaning of the actions. We will introduce briefly three authentic attitudes: solidarity, opposition, and dialogue. Later, we will look at two non-authentic attitudes, which are conformity and evasion.

Solidarity is "a constant disposition to accept and fulfill the part which falls to each one as participant in a specific community."[22] One does what the community expects him to do as a member of the group, having in mind the benefit of all: for the common good. The member who shows solidarity sees not only his own part of the task, but also the common benefit of the other members' parts.

What is highlighted above all in solidarity is "complementarity," more than the division of parts, since one must evaluate and be disposed to complete what other members of the community do. This complementarity is an intrinsic feature of participation and allows it to be seen why solidarity is one of its manifestations. "In virtue of this attitude the human being finds his own realization in realizing others."[23] A person always needs the support and help of other members of the community and vice versa. This disposition forms part of acting "together with others" and, as will be seen later, this

21. See PA, 403; OC, 322; AP, 283.   22. PA, 405. See OC, 323; AP, 285.
23. PA, 406. See OC, 324; AP, 285.

disposition is more easily acquired when we discover the meaning of the concept "neighbor."

Solidarity does not mean doing the other's part, as if that were the important thing. Quite the opposite: solidarity establishes parts wherein each member must carry out his own part and, at the same time, respect the parts belonging to others, because it is in these where participation takes place. "To take over that part of the obligations that do not belong to me is fundamentally contrary to community and participation."[24] In any case, we need not be radical. We must take into account that, under certain circumstances, collaboration could be necessary, and, in this case, devoting oneself exclusively to his own part could constitute a lack of solidarity. The framework for action is given by the common good; with this pattern, one can evaluate the way of acting in solidarity. All of this can help judge which is the adequate way of participation by members of the community.

Opposition, in the sense of an authentic attitude, accompanies solidarity. It is a manifestation by a member of the community who does not agree with the methods being used to reach the common good; he does not, however, on that account reject his condition as a member of the community. An attitude of authentic opposition manifests one's search for a place within the community, the search for some type of participation and common good that allow him to improve and deepen what is his own. We may consider the examples of disagreement between parents relating to their children's education or among politicians who oppose each other because they consider that their proposals are better for the welfare of the state. These are forms of "constructive" opposition, and legitimate in themselves, because it is normal that there are differences in points of views and in the alternative solutions to problems. The action is carried out among free and intelligent people where there can be numerous forms of addressing the common good. "The human

24. Ibid.

community possesses a proper structure when just opposition not only has the right of citizenship in it, but also the efficacy that the common good and the right of participation require."[25] To resolve these situations of solidarity and opposition, another authentic attitude is necessarily suggested—that is, dialogue.

Dialogue has several meanings, one of them being the way of acting that serves "to constitute and consolidate human solidarity, even by way of opposition."[26] Since the common good is something dynamic, it has to support the attitude of solidarity without denying opposition. Therefore, dialogue is presented as the most appropriate attitude to arrive at what is best. Opposition cannot be such that it hinders coexistence or cooperation among men. It is very easy to fall into confrontations and disputes, but when seeking for goodness and truth it is possible to bring forth ideas appropriately. Here, dialogue has an important function: pave the way toward the realization of the common good.

For the attitudes mentioned to be really authentic, they need to be supported by participation and transcendence of the acting person. The solidarity and opposition are authentic if they respect the personalistic value that is always dynamically subordinated to the truth. Verification of the personalistic value occurs in the upright moral conscience "which guarantees the dynamic and vitality of participation to the common good."[27]

On the other hand, we cannot deny or close our eyes to the threats that undermine the authenticity of attitudes of solidarity or opposition. Wojtyła calls these other attitudes "non-authentic."[28] The non-authentic attitudes arise out of deviating from solidarity and opposition, for they lack the intrinsic principles that allow participation and the personalistic value. Through the non-authentic attitudes, solidarity becomes conformism and opposition turns into a lack of commitment or evasion. In both cases, the authenticity is broken.

"In general, the term 'conformism' expresses the resemblance or

---

25. PA, 407. See OC, 325; AP, 287. 26. PA, 408. See OC, 325; AP, 287.
27. PA, 409. See OC, 326–27; AP, 288.

assimilation to the others, which is in itself a natural process and in particular conditions is positive, as well as creative and constructive."[29] The problem arises when it begins to be oriented toward servility; it then comes to have a negative sense, and we are dealing with a lack of solidarity and an elimination of opposition. In this change of attitude, the human being stops participating in the community and rather allows himself to be carried along by the crowd. It can be said that he stops being an "acting person" and becomes a "subject of what happens." The attitude is non-authentic because, with it, personal transcendence weakens, owing to the lack of self-determination and choice. The problem lies not in the submissive attitude but in the fundamental rejection of realizing oneself by acting "together with others"; through this rejection, the "man-person in a way consents to the community's depriving him of himself."[30]

In conformity we see a renouncing of true participation in the community; the person loses the opportunities to intervene creatively. His acting together with others is superficial and external, and he does not adopt positions of conviction, and of course he is not geared toward his own self-realization, nor toward that of others. The individual does not act in a truthful manner but adopts masks, in order to go unnoticed in the community, and performs individualistically. This individualism leads him to take immediate advantages from his action in the community, limiting himself to his own advantage, which eventually ends up harming the common good and even his own fulfillment.

For its part, evasion is the attitude of absence of commitment and is related to conformity. If conformity evades opposition, evasion "evades" conformity—in a negative sense. It is a "withdrawal" that initially can seem an attitude of protest and nonconformity; but in reality it does not reach that because it does not care for participation or the community.[31]

28. In Polish, "nie-autentyczne."   29. PA, 410. See OC, 327; AP, 289.
30. PA, 411. See OC, 328; AP, 290.
31. Wojtyła also analyzes the case in which that evasion is presented as a kind of re-

Neighbor and Love

At this point, after analyzing authentic and non-authentic attitudes, Wojtyła leads us to an even deeper and more radical stratum of participation of the person who acts "together with others." We have seen the characteristic of the person as a "member of the community" relative to participation, but there is still another form of participation, in which the person's action "together with others" is more absolute. To understand this we must unravel the significance of the concept "neighbor." This concept "makes us notice and value in the human being that which does not depend on his belonging to any kind of community. It brings us to notice and value in him something more absolute."[32]

When speaking about "neighbor" we have to prescind from all the person's relations with any particular community to embrace a type of relation that acquires a universal meaning. Let us explain the reason. Through this concept we realize that the "humanity of man" that every human being possesses is the same as one's own. Therefore, the relation that I have with another is based not in the common aims of a community but in the common nature of the community members. From this point of view, every frontier that tries to delimit one or another community is eliminated, for there is no separation; the neighbor is every man, because the common character of mankind is stressed.

How does participation figure in speech about our neighbor? The neighbor's participation shows that man is able to participate not only in a community but in the humanity of others. "Every participation in a community is based on this and, at the same time, finds its personal meaning through the capacity to participate in the humanity of every human being. And it is precisely this that the concept 'neighbor' indicates."[33]

jection of the social system in the form of a "withdrawal"; ultimately, though, evasion leads one to stop seeking his realization in community and rather to distance himself from it. See PA, 412–13; OC, 328–29; AP, 291.

32. PA, 415; OC, 329–30; AP, 293.   33. PA, 416. See OC, 331; AP, 294.

The concept "member" of a community shows a specific form of participation when the person acts "together with others"; the concept "neighbor" makes us see clearly the entire meaning of participation. Both concepts express, in different ways, the personal and social nature of man. It is not appropriate to consider them as independent terms, for they point to intimately related concepts. "Member" and "neighbor" name types of participation that manifest different aspects of the human social condition and are, at the same time, both based in man's social nature. For this reason, in the consideration of the participation of the person who acts "together with others" these concepts complement each other.

This co-penetration in the subjective order of participation has a special significance. Let us see briefly how our author expounds this. Participation as a person's dynamic property manifests itself in the execution of actions "together with others." In participation, cooperation and coexistence contribute to the person's realization, because participation is associated with the community and with personalistic value. It therefore manifests the membership of a community and then, thanks to that membership, it reaches the humanity of each human being. "Only through this interrelationship in humanity itself, to which the concept 'neighbor' refers, does the dynamic property of participation attain its personal depth and universal dimension."[34] It is then when participation serves the individual person's realization and the realization of the other persons within the community, "thanks to" their condition as community members. This dynamic can be extended to any community in which men act and exist.

Regarding the reflection on the neighbor, Wojtyła finishes his work by referring to "the commandment of love." This consideration does not have as an objective to show any ethical or theological meaning, but arises naturally when one notices how the status of "neighbor" sustains the authentic status of community "mem-

34. PA, 417. See OC, 332; AP, 295.

ber." He proposes to show "in a sufficiently expressive and coherent way that, in any acting and existing 'together with others,' the system of reference 'neighbor' is of fundamental significance."[35] This is achieved when the words neighbor and "I" are juxtaposed: you shall love "your neighbor as yourself."

The focus of the concept "neighbor" surpasses any other foundation of the human community, because of its scope, simplicity, and depth. It allows the concept of "participation" not to be left on the threshold of community "member" but to be universally extended. This shows that the idea of "neighbor" is prior to, superior to, and transcendent in regard to "member" inasmuch as it points out the adequate hierarchy of values according to the principle of humanity, something that does not happen with the idea of member. All of this is indirectly contained in the evangelical commandment of love.[36] "The commandment 'you shall love' has a thoroughly communitarian content. It treats of what conforms to the community, but above all reveals what makes the community fully human. It treats of what makes participation particularly alive."[37]

So, we see how there is highlighted the co-penetration that there has to be in the condition of neighbor and of member of a community. Their complementarity is necessary, and their separation is inadmissible, because it could lead to total alienation. Karol Wojtyła's experiences under totalitarian regimes are revealed in his reflection about alienation and his profound concern for the "social question." His deep concern would not allow him to detach the latter part of his work from the anthropological framework to point out its intimate connection with the social aspect, so convinced was he that personal realization can be achieved only in a community that recognizes the personalistic value, and not to do so only favors opportunities for alienation.

Our author recalls that philosophies from the nineteenth and

35. Ibid. See OC, 333; AP, 295.   36. See PA, 418. See OC, 333; AP, 295.
37. PA, 418. See OC, 333; AP, 295.

the twentieth centuries have interpreted alienation as the separation of man with respect to humanity; in this work alienation is understood in terms of personalistic value. The participation in the other's humanity becomes clouded when the idea of neighbor is blurred. The main causes of the dehumanization that leads to alienation come from (a) forgetting the real depth of participation that the term "neighbor" indicates and (b) forgetting the idea of the interrelation and mutual subordination of human beings in their humanity, rather than in different theses on "nature," "the production system," or "civilization."[38] Alienation can be avoided and the community strengthened if the ultimate criterion for the development of coexistence and cooperation of men is "neighbor."[39] If this aspect is neglected, first the person will be affected and then the damage will inevitably be extended to the whole community. The commandment of love emphasizes these ideas in relation to participation when it focuses on the "neighbor"; at the same time, the idea of neighbor displays the adequate foundation for the relation between person and community, as well as the truth in the affirmation of the social nature of the human being.

Finally, it is appropriate to note synthetically that participation, as a propriety of the acting human being, is at the root of two different dimensions of human intersubjectivity:

The first of these [dimensions] is that which we find in the "person to person" relationship [I-thou, soi-autrui]; the second is that which we find in the "we" relationship [community, Gemeinschaft]. Each of these forms of intersubjectivity requires its own analysis, because participation understood as the simple capacity for participating in the humanity of another person [neighbor] is one thing, and another is participation as being regularly a member of distinct communities [societies] in which the human being has to exist and act "together with others."[40]

The commandment "you shall love" sheds light on the reality of the human being who participates in the community and is thus also

38. See PA, 419–20; OC, 334; AP, 350.
39. See ibid.; OC, 334; AP, 351
40. PA, 420n4. See OC, 334n76; AP, 297 and 354n79.

presented as a task that must be carried out by every person and every community if they are to attain their realization.

In the "concluding words" of *Person and Act*,[41] our author notes that he is aware that this last chapter about the "Intersubjectivity by participation" is an outline and not a fully developed conception. However, he wished to include it in order to point out the necessity of showing the experience of the man who acts "together with others" in a wider conception of the acting person. He leaves open the study of approaches different from his for investigating the acting person's participation or for discovering new personal dimensions.

Lastly, he mentions that there are other "troubling" issues that deserve careful consideration, such as the "existential condition" of man, his condition of being or existing, and the truth about his limitations and his ontic contingency. In any case, his intention was not to develop a metaphysical conception of man, a theory of the person as being. "And yet, the human being who is manifest as a person in the way that we have intended to show in these analyses so far seems sufficiently to confirm that his ontological 'status' does not exceed the boundaries of contingency: *esse contingens*."[42]

Of course, what he has made clear is the profundity of study of the person that can be attained from the perspective of the action.

41. See PA, 423; OC, 337–38; AP, 299ff. and 355ff.
42. PA, 425. See OC, 338; AP, 300.

BIBLIOGRAPHY

Works of Karol Wojtyła

Aby Chrystus się nami posługiwał. Kraków: Wydawnictwo Znak, 2009.

The Acting Person. Edited by Anna-Teresa Tymieniecka. Translated by Andrzej Potocki. Boston, Mass.: D. Reidel, 1979.

El don del amor. Escritos sobre la familia. Edited by Alejandro Burgos. Translated by Antonio Esquivias and Rafael Mora. Madrid: Palabra, 2001.

El hombre y su destino. Ensayos de antropología. Translated by Pilar Ferrer. Madrid: Palabra, 2003.

"In Search of the Basis of Perfectionism in Ethics." In *Person and Community: Selected Essays,* translated by Teresa Sandok, 45–46. New York: Peter Lang, 1993. Originally published as "W poszukiwaniu podstaw perfekcjoryzmu w etyce." *Roczniki filozoficzne* 5, no. 4 (1955–1957): 303–17. SPANISH EDITION: "En busca de una base para el perfectivismo en la ética." In *Mi visión del hombre. Hacia una nueva ética,* translated by Pilar Ferrer, 135–152. Madrid: Ediciones Palabra, 2003.

Lecciones de Lublin. Translated by Rafael Mora. Vol. 1. Madrid: Ediciones Palabra, 2014.

Love and Responsibility. Translated by H. T. Willetts. San Francisco, Calif.: Ignatius Press, 1993. SPANISH EDITION: *Amor y responsabilidad.* Translated by Jonio González and Dorota Szmidt. Madrid: Palabra, 2008.

Lubliner Vorlesungen. Translated by Anneliese D. Spranger and Edda Wiener. Stuttgart-Degerloch: Seewald Verlag, 1981. Originally published as *Wykłady Lubelski.* Lublin: Towarzystwo Naukowe KUL, 2006.

Max Scheler y la ética cristiana. Translated by Gonzalo Haya. Madrid: BAC, 1982. Originally published as *Ocena możliwości zbudowanie etyki chrześcijańskiej: przy założeniach systemu Maksa Schelera.* Vatican City: Librería Editrice Vatiana, 1980.

Metafisica della persona: Tutti le opera filosofiche e saggi integrative. Edited by Giovanni Reale. 3rd ed. Milan: Bompiani, 2005.

Mi visión del hombre. Hacia una nueva ética. Translated by Pilar Ferrer. Madrid: Ediciones Palabra, 2003.

"On the Metaphysical and Phenomenological Basis of the Moral Norm." In *Person and Community: Selected Essays*, translated by Teresa Sandok, 73–94. New York: Peter Lang, 1993.

Osoba i czyn: oraz inne studia antropologiczne. Lublin: Towarzystwo Naukowe KUL, 2000.

Perché l'uomo. Scritti inediti di antropologia e filosofia. Vatican City: Librería Editrice Vaticana, 1995.

Person and Community. Selected Essays. Translated by Teresa Sandok. New York: Peter Lang, 1993.

"Person: Subject and Community." In *Person and Community: Selected Essays*, translated by Teresa Sandok, 219–24. New York: Peter Lang, 1993. SPANISH EDITION: "La persona: sujeto y comunidad." In *El hombre y su destino. Ensayos de antropología*, translated by Pilar Ferrer, 41–109. Madrid: Palabra, 2003.

"Persona e Atto." In *Metafisica della Persona. Tutte le opere filosofiche e saggi integrativi*, edited by Giovanni Reale and Tadeus Styczen, 829–1216. 3rd ed. Milan: Bompiani, 2005.

Persona y acción. Translated by Jesús Fernández Zulaica. Madrid: BAC, 1982.

Persona y acción. Edited by Juan Manuel Burgos and Rafael Mora. Translated by Rafael Mora. Madrid: Ediciones Palabra, 2011.

"The Personal Structure of Self Determination." In *Person and Community: Selected Essays*, translated by Teresa Sandok, 187–95. New York: Peter Lang, 1993.

"The Problem of Experience in Ethics." In *Person and Community: Selected Essays*, translated by Teresa Sandok, 114–25. New York: Peter Lang, 1993.

"The Problem of the Will in the Analysis of the Ethical Act." In *Person and Community: Selected Essays*, translated by Teresa Sandok, 3–22. New York: Peter Lang, 1993.

Sign of Contradiction. New York: Seabury Press, 1979.

"Subjectivity and the Irreducible in the Human Being." In *Person and Community: Selected Essays*, translated by Teresa Sandok, 209–17. New York: Peter Lang, 1993. Originally published as "La soggettività e l'irreducibile nell'uomo," *Il Nuovo Areopago* 1 (1978): 7–16. SPANISH EDITION: La subjetividad y lo irreductible en el hombre." In *El hombre y su destino. Ensayos de antropología*, translated by Pilar Ferrer, 25–39. Madrid: Palabra, 2003.

Works of John Paul II

Apostolic Letter Mulieris Dignitatem. Vatican City: Librería Editrice Vaticana, 1988.

Apostolic Letter Salvifici Doloris. Vatican City: Librería Editrice Vaticana, 1984.

Encyclical Fides et Ratio. Vatican City: Librería Editrice Vaticana, 1998.

Encyclical Veritatis Splendor. Vatican City: Librería Editrice Vaticana, 1993.

Man and Woman He Created Them: A Theology of the Body. Translated by Michael Waldstein. Boston, Mass.: Pauline Books and Media, 2006.

Mężczyzną i niewiastą stworzył ich: Odkupienie ciała a sakramentalność małżeństwa. Lublin: KUL, 2008.

Rise, Let Us Be on Our Way. Translated by Walter Zięmba. New York: Warner Books, 2004.

Uomo e donna lo creò. Rome: Città Nuova, 2011.

Books and Articles

Acosta, Miguel. "La intentio como clave de la transobjetividad de la inteligencia en la filosofía realista." In *Filosofía de la Inteligencia*, edited by Manuel Oriol, 79–102. Madrid: Ediciones CEU, 2011.

———. *Los afectos inferiores.* Madrid: Publicep, 2006.

Aristotle. *Complete Works of Aristotle: The Revised Oxford Translation.* Edited by Jonathan Barnes. 2 vols. Bollingen Series. Princeton, N.J.: Princeton University Press, 1995.

Benatar, David. *Better Never to Have Been: The Harm of Coming into Existence.* Oxford: Oxford University Press, 2006.

Brown, Helen G. *Sex and the Single Girl.* New York: B. Geis Associates, 1962.

Buch Camí, Emmanuel, Pilar Ferrer, and Ildefonso Murillo. *Personalismo teológico. Brunner, Wojtyła, von Balthasar.* Madrid: Fundación Emmanuel Mounier, 2007.

Burgos, Juan Manuel. *El Personalismo.* Madrid: Palabra, 2000.

———, ed. *La filosofía personalista de Karol Wojtyła.* Madrid: Palabra, 2007.

———. "La antropología personalista de Persona y acción." In *La filosofía personalista de Karol Wojtyła*, edited by Juan Manuel Burgos, 117–43. Madrid: Palabra, 2007.

Buttiglione, Rocco, Carlo Fedeli, and Angelo Scola, eds. *Karol Wojtyła. Filosofo, Teologo, Poeta.* Vatican City: Librería Editrice Vaticana, 1984.

———. *Karol Wojtyła: The Thought of the Man Who Became Pope John Paul II.* Translated by Paolo Guietti and Francesca Murphy. Grand Rapids, Mich.: Eerdmans, 1997.

Choza, Jacinto. *Conciencia y afectividad (Aristóteles, Nietzsche, Freud).* Pamplona: Eunsa, 1991.

———. *Manual de Antropología Filosófica.* Madrid: Ediciones Rialp, 1988.

Conan Doyle, Arthur. *The Complete Adventures and Memoirs of Sherlock Holmes.* New York: Bramhall House, 1975.

Darwin, Charles. *The Descent of Man*. Great Books of the Western World, edited by Robert M. Hutchins, vol. 49. Chicago: Encyclopedia Britannica, 1952.

Descartes, René. *Meditations on First Philosophy*. Translated by Donald. A. Cress. Indianapolis, Ind.: Hackett Publishing Company, 1993.

Dennett, Daniel. *Consciousness Explained*. Boston, Mass.: Little, Brown, 1991.

Ferrer, Pilar. Introduction to *Mi visión del hombre. Hacia una nueva ética*, by Karol Wojtyla, 7–22. Madrid: Ediciones Palabra, 2003.

Franquet, María José. *Persona, Acción y Libertad. Las claves de la antropología de Karol Wojtyla*. Pamplona: Eunsa, 1996.

Frossard, André. *"Be Not Afraid": Pope John Paul II Speaks Out on His Life, His Beliefs, and His Inspiring Vision for Humanity*. Translated by J. R. Foster. New York: St. Martin's Press, 1984.

García Cuadrado, José Angel. *Antropología Filosófica. Una introducción a la Filosofía del Hombre*. 6th ed. Pamplona: Eunsa, 2014.

Gilson, Etienne. *Being and Some Philosophers*. Toronto: Pontifical Institute of Mediaeval Studies, 1952.

Grygiel, Stanisław. Preface to *L'amore e la sua regola: Karol Wojtyła e l'esperienza dell' "Ambiente" di Cracovia*. Edited by Stanislaw Grygiel and Przemysław Kwiatkowski. Siena: Edizione Cantagalli, 2009.

Guerra López, Rodrigo. "El aporte filosófico de Juan Pablo II. Homenaje al Papa en el XXV aniversario de su pontificado." Boletín CELAM, no. 302 (2003): 1–10.

———. *Volver a la persona. El método filosófico de Karol Wojtyla*. Madrid: Caparrós Editores, 2002.

Guzowski, Krzysztof. "El personalismo de comunión en Karol Wojtyła." In *La filosofía personalista de Karol Wojtyla*, edited by Juan Manuel Burgos, 195–209. Madrid: Palabra, 2007.

Halberstam, David. *The Best and the Brightest*. New York: Random House, 1972.

Hawthorne, John. *Metaphysical Essays*. Oxford: Oxford University Press, 2006.

Howorth, Henry H. *History of the Mongols from the 9th to the 19th Century*. Vol. 1, *The Mongols Proper and the Kalmyks*. New York: Cosimo, 2008.

Hume, David. *Hume's Ethical Writings*. Edited by Alasdair MacIntyre. New York: Collier Books, 1965.

———. *An Inquiry concerning Human Understanding*. Indianapolis, Ind.: Bobbs-Merrill, 1955.

Ingarden, Roman. *Über die Verantwortung. Ihre ontischen Fundamente*. Leipzig: Philipp Reclam, 1970. Polish edition: *O odpowiedzialności i jej podstawach ontycznych*. Kraków: Książeczka o człowieku, 1973. Spanish edition: *Sobre la responsabilidad*. Translated by Juan Miguel Palacios. Madrid: Caparrós Editores, 2001.

James, William. *Pragmatism*. Buffalo, N.Y.: Prometheus Books, 1991.

Kant, Immanuel. "Grundlegung zur Metaphysik der Sitten." In *Kants gesammelte Schriften*. Vol. 4. Berlin: Druck und Verlag von Georg Reimer, 1911. English edition: *Grounding of the Metaphysics of Morals*. Indianapolis, Ind.: Hackett Publishing, 1993.

Köchler, Hans. "Karol Wojtyła's Notion of the Irreducible in Man and the Quest for a Just World Order." In *Karol Wojtyła's Philosophical Legacy*, edited by Nancy Mardas Billias, Agnes B. Curry, and George F. McLean, 165–82. Washington, D.C.: The Council for Research in Values and Philosophy, 2008.

Kupczak, Jarosław. *Destined for Liberty: The Human Person in the Philosophy of Karol Wojtyła/John Paul II*. Washington, D.C.: The Catholic University of America Press, 2000.

LeDoux, Joseph. *Synaptic Self: How Our Brains Become Who We Are*. New York: Viking, 2002.

Llano, Alejandro. *Gnoseología*. Pamplona: Eunsa, 2000.

Lorda, Juan Luis. *Antropología. Del Concilio Vaticano II a Juan Pablo II*. Madrid: Palabra, 1996.

Marías, Julián. *Persona*. Madrid: Alianza Editorial, 1996.

Merecki, Jarosław. "Las fuentes de la filosofía de Karol Wojtyła." In *La filosofía personalista de Karol Wojtyła*, edited by Juan Manuel Burgos, 13–24. Madrid: Palabra, 2007.

Millán-Puelles, Antonio. *La estructura de la subjetividad*. Madrid: Rialp, 1967.

Ocáriz, Fernando. "Rasgos fundamentales del pensamiento de Santo Tomás." In *Tomás de Aquino, también hoy*, edited by Cornelio Fabro et al., 49–94. Pamplona: Eunsa, 1990.

Plato. *The Collected Dialogues*. Edited by Edith Hamilton and Huntington Cairns. Princeton, N.J.: Princeton University Press, 1980.

Poltawski, Andrzej. "The Epistemological Basis of Karol Wojtyła's Philosophy." In *Karol Wojtyła. Filosofo, Teologo, Poeta*, edited by Rocco Buttiglione, Carlo Fedeli, and Angelo Scola, 79–91. Vatican City: Librería Editrice Vaticana, 1984.

Reale, Giovanni, and Dario Antiseri. *Historia del Pensamiento Filosófico y Científico*. Vol. 1, *Antigüedad y Edad Media*. Barcelona: Herder, 2001.

Reale, Giovanni. "Introductory essay" [in Italian] to *Metafisica della persona: Tutti le opera filosofiche e saggi integrative*, by Karol Wojtyła, vii–ciii. 3rd ed. Milan: Bompiani, 2005.

Reimers, Adrian J. "Karol Wojtyła's Aims and Methodology." In *Christian Wisdom Meets Modernity*, edited by Kenneth Oakes. New York: Bloomsbury Academic Press, forthcoming.

———. "La antropología personalista de Karol Wojtyła." In *Propuestas antropológicas del siglo XX*, edited by Juan Fernando Sellés, 2:309–28. Pamplona: Eunsa, 2007.

———. *Truth about the Good: Moral Norms in the Thought of John Paul II*. Ave Maria, Fla.: Sapientia Press of Ave Maria University, 2011.

Ritter, Cezary. Afterword [in Polish] to *Mężczyzną i niewiastą stworzył ich: Odkupienie ciała a sakramentalność małżeństwa*, by Karol Wojtyła, 399–400. Lublin: KUL, 2008.

Ryle, Gilbert. *The Concept of Mind*. New York: Barnes and Noble, 1949.

Sagan, Carl, and Ann Druyan. *Pale Blue Dot: A Vision of the Human Future in Space*. New York: Ballantine Books, 1994.

Second Vatican Council, *Gaudium et Spes [Pastoral Constitution on the Church in the Modern World]*. Vatican City: Librería Editrice Vaticana, 1965.

Scheler, Max. *Der Formalismus in der Ethik und die materiale Wertethik: Neuer Versuch der Grundlegung eines ethischen Personalismus*. Bern: Franke Verlag, 1966.

———. *The Human Place in the Cosmos*. Translated by Karin S. Frings. Evanston, Ill.: Northwestern University Press, 2008.

Schmitz, Kenneth. *At the Center of the Human Drama: The Philosophical Anthropology of Karol Wojtyła/Pope John Paul II*. Washington, D.C.: The Catholic University of America Press, 1993.

Scola, Angelo. "Gli interventi di Karol Wojtyła al Concilio Ecumenico Vaticano II. Esposizione ed interpretazione teologica." In *Karol Wojtyła. Filosofo, Teologo, Poeta*, edited by Rocco Buttiglione, Carlo Fedeli, and Angelo Scola, 289–306. Vatican City: Librería Editrice Vaticana, 1984.

Searle, John R. *Minds, Brains and Science*. Cambridge, Mass.: Harvard University Press, 1984. Spanish edition: *Mentes, cerebros y ciencia*. Madrid: Ediciones Cátedra, 1994.

———. *The Rediscovery of the Mind*. Cambridge, Mass.: MIT Press, 1992.

Serretti, Massimo. "Invitation to Read" [in Italian] to *Perché l'uomo. Scritti inediti di antropologia e filosofia*, by Karol Wojtyła, 5–10. Vatican City: Librería Editrice Vaticana, 1995.

Shakespeare, William. *The Complete Works of Shakespeare*. Edited by W. J. Craig. New York: Oxford University Press, 1919.

Simpson, Peter. *On Karol Wojtyła*. Belmont, Calif.: Wadsworth, 2001.

Singer, Peter. "Should This Be the Last Generation?" *New York Times*, June 6, 2010. New York edition. http://opinionator.blogs.nytimes.com/2010/06/06/should-this-be-the-last-generation/

Smart, John J. C. *Philosophy and Scientific Realism*. London: Routledge and Kegan Paul, 1963.

Smith, Christian. *What Is a Person*. Chicago: University of Chicago Press, 2010.

Sperry, Roger W. "Consciousness and Causality." In *The Oxford Companion to the Mind*, edited by Richard L. Gregory, 164–66 Oxford: Oxford University Press, 1987.

Stanford, Craig. *Significant Others: The Ape-Human Continuum and the Quest for Human Nature*. New York: Basic Books, 2001.

Styczeń, Tadeusz. "Introduction" [in Spanish] to *Mi visión del hombre. Hacia una nueva ética*, by Karol Wojtyla, 117–34. Madrid: Ediciones Palabra, 2003.

Tatarkiewicz, W. *Analysis of Happiness*. Translated by E. Rothert. The Hague: Martinus Nijhoff, 1976. Originally published as *O szczęściu*. Warsaw, 1962.

Tattersall, Ian. "How We Came to Be Human." *Scientific American* 16, no. 2 (2006): 66–73.

Thomas Aquinas. "Opera omnia S. Thomae." In *Index Thomisticus*. Edited by Roberto Busa, Eduardo Bernot, and Enrique Alarcón. http://www.corpusthomisticum.org/it/ index.age

Twain, Mark. *Life on the Mississippi*. Chapel Hill: University of North Carolina at Chapel Hill, 1999, 188–21.

Urabayen, Julia. "Emmanuel Lévinas y Karol Wojtyla: Dos comprensiones de la persona y una misma defensa del ser humano." *Persona y Derecho* 56 (2007): 409–42.

———. "Gabriel Marcel: Una imagen digna del hombre." In *Propuestas antropológicas del siglo XX*, edited by Juan Fernando Sellés, 1:327–43. Pamplona: Eunsa, 2006.

Van Inwagen, Peter. *Metaphysics*. Boulder, Colo.: Westview Press, 1993.

———. *The Problem of Evil: The Gifford Lectures Delivered in the University of St Andrews in 2003*. Oxford: Clarendon Press, 2006.

Wais, Kazimiers. *Ontologija czyli Metafizyca ogólna*. Lwów: Bibljoteka Religijna, 1926.

Waldstein, Michael. Introduction to *Man and Woman He Created Them: A Theology of the Body*, by John Paul II, 3–11. Translated by Michael Waldstein. Boston, Mass.: Pauline Books and Media, 2006.

Weigel, George. *The Final Revolution: The Resistance Church and the Collapse of Communism*. New York: Oxford University Press, 1992.

———. *Witness to Hope: The Biography of Pope John Paul II*. New York: Harper Collins, 1999.

Wittgenstein, Ludwig. *Tractatus Logico-Philosophicus*. Translated by David Pears and Brian McGuinness. London: Routledge and Kegan Paul, 1961.

INDEX

ability, 58, 80, 101, 121, 200–1, 209, 221–22
absolute, 56, 72–73, 83, 98–99, 124, 202, 230n13, 239
abstract, 90, 94, 128, 164
abstraction, 88–90, 109, 183
act, 7, 22, 24, 27, 29, 42, 46–47, 49–50, 53, 56, 58n44, 60, 67, 75, 80–81, 99, 101, 106, 111–13, 116–19, 121, 125n1, 126–37, 139–45, 147–50, 151n77, 152–53, 156–61, 162n21, 163–72, 174–79, 181–86, 189, 192, 194–95, 197, 200–201, 205–206, 209–12, 215–17, 219, 222–23, 225–28, 232–33, 235, 238, 240, 242
action, 7, 14–15, 32, 33n2, 35, 47–49, 51, 54, 61, 64–65, 67–68, 71, 78–79, 82, 95, 106, 109, 111, 115, 117, 119–20, 122–23, 126, 129–31, 133, 139, 141–46, 148–49, 151–52, 156, 158n9, 161n20, 162n21, 163, 165, 170–75, 182, 186, 190–201, 203, 207, 211, 215, 217–19, 220n76, 221–36, 238–40, 243
activation, 144, 147–49, 151–53, 156, 163, 166n35, 167, 175, 191, 213, 217
actor, 145
aesthetic, 60, 85, 88, 125n1, 173n53
affectivity, 120–22, 132n24, 183, 220
agent, 47–48, 54–55, 69, 75, 100, 117, 129–30, 144–45, 149, 160, 169, 171, 177, 190
alienation, 55n35, 69, 241–42
anger, 64, 218
animal, 25, 44, 51, 70–71, 78, 96, 101, 146, 163, 180, 193, 197, 205n39
anthropological, 3, 5n5, 13, 18, 25, 27, 29, 38, 105, 113, 137, 151, 186, 193n14, 195, 196n22, 206, 211, 219, 221, 222n79, 225, 231, 241

Anthropological Philosophy. *See* Philosophical Anthropology
Anthropology, 6, 8–9, 17–19, 21–22, 27, 29–30, 32–35, 38, 41, 65, 93, 105–8, 110–16, 127, 129–30, 141, 143, 145, 151, 154, 164–65, 180, 189, 192–94, 196, 200, 204–5, 206, 207n42, 221–22, 224, 226–27
antipersonalistic, 231
appetite, 49–51, 57–58, 162n23, 212–13, 217
a priori, 127
art, 14, 56, 125n1, 173n53
Aquinas, 16, 19, 21, 33, 38, 67n1, 75, 82, 90, 106n1, 126n5, 128n9, 131, 142, 150n74, 157n5, 193, 212n56
Aristotle, 21n21, 68, 106n1, 125, 128n9, 130n19, 131, 132n24, 144n59, 179, 186n86, 193–94, 217, 225n1
Augustine, 16
authentic: act, 119, 168, 232; attitudes, 123, 170, 211, 233, 235–39; common good, 83; communion, 101; community, 235, 240; experience, 43, 116; love, 97–98, 101–2; revelations, 72; value, 90
autonomy, 80, 90–92, 162n22, 172
aversion, 121
axiology, 226

beatitude, 178n68, 180
beauty, 41, 51–52, 59, 61, 68, 76, 85, 173n53, 207
behavior, 51, 58–60, 63, 65, 71, 102, 119, 176–78, 205, 230
belief, 2n3, 44, 57, 81
Benedict XVI, 4
Bentham, Jeremy, 92, 181

education, 93, 122, 154, 220–21, 236

effect, 3, 6, 20, 24, 47, 54, 63–64, 91, 96, 106, 113, 121, 126, 130n16, 145, 153, 159, 169n44, 171, 179, 184, 187n86, 204n37, 206, 210, 213–14, 217–18, 224, 226

elation, 212–15

emotion, 7, 58, 61–66, 74, 78, 91, 97, 101, 107, 113, 121–22, 137, 153, 181, 204–6, 207n42, 210–12, 214–21

emotionalization, 63, 122, 137, 210n49, 218–20

emotivity, 121–22, 204–8, 210–11, 217, 219, 222

empirical science, 90–91

empiricist, 37, 42, 48

encounter, 20, 33, 62, 73, 82, 96, 116, 118, 126, 128, 130, 137, 180, 200, 230

end, 2–3, 6n8, 22, 25, 27–28, 38, 47, 51, 69, 86, 90, 97, 110, 112, 120, 123, 160–61, 162n22, 162n23, 164–67, 170–72, 182, 197, 203, 238

energeia, 142

environment, 7, 43–44, 53, 58, 68, 94, 175n61, 177, 207n42

epistemology, 21n23, 38, 42

error, 46, 88, 90–91, 99, 101, 167, 170n46, 174, 211

essence, 37, 42, 44, 50, 82–83, 99, 145–46, 156n4, 170n46, 220n76, 226

essentialism, 128n11

ethics, 7, 16, 17n9, 18–19, 21–23, 26, 29–30, 38, 47, 48n17, 67n1, 92, 105, 107, 122, 127, 129–30, 172, 174n56, 179n70, 221–22

evasion, 235, 237–38, 239n31

evidence, 55–56, 167

evil, 2, 27, 29, 54n30, 63, 71, 85, 94–95, 99, 119, 142, 153, 167, 172–73, 175, 182, 215, 221, 226, 231

evolution theory, 43–44, 60, 197

excitability, 7, 212–14

excitement, 207n42, 212–16, 218–19

existence, 1, 14, 19–20, 48, 50–51, 76, 89–91, 94n23, 110, 121, 123, 126, 129, 132, 138–39, 141, 145–46, 149–50, 155, 159n13, 171, 183n80, 184–85, 202–3, 219, 231–34

existential, 13, 21n23, 34–35, 51, 93–94, 106, 111, 172, 184–85; condition; level, 203

experience, 2, 4–5, 7, 15, 20, 21n22, 25, 27–28, 31, 33, 37, 41–66, 67n1, 72, 74, 78–80, 98, 100–1, 105–6, 111–12, 115–21, 125–31, 133–45, 148–49, 151–53, 159–61, 168–69, 173–74, 177, 180, 182, 184, 186–87, 189–90, 192, 198, 202, 204, 207–16, 218–20, 222–23, 230, 241, 243

experiment, 2, 24, 89

exteriority, 74, 161n20, 194

faculty, 15n6, 21n23, 27, 44, 48, 105–6, 112, 118, 132, 151–52, 157–58, 161–62, 165–66, 169n44, 186, 198, 206n40, 226

faith, 1–2, 14, 16–17, 19–20, 23, 39, 66, 80, 174, 184n80

falsity, 167, 168n41, 173

family, 2, 13, 24, 70, 83, 95, 123, 203, 231–32, 234

feelings, 41–43, 121, 207n42, 208–11, 215n66

felicity, 178–83

Fides et Ratio, 1n1, 6, 16n8, 17n11, 23, 24n32, 57n39, 67n1, 80, 88, 91n14, 93n16, 94n19, 94n22, 98n31, 98n32, 102

form, 14–16, 20, 22, 23n30, 26, 29, 42–43, 49, 52, 54, 70, 72, 78, 82, 88, 91–92, 95, 110, 112, 116, 118, 127, 128n9, 142–43, 146, 149, 151–53, 155, 161, 167n40, 168, 169n44, 171–74, 176, 182–84, 186, 188, 190, 193, 198, 200–3, 207, 215–16, 221, 231, 234–36, 239–40, 242

freedom, 7, 15, 23n30, 26–27, 33n2, 35, 53–57, 66, 69, 73, 80, 96, 102, 113, 118–19, 123, 156–57, 161–65, 167, 171–72, 174–75, 179, 182, 184–86, 189, 195, 211, 230–31

friendship, 15, 51, 60, 92, 98, 102, 179, 207n42

Frossard, André, 2n3, 19n14

fulfillment, 119, 155, 174, 182–83, 194, 229, 238

gift, 24, 69, 76, 80, 96–97, 99–102

God, 3, 14–16, 20, 25, 27, 42, 69, 71–72, 77, 79–80, 82–83, 86–88, 90, 97–102, 178n66, 180, 184n80

suppositum, 30n53, 48, 116, 118, 131, 138–40, 140n48, 141, 145–46, 149–50, 164, 192, 198
Swieżawski, Stefan, 21n23, 23
Szostek, Andrzej, 15n5

Tartarkiewicz, Władisława, 180n74
Tattersall, Ian, 58n42
theology, theological, 2, 6, 13–14, 16–17, 19–20, 27–28, 31, 69, 72, 87–88, 100, 102, 107, 111, 178nn66–68, 184n80, 227, 240
theology of the body, 6, 17, 71, 75, 178n68
Thomism, Thomistic, 19–20, 21n23, 23, 25, 28–30, 30nn52–53, 33–35, 38, 67, 107, 127, 128n9, 129–30, 150n74, 157n5, 189, 206n40, 207n42, 212
Tischner, Józef, 36
totalitarianism, totalitarian, 123, 229–31, 241
transcendence, 7, 14, 49, 53, 77, 87, 96, 100–101, 112, 118, 145, 150, 151n77, 155, 164–65, 167–68, 170, 172–73, 176, 178, 181, 183–86, 188–91, 194, 206, 211, 218, 220, 222–23, 225, 228, 230n13, 237–38; horizontal transcendence, 7, 49–50, 52–53, 57, 94, 118, 155, 162n23, 164, 190, 226; vertical transcendence, 7, 53, 57–59, 118–19, 122–23, 155, 162n23, 164, 226
truth, 1–2, 4, 7, 14, 16–17, 19, 22, 24n32, 27–28, 37, 41–42, 44, 46, 51, 53, 56–57, 61, 66, 67–70, 72, 76–77, 81–83, 85–86, 88–89, 91, 94, 97, 99–100, 102, 113, 118–19, 126–27, 162n21, 166–70, 170n46, 172–77, 179, 180 n73, 183–84, 186, 194–96, 207, 210–11, 215, 220–21, 237–38, 243

Twain, Mark, 52
Tygodnik Powszechny, 17n9, 28, 32n1
Tymieniecka, Anna-Teresa, 9, 130n16

understanding, 19, 32–33, 38, 52–53, 66–68, 75, 80–82, 94, 97, 102, 109–10, 112, 114, 127–28, 132–34, 135n35, 136, 141,147n65, 153n81,157n5, 166, 169, 169n44, 192–93, 195, 205, 223, 225, 228, 230n13, 231
Urabayen, Julia, 196, 230n13
urge, 50–51, 60, 121, 197, 201n31, 203
utilitarianism, 6, 88, 92–95, 99, 181, 196

value, 7, 16, 21n22, 49–50, 52–54, 58–64, 87, 90–92, 99–100, 102, 118–19, 121–24, 128n11, 137, 160–61, 166, 168, 170–77, 185, 195, 201–2, 207–8, 210, 210n48, 211–14, 216, 219–20, 225–28, 231, 235, 237, 239–42
Van Inwagen, Peter, 53–54, 55n33
Vatican Council II, 3, 23, 26, 69, 86, 100
volition, 119, 157n5, 158–60, 164, 165, 167, 168n43, 226

Wais, Kazimierz, 19n14
Weigel, George, 3n4, 15n6, 20n18, 21n23, 22n26, 23n31, 24, 27n43, 28n48, 29n49, 30n54, 31n56, 106n2
will, 27, 47–48, 53–54, 56, 60, 62, 97, 100, 113, 118–19, 121–22, 142, 156–58, 160–66, 166n35, 167–68, 169n44, 170, 172–73, 176–77, 185–86, 189–90, 197–201, 212n56, 217–19, 226
Wittgenstein, Ludwig, 68
Woznicki, Andrew N., 34
Wyszyński, Stefan Cardinal, 3